Christ as Sacrament and Example

Luther's Theology of the Cross and its Relevance for South Asia

Jhakmak Neeraj Ekka

Lutheran University Press
Minneapolis, Minnesota

Christ as Sacrament and Example
Luther's Theology of the Cross and its Relevance for South Asia
Jhakmak Neeraj Ekka

Copyright 2007 Luther Seminary. All rights reserved. Published by Lutheran University Press, an imprint of 1517 Media. Except for brief quotations in articles or reviews, no part of this book may be reproduced in any manner without prior permission from the publisher.

Encounters in World Christianity is published in partnership with Luther Seminary with funds from the Global Mission Institute and the Justice and Christian Community Program.
The series editorial team is:
    Dr. Charles Amjad-Ali
        The Martin Luther King, Jr., Professor of Justice
            and Christian Community
        Director, Islamic Studies Program
    Dr. David Lose
        Academic Dean
    Dr. Frieder Ludwig
        Associate Professor of Mission & World Christianity
        Director, Global Mission Institute

    Library of Congress Cataloging in Publication data

Ekka, Jhakmak Neeraj, 1962
   Christ as sacrament and example : Luther's theology of the cross and its relevance for South Asia / Jhakmak Neeraj Ekka
      p.cm.
   Includes bibliographic references.
   ISBN-13: 978-1-932688-24-5 (perfectbound : alk. paper)
   ISBN-10: 1-932688-24-1 (perfectbound : alk. paper)
   eISBN: 978-1-942304-48-7
   1. Luther, Martin. 2. Theology of the Cross. 3. Christianity—South Asia.
I. Title.
   BR333.5.C72E35 2007
   230'.41092—dc22
                                        2007002890

Table of Contents

Foreword 7
Preface 8
List of Abbreviations 10
1. The Context Delineated 11
   Survey of the World of South Asia 11
      Mass Poverty: A Pervasive Reality 12
      Multi-religiosity: A Distinctive Characteristic of South Asia 14
      Conclusion 21
   Survey of the Theology of the Cross 22
      Scripture 23
      Patristic Period 26
      Medieval Period 28
      Modern Period 33
      Conclusion 37
2. Luther's *Theologia Crucis* 39
   Background 39
   Martin Luther's *Thelogia Crucis* 43
   Theology of the Cross as Theology of Revelation f
      or Salvation 56
   Vulnerability of God 58
   Theology of Incarnation 65
   Hidden and Revealed God 65
   Theology of Faith 67
   Magnificat 68
   Discovery of the New Meaning of the Righteousness
      of God 70
   Church Postils 72
   Conclusion 74
3. The Present Debate on the Theology of the Cross 77
   Walter von Loewenich 77
   Paul Althaus 81
   Gerhard Førde 85

	Regin Prenter	90
	Jürgen Moltmann	95
	Conclusion	101
4.	South Asian Theologicans and the Theology of the Cross	102
	M.M. Thomas	102
	Aloysius Pieris	116
5.	The Theology of the Cross Amidst Many Religions and Many Poor	131
	Preparatio Evangelica	137
	A New Grammar to Talk about God	142
	Uniqueness Reconsidered	143
	The Thing What It Is	145
	A New Grammar for Dialogue	147
	Theology of the Cross among the Poor	148
	Conclusion	152
6.	Markers of a South Asian Theology of the Cross	154
	Theology of the Cross as Theology of Perpetual Self-Criticism	154
	Finality of the Cross: Revelation of the Crucified God	156
	Uniqueness of the Cross: Vulnerability	157
	Way of the Cross: Scandal and Foolishness	160
	Power of the Cross: For the Sake of the Other	161
	Theology of the Cross vs. Incarnational Life	166
	Constructive Proposal: Theology of the Cross as Theology of the Way	169
7.	Conclusions	173
	Acknowledgments	181
	Bibliography	183
	Endnotes	194

TO MY PARENTS
Rev. Niranjan and Manoranjini Ekka
for their decisive role in discerning my calling,
with immense gratitude, I dedicate this book.

Foreword

This book explores the significance of Luther's *theologia crucis* as a viable resource for contextual theology amidst plurality of faiths and the massive poverty in South Asia. Against the pluralistic theological position that denies uniqueness and finality to Jesus Christ, this thesis argues that the concerns of genuine sensitivity towards other religions, liberation, justice, and peace can be adequately addressed within the framework of Luther's theology of the cross. As such the uniqueness and finality of Jesus Christ may not be compromised but rather be understood as the very foundation for openness and commitment to the other, based on its intrinsic soteriological intention and inevitable epistemological implications.

Luther's theology of the cross understands Jesus Christ as the sacrament and example. The orthodoxy of salvific understanding of the cross, to be confessed and proclaimed cannot be devoid of ortho-praxis of the cross, understood and practiced with reference to ever deepening vulnerability of God on the cross. A critical conversation between Luther's theology of the cross and two prominent South Asian theologians, (namely, M. M. Thomas and his emphasis of salvation as humanization, and Aloysius Pieris' and his insistence on liberation as *raison d'etre* for theology and inter-religious dialogue in South Asian context) broadens and deepens the expanse of the theology of the cross to include incarnational life of Jesus Christ.

Luther's uncompromising claim that Jesus Christ is the final revelation of God on the cross for the sake of salvation and the inevitable implication of the cross enable believers to be open towards other faiths and seek existence only in reference to that of God's vulnerability. Thus, it is my constructive proposal that the dual dimensions of sacrament and example could meaningfully be accounted for in the understanding of the theology of the cross as the theology of the way with characteristics of inbuilt self-criticism; conscious existence in vulnerability; finality of the crucified God; uniqueness of the scandal and foolishness; and its power for the sake of the other.

Preface

It is a theological imperative to face the issues of plurality of religions and poverty of the masses in South Asia. The questions of what does it mean to be a Christian and what is the relevance of church in this context are not merely matters of academic concern, but they are part of and parcel of my struggle in faith reflection. Probing further into these questions would inevitably lead to the question of who is this Jesus for me and others in South Asia.

My journey that finds expression in the following pages began one evening with an informal sharing with some friends. As I spoke of the deep crisis in the Gossner Evangelical Lutheran Church in India in 1914, which was precipitated due to the abrupt departure of German missionaries from India then a British colony, as the Germans and the British were fighting against each other in the First World War. In 1919 the Lutheran church opted for autonomy over easy and quite enticing solution of merging with the Anglican church. As I shared this apparent crisis with friends, something struck deep within me. A question arose in my guts as to why the simple members of the church would want to remain Lutheran as it only forebode suffering due to uncertain future. This question became much more poignant as the days went by and forced me to search deep within Lutheran tradition for God and his relation with suffering. More than just an issue of one church and its existence in the reality of suffering, now it became the basis to reflect on the present manifestations of the theological basis of the Church of Jesus Christ in South Asia. It was not merely a historical question but rather a theological one with very serious consequences both for the identity and relevance of the church. As I have always been deeply convinced about the continuing task of contextualizing theology, it finally led me to reflect on the relevant theology for South Asia, a context alive with living faith traditions and marred with debilitating poverty of the masses. When I encountered the God on the cross in Luther's *theologia crucis*, my heart jumped once more with profound curiosity and hope.

I began a journey to explore contextual possibilities in Martin Luther's theology of the cross. The issues and controversies of Luther's day and the serious theological stake in Luther's position kept me motivated in this inquiry. I was struck to find an unknown and insignificant professor Luther's conviction of God's grace on the cross of Jesus Christ. Luther's theology of the cross testified to the courage of the one who is gripped by the sheer grace of our Lord as he countered the official theology of the time that robbed God of his power and people of their money and true posture in the sight of God. His unified vision of Christ as the sacrament and an example in dialectical relationship kept me hopeful and creative for a contextual theology for South Asia. The following reflection, in some significant way, is about faithful response to Christ the sacrament, a relation initiated by God and a grateful affirmation of the same in Christ the example in relation to the other.

List of Abbreviations

CISRS	Institute for the Study of Religion and Society
LW	*Luther's Works*, American Edition
NRSV	New Revised Standard Version
SCM	Student Christian Movement
WA	Martin Luthers Werke. Weimarer Ausgabe
WCC	World Council of Churches
WSCF	World Student Christian Federation

CHAPTER 1

The Contexts Delineated

This introductory chapter is divided into two parts. The first delineates the context of South Asia and the second part is a survey of the major discussions of the theology of the cross.

Survey of the World of South Asia

The term South Asia refers to seven countries located in the Indian peninsula. They are India, Pakistan, Bangladesh, Sri Lanka, Nepal, Bhutan and Maldives.[1] The region of South Asia is important for many reasons, but for the purpose and scope of this study our general description of the context of South Asia is restricted to the rich religio-cultural traditions on the one hand and the mass poverty on the other. A brief introduction to the region will provide an overall understanding as well as highlight some of the reasons why the region of South Asia is significant for the theological discourse itself. Firstly, it accounts for a large number of populations of the world.[2] Further, according to the World Bank data, South Asia, in terms of population, has been the second fastest growing region in the world after East Asia.[3] Secondly, South Asia truly and intensely represents a context of many religions in the world. Besides being the place of origin for Hinduism, Buddhism, Jainism, Sikkhism and other primal religions, the majority of all the Hindus and Muslims in the world are found in this region. In fact, India alone has the second largest Muslim population in the world only next to Indonesia. Further, whatever little is left of Zoroastrian religion with its origin in Persia is now exclusively found in South Asia. Whereas Buddhism is the dominant religion of Sri Lanka and Bhutan, Hinduism is dominant in India and Nepal. Islam is predominant in Pakistan, and Bangladesh. Thirdly, racially also this is a unique region as there are people of Aryan, Dravidian and Mongolian races that have lived there together for centuries. Fourthly, unlike many parts of the world its cultural and religious history dates as far back as at least 3500 years B.C.E. This provides the region with a well-defined and long history of peoplehood. Fifthly, it is also one of the poorest regions of the world as 45% of the population live below the international poverty line of $ 1 a day. They comprise about 40% of world's poor.[4]

The significance of this region is undeniably great for theological enterprise in addition to economic and geo-political reasons.[5] Thus, we should keep in mind that the South Asian reality is very complex and multi-faceted and this reality is especially critical while doing theology in this region.

Mass Poverty: A Pervasive Reality

Poverty is displayed in helpless destitution, daily misery, and constant squalor of the masses in this region. The western standards for poverty and daily count of calorie has no meaning for the poor in South Asia, where it is a matter of extreme struggle to even find something/anything to eat. Thus, for a large number of people poverty is simply an issue of survival. What C. T. Kurien says of India is equally true for the whole of South Asian situation. It is qualitatively and analytically different from the pocket poverty existing in other parts of the world.[6] The sheer number of people reeling under poverty make it an overwhelming ocean of poverty.

There are many factors contributing to the poverty in South Asia, which include colonial history, religious traditions, globalization, etc. Colonial powers, especially the British *Raj*, destroyed the indigenous economy, hastening the process of impoverization. With its extended period of rule of exploitation and subjugation, the British *Raj* must bear the brunt of this allegation as it facilitated 19th century globalization.[7] The fatalistic attitude found among certain Asian religions has further contributed to poverty.[8] Notwithstanding its many blessings the globalization process along with domestic policies such as liberalization (delicensing), privatization (denationalization), and marketization (deregulating) seems to have pushed the poor and the marginalized further in to the situation of desperation.[9] Ironically, the countries of South Asia have achieved growth in production of food grains, recorded higher industrial production, and helped increase per capita income; yet, the majority of the people still live in extremely poor or even in subhuman conditions.[10] For a critical eye, the question as to who is benefiting from this is inescapable. The comment by John Desrochers is indicative:

Moghal India, colonial India, and India since independence have all conferred benefits and favours on the upper income groups in society, while all through these ages the poor half of the population has continued in dire poverty and squalor.¹¹

For a long time, even the planners of economic development assumed that the benefits of economic growth would trickle down to impact the lives of the poor. While the vast majority of the population struggles to make ends meet, a small percentage of the population controls the resources of food and security of life. Most of the development programs have heavily tilted towards favoring the rich and the powerful.¹² The much praised and unceasingly promoted globalization agenda has only helped perpetuate this unfortunate and anti-poor trend in South Asian countries. Consequently, even after so many decades since independence, not without so-called valiant efforts at poverty eradication, the destiny of the masses remains that of much misery and desperation.

Many South Asian theologians have rightly denounced structural injustice as the cause of poverty in the countries of the region.¹³ Few will doubt that the South Asian context represents a world that is marred with acute and inhuman poverty, infested with humanly perpetuated unjust religious, political and economic structures. Further, it would not be far from the truth to say that the religiously sanctioned if not ordained caste system with its deep and overarching structures of indignity and injustice institutionalized the problem of poverty and suffering for the vast majority. Notwithstanding the constitutional illegality of caste system (especially its inevitably abominable practice of untouchability) in India, it is still prevalent especially among Hindu community that impacts other communities as well. With insignificant place accorded to this in national discourse of the middle class, the caste system is concealed behind the garb of democracy, yet its pervasive menace is as potent as ever. Thus, George Soares Prabhu concludes about caste system, "Except for *apartheid* in South Africa, which it closely resembles, I know no other system in the world as oppressive and dehumanizing as this."¹⁴

The church in South Asia has generally failed to respond to the context of poverty and suffering, and hence has had to face the condemnation of the theologians in recent years. Aloysius Pieris criticizes the church as the western church in Asia, which lacks the idiom, content and liberating spirituality of Asian religions.[15] The Asian church, shaped and driven by the western model is yet to find her true manifestation as the church of Jesus Christ in Asia. In the concept of mission-compound Christianity, the church developed a Christian life of aloofness and distance rather than involvement and invitation to the world. Thus, Tissa Balasuriya describes the theology of the church as a " theology which is imported from the west, individualistic in morality, socially uncritical, and heavily weighed on the side of the preservation of the status quo. We have a theology in essence, of a certain immobility in which the highest priority has been the building and preservation of the church itself."[16]

Moreover, in the critique of the church the fundamental question about the authenticity of the church in terms of the concern for justice and the God of righteousness of the Bible is raised both as issue of identity and relevance. Based on these twin aspects, the Christian theological task is defined and redefined in poverty stricken South Asia. Thus, Samuel Ryan understands the theological task as a quest for "a just, participatory, inclusive, sustainable society,"[17] while Pieris articulates the same vision in terms of liberation.[18] After the constitution of the Ecumenical Association of Third World Theologians (EATWOT) in 1976, these concerns have been given sharp expression as profound theological issues.

Multi-religiosity: A Distinctive Characteristic of South Asia

The South Asian context thrives with spiritual energies of various faith traditions. The fact of its dynamic and throbbing pluralism of faiths gives the region not only a unique characteristic, but, also makes the reality much more complex and the task of any theological reflection much more challenging. A glimpse of percentage of different religions in South Asian countries will provide the contemporary picture:[19]

	Hindu	Muslim	Christian	Buddhist, Sikh, Parsi	Others
India:	83.3%	12%	2.3%	2.5%	
Pakistan:	3%[20]	97%[21]			
Sri Lanka:	15%	7%	8%	70% (only Buddhist)	
Nepal:[22]	86.2%	3.8%			2.2%
Bhutan:	25%			75%[23]	
Maldives:		100%[24]			

It is not simply the presence of different religions that provides South Asian context a distinctly unique quality but the fact that this region has been a veritable birthplace for so many of the world religions brings a religious sensibility, pervasiveness and spiritual depth hardly found anywhere else in the world.[25] Apart from Hinduism, Buddhism, Jainism, Sikkhism, and tribal religions that originated in South Asia, Islam and Zoroastrianism have been a major part of socio-cultural history of the region for many centuries. In fact, the largest numbers of Muslims are found in South Asia. Even Christian faith has been present in Indian subcontinent for almost as long as Christianity's existence.[26]

The histories of all these religions have had a very interesting and intriguing past and they continue to exert profound influence upon the socio-cultural ethos in addition to decisive impact upon their followers. Hinduism is one of the oldest religions of the world, which developed a very complex philosophical-theological system of God, life, world, and salvation. By and large India and Nepal have been shaped by Hinduism with its millions of gods and goddess, metaphysics, caste systems, world-views, etc. Buddhism, though it originated in India, did not flourish there but became the dominant religion of other Asian countries as it attracted many with its mission emphasizing the principles of asceticism and compassion. Jainism's extreme position on non-violence made it difficult to become a popular religion, yet there are adherents whose religiosity have immense depth of the understanding of the transcendence. Zoroastrian religion is more or less extinct except for the few but wealthy exceptions found in South Asia. Sikkhism has acquired special distinction of its own because of its unrelenting emphasis on equality and community dimensions of religious life. Islam's strong presence has been a result of both the mystic mission from late 7th century and the Moghul invasion in 13th century culminating in the Moghul rule for many centuries. Christianity's presence (excluding the early presence of Syrian Christianity) is primarily due to the mission work of 18th, 19th and early 20th centuries, especially during the considerable length of British colonial rule. Thus, this long history of the presence and interaction of religions has resulted in the deep religious and spiritual roots, which further helped to define their Asianness in a unique way. Unfortunately, it has also led to the palpable tension between religions, e.g., Hindu-Muslim in India, Hindu-Christian in Northern India, Muslim-Christian in Pakistan, lower-caste Hindu and high-caste Hindu, etc. The deep religious consciousness and identity is underlined in the fact that the religious faiths are not only lived out but defended, fought, killed, and died for. The religious world of South Asia then, is dynamic, vigorous and full of ambiguity.

Thus, the theological grammar, idioms, and religious symbols in South Asia are different from that of Latin America, though it shares the struggle against injustice and crippling poverty. Unlike the so-called Christian west, religions in South Asia remain a major influence in people's lives. Its powerful force is to be reckoned with in all aspects of human activity.[27] Thus, emphasizing the synthesizing value of religion in the third world context, Charles Amjad-Ali states that "religion still constitutes the core value for integrating society, providing coherence to their intersubjective activity,....."[28] Thus, when we speak of religions in South Asia, we do not mean some benign and irrelevant reality but rather a highly determining and consequential power.

As with Asia's ocean of poverty, the theologians have also reflected on the reality of pluralism. There are many reasons as to why the issue of plurality of religions has taken the prominent place in the theological debate of our time. The concept of a global village has made it clear that no country or society is an island and consequently emphasized the increasing proximity and interaction of people of diverse backgrounds of the world. Further, the theological urgency as to how Christian faith should understand the place and value of other faiths is felt with increasing intensity. The concern for peace in the world and for the integrity of creation has also led theologians of all religions to address the question of many religions.

More than anything else, for an incarnational faith like that of Christianity, it amounts to a theological mandate to understand itself in the light of, and also in relation to, the soil and surroundings in which it exists. The Christian faith as a missionary religion is always on the move, must be born and rooted in its context of existence. Many theological positions articulated under the paradigm of exclusivist, inclusivist and pluralist positions[29] have been put forth as a way to respond and account for religious diversity. Certainly such attempts have energized the theological articulation of the nature, rationale, mandate, and phenomenon of religious pluralism.

In a world of increasing plurality of faiths, an obvious question for Christianity that will not go away is why Christianity cannot accept such plurality as a matter of course. Arguing against Ramakrishna

Paramhansa's Neo-Hinduism approach to religions as different means to the same goal and John Hick's conclusion of different religions as 'expressions of the diversities of human types and temperaments and thoughts forms,' O. V. Jathanna says:

> To relegate all the differences to the sphere of mere expression, personal disposition, cultural variation and the like is not realistic enough. In a genuine religious conversion, which is not a side-issue but an integral part of all historically founded religions, especially of the non-ethnic type, a person comes to accept a different religion, not as a matter of personal taste, but primarily as a matter of truth and of conviction even at the risk of his or her life.[30]

Thus, the question of truth should remain the most fundamental issue in pluralistic conversation. However, any temptation to arrogance and superiority must be consciously banished as utterly unchristian. The cultural explanation of different religions as different expressions of the same truth will be proved to be inadequate for two reasons: one, all religions arose amidst other religions; and two, at least Buddhism and Christianity flourished in places other than their origin. Even many centuries of co-existence of Hinduism, Buddhism, Islam, and Christianity has not superseded their differences. We agree with O. V. Jathanna when he speaks of Christian faith's obligation to take other religions seriously for the following reasons.[31] First, the Christian faith as the self-communication (revelation) of God is bound to take the issue of truth seriously. Second, rooted in the historical event, i.e., the life, death and resurrection of Jesus Christ, it establishes a particularity for the salvation of the world. Third, Christian faith came into existence amidst other religions and its decisive significance cannot be diluted in present day debate over plurality of faiths. Fourth, the missionary dimension (both in terms of proclamation and praxis), which is integral to Christianity, necessitates reflection over the relationship with other religions of the world.

Faced with positive and powerful faith traditions in which the profound awareness of the mystery and revelation of God is both sublime and salutary, many theologians have found theocentric assertion to the neglect of the Christological particularity most helpful. However, any Christian appropriation of the understanding of God cannot, by definition, avoid Jesus of Nazareth. The central assertion of the Biblical faith tradition is that Jesus is wholly God even though it must at the same time be recognized that he is, with his historical contingencies and particularities, not the whole of God. Nonetheless, the fact of the Christian claim remains that the truth of God can historically be understood only in the facts of the life, death and resurrection of Jesus Christ. Thus, the Christological question is, beyond doubt, at the center of inter-religious relationships. Hans Küng's answer to the question 'what is Christianity' points to this:

> We may distinguish it (Christianity) from the modern humanisms, from the world religions or from Judaism: the distinguishing Christian factor is this Christ, who, as we saw, is identical with the historical Jesus of Nazareth. Jesus of Nazareth is what makes Christianity what it really is.[32]

While Christology is at the heart of Christian assertion, the cross is at the heart of this Christology. It is on this basis the theology of the cross must engage with and facilitate a discussion on relevant and contextual theology in a context of multi-religiousness. Thus, questions such as the following are important: What does it mean to confess Jesus to be the Lord and Savior in South Asia? Is it possible to forsake the theology of the cross for the sake of contextual validity? How does theology of the cross provide resources for doing contextual theology? Why and how can Luther's theology of the cross with its claim of finality remain helpful for Christians in a multi-religious situation? Given the particularities of all religions, Pilate's proverbial question while facing Jesus—what is truth?—(John 18:38) is not to be undermined amidst many claims of truth in many religions. As important as this question is, the philosophical-theological debate over the issue of truth lies outside the scope of this project. However, the normative truth of God understood in terms of Luther's theology of the cross will find serious consideration in this project.

However, speaking of the faith traditions of South Asia only in the general category of religion (the dominant trend in the west) without a careful and critical attention to the ambiguities and complexities both in terms of intra-religious differences and dynamics as well as the inter-religious relationships is to completely misjudge the real nature and possibilities of the issue. In addition, multiple ethnicity and hundreds of languages add to the complexity of the nature of religious pluralism in South Asia. Any pluralistic concern without insights into such complexities will only confuse the matter. The creation of Bangladesh in 1971, to a large extent, can be explained in terms of the power of ethnic and linguistic categories over religious commonalities and unities.[33] The ethnic conflict of Sri Lanka and caste wars between different Hindu communities are other examples of the same dynamics. Moreover, factors like language and ethnicity have direct impact upon the political equation of a country. Thus, D. L. Sheth argues "The state rather than addressing itself to the creation of civil society, becomes largely a mediator of ethnic political equations."[34] Thus, many levels and complex nature of religions in South Asia, should at the very least, keep us from making any easy blanket statement about them.

Related to the challenges of poverty and pluralism of faiths are the issues of conversion and corruption in South Asia.[35] The issue of conversion has been a bone of contention for a very long time. This has found central stage in national debate in recent years in India soon after the murder of an Australian medical missionary in North India in 1999.[36] Even the then Prime Minister of India invited discussion and debate over the issue of conversion. In the debate of pluralism, the issue of conversion remains a major contentious subject, which must not be ignored for the following reasons. Firstly, the presence of large and imposing number of followers of different religious faiths can only be explained adequately in terms of conversion in the past. In fact, this phenomenon is to be recognized to account for steady growth of not only Christianity but also Buddhism and Islam. Secondly, a contextual theology must take this phenomenon into consideration to understand it theologically. Thirdly, within the scope of our study it will be important to investigate the compatibility of conversion with the theology of the cross.

Though Christianity is generally held responsible for a negatively understood issue of conversion; mostly as western conspiracy, it is, by no means, the only missionary religion in this sense. In fact, most other religions owe their growing population to the conversion.[37] This phenomenon is far from over as India witnessed an interesting and rather intriguing mass conversion of Dalits to Buddhism in a rally organized in the heart of the capital city of Delhi as recent as 2001.[38] Thus, any discussion on theology in South Asia can only afford to ignore the issue of conversion at the risk of being naive and ignoring the reality on the ground.

Further, the issue of corruption is seldom taken to be important enough to consider in theological reflection. However, in the light of recent recognition of this phenomenon as alarming and detrimental to the overall health of the countries of South Asia we believe that an exercise in contextual theology will be seriously amiss in ignoring this. The extent of corruption may be gauged by the recent report by Transparency International, which surveyed 146 countries in the world for a corruption perception index. Sri Lanka ranked 67 whereas India and Nepal ranked 90. Pakistan and Bangladesh were found to be two of the most corrupt countries as their ranks were 129 and 145, respectively.[39] Caught in the snares of corruption, the defaming face of the Asian church is only a further warranty for theological inquiry. The institutional model of a hierarchical church and an unbridled power of the bishops and the heads of the church with rare accountability and transparency coupled with an unrepented sense of the self and self-aggrandizement, shows clearly that the church has not been able to withstand the temptation of corruption found in the societies around it.[40] It can be said without hesitation that the problem of corruption has become one of the major crises of the church, which erodes its credibility as the vehicle of God's mercy and truth.

Amidst a context so poignantly marked with complexities of religions, so desperate with crippling poverty, and sinking ethical values manifestly visible in the ever-growing phenomenon of corruption, the challenge for the church is to constantly evaluate both its theological assertions as well as its piety. Many of the studies are one-sided, as they seem to emphasize the importance of Christian identity over against Christian witness and relevance. There are others with just the opposite claims. Though they are all valuable sources for doing theology in South Asia, there is hardly any mention of the theology of the cross in this context and particularly that of Luther's theology of the cross. It is in the light of this that a fresh theological attempt is indeed needed to understand what it means to live a Christian life as well as the meaning of existence of the church in South Asia. Thus, the questions of the identity of Christian faith among many faiths and its relevance amidst the poor are inevitable. In other words, the same questions can be formulated differently: what is the relevant contour of Christianity that is adequate both for a unique identity while remaining truly open to the other who follow a different faith; and how is this perception of the uniqueness to be understood regarding genuine concern for the neighbor who is poor.

In this study two perennial questions are investigated and a response is offered with a definite objective of speaking about a relevant and contextual theology for South Asia today. In order to approach this task, we propose the paradigm of Martin Luther's theology of the cross. The assumption of this study is that Luther's theology of the cross provides an adequate theological epistemology to address the many issues of this region, particularly the reality of many faiths and the poverty of the masses.[41] Thus, it is in the affirmation of the uniqueness and finality of the cross of Jesus Christ that one is truly open to the other and genuinely concerned for the neighbor. This could be realized in thinking of the theology of the cross as theology of the way. As such, we will argue that this stands in sharp contrast to the traditional pluralistic stance in contemporary Christian theology. Yet, the pluralistic concern will seriously occupy our attention within the paradigm of the theology of the cross to argue that the question of how and why religions other than one's own can be given not only legitimate space but also are to be understood in terms of expanding the understanding of the theology of the cross. What paradigm does the theology of the cross afford to develop a contextual theology that will be helpful both to the ones theologizing and to those among whom this is being done? Further, the enforced poverty of the masses challenges our thesis to articulate its relevance for those who are yet to become the subject of God-talk? What resources does the theology of the cross promise for making theology an exercise, which enables one to break free from the bondage of self-centeredness to move to one's neighbor in utter giving?

Conclusion

We have seen both the diverse and complex world of religious faiths as well as extreme and ubiquitous presence of the poor in South Asia. Many factors such as ethnicity and languages are highlighted to be of utmost importance for genuine appreciation and true evaluation of this situation. We have also noted that the issues of corruption and conversion, though, not dealt within theology in any significant way, further intensify complexities in theological reflection and religious sensibilities. The need of a fresh look, hence, is not only desirable but also an imperative to the ongoing process of theological vocation in South Asia. Even a short introduction is adequate to warrant this. Thus, the following theological questions are inescapable: What does the church do with these realities? How does the theology of the church understand them in relation to its existing theology? How and why Luther's theology of the cross could relate to these realities as an integral part of Christian theology? In what way does Luther's theology of the cross with its inherent exclusiveness remain a viable paradigm for contextual theology? Why and how the theological implications of the scandalous nature, vulnerability, and self-criticism in the cross reorient and reshape the theological task?

Our exercise of a fresh look at these issues will hopefully find adequate expression in the exposition and contextualization of Luther's theology of the cross. In many theological attempts at contextualization either the sacramental aspect of Christian faith on the cross (identity) is given precedence over the exemplary dimension of Christ's crucifixion (relevance). Since both of these aspects are indispensable for faith in Jesus Christ of Nazareth, our task is to hold them in dialectical relationship as understood in Luther's theology of the cross. In order to develop a theology in the context of many faiths, which is truly open for the people of other faiths and, in the face of crippling poverty, is genuinely concerned for the welfare of the poor neighbor, this writer assumes Luther's theology of the cross is both adequate and relevant and may provide us some new and fresh insights. Against both the notion that Christianity is inadequate to deal with the phenomenon of religious pluralism in South Asia, as well as against the view that the Christian faith can be relevant without tackling the question of poverty,[42] we defend the thesis that it is in the affirmation of Luther's theology of the cross, with its exclusive claims of God's final revelation in the vulnerability of the cross of Jesus Christ of Nazareth, one is able to be truly open to the other faith as well as become genuinely concerned for the poor people. Thus, this is to be an exercise in exploring and affirming the valuable insights of the theology of the cross in the context of both the complex world of many religions and the many poor. We now turn to the theology of the cross in the history of doctrine, followed by Luther's understanding of the theology of the cross.

A Survey of the Theology of the Cross

Though the significance and centrality of the cross for Christian faith cannot possibly be overstated, yet it is also perplexing to note that theology of the cross, in general, has been on the periphery of theological inquiry in the history of theology. In recognition of this

Douglas John Hall concludes that the theology of the cross is a thin tradition in the history of doctrines.[43] However, there is hardly a theologian who would not consider the importance of the cross for theological reflection. Our task in this section is to survey the major discussions about the cross, and the theology of the cross, in the history of the doctrine as antecedents and precedents to understand Luther's theology of the cross as basis of contextual theology for South Asia.

The theological traditions have always considered the cross and the resurrection of Jesus within the horizon of soteriology. Though there are obvious variations of each theory, the three types cited by Gustaf Aulén remain the most prominent.[44] Seen against the theology of the cross, Luther understands *Christus victor* to be more than a simple soteriological proposition. On this foundation Luther builds a theological structure that would turn the theological thinking upside down to establish the cross as the center of human being's existence.

Though Luther has been the pioneer in terms of making the theology of the cross the basis of all theologies and a measuring rod for all true theologians, the history of the theology of the cross does not begin with Luther. Because of Luther's groundbreaking theological propositions and his enormous influence on subsequent generations of theologians with regard to the theology of the cross, the following discussion will refer to Luther's understanding and interpretation of the theology of the cross as a critical partner in conversation.

Scripture

No other source can replace scripture for the basis of Luther's theology of the cross. As the foundation of the theology of the cross, the word of God determines all aspects of his theology. Any attempt to expound Luther's *theologia crucis* apart from his close reading of the scripture would be bound to fail.[45] Moreover, the scriptural witness provides a foundation in terms of originality, antiquity, and rootedness in Christian tradition. It is during the study of scripture, especially, during the lectures on the psalms and the epistles of Paul that Luther came to discover the radical meaning of the righteousness of God.[46] Consequently, under the power of the newfound mercy of God he would understand themes of grace, faith, gospel, the Word of God in a non-conventional way, which would be fundamental to the content of his theology of the cross.

Paul's Epistles

Paul's understanding of the theology of the cross is based on his assertion found in 1 Corinthians 1: 18-2:5. After his extensive study of Pauline letters, Charles B. Cousar concludes that for Paul "theological reflection begins with the message of the crucified Messiah."[47] The selected verses will bear the truth of Paul's theology of the cross.

1 Corinthians 1:18-2:5 is probably the most succinct exposition of the theology of the cross in Paul's writings. The foundational character of the text is obvious as the message about the cross is said to be foolishness to wisdom-seeking Gentiles (Greeks) and a stumbling block to sign-demanding Jews. It is a stumbling block because it rejects attempts "to logically deduce from sign" any *a priori* understanding of "how God ought to behave in a saving event" or foolishness, "since it rejects all attempts to force a logical system, based on a human interpretation of reality, upon the cross."[48]

Cousar points out four things in this passage. First, all theological reflection begins with the cross.[49] Second, the cross reveals God who does not "look and act as a responsible God ought to look and act."[50] God is known through the shameful and scandalous event of the cross. Third, the message about the cross is to be understood in terms of an event of atonement: "to those who are being saved, it is the power of God" (Corinthians 1:18). Fourth, God's chosen ones, though foolish, weak, low and despised, are to be in the world. Wolfhart Pannenberg states, "The cross does not provide the spiritual power to become independent of the world. That is its weakness."[51]

Further, besides the Corinthians passages there are other Pauline writings that underline Paul's theology of the cross. For example, Roman 3:21-26 becomes the basis of epistemology for Paul[52] and Romans 6:1-11 underlines the connection between Christ's death and crucifixion with baptism and discipleship. Thus, Paul suggests that the cross of Christ for its followers mandates involvement. However, one must remember that Paul's theology of the cross is not theology about the cross but rather a theology of the cross. This would imply that it calls for involvement rather than analysis as it denies any reflection in isolation. Another important aspect of his theology of the cross is that though it speaks of the cross: a symbol of shame, brokenness and death, yet, Paul is speaking of God. Thus, Ulrich Luz resonates with Paul when he asserts that, "Es geht also Paulus in seiner Kreuzestheologie um die Gottheit Gottes."[53] Interestingly, Paul is responding to the crisis of unity among the Corinthians, albeit, Luther's theology of the cross also developed in response to the concrete pastoral and theological situation of 16th century church in Germany.[54]

Understandably, Paul is considered to be the source of much of the theology of the cross. The crucified Christ is the focal point in Pauline writings. Paul's message begins and ends in "we proclaim Christ crucified" (I Corinthians 1:23). No reason exists for boasting other than the cross "by which the world has been crucified to me and I to the world" (Gal. 6:14). This is what Luther found so compelling in Paul and what led him to oppose the rationalism of the scholastics. Ernst Käsemann has concluded that Paul's understanding of the cross is dominated by the concept of justification by faith (Galatians) and the cross as criterion (Corinthians) for authentic living. Käsemann's study is important because he goes beyond the tradition of interpreting the cross as an act of God's love and grace where sin was defeated for good. He perceives in the cross "the divinity of God revealed."[55] Thus, its theological significance is not to be extenuated but rather accentuated. Because of this the cross is not a "chapter in the theology of the Resurrection," but as Käsemann famously puts it, remains always "the signature of the one who is risen."[56]

Luther's indebtedness to Paul is affirmed in Walter von Loewenich's conclusion that "Paul is the father of Luther's theology of the cross."[57] However, one important aspect to note in Paul's theology of the cross is his two seemingly opposing perceptions of the cross: (1) the foolishness for the world, and (2) power of God. Paul distinguishes them at the very beginning of his profound understanding of the cross in relation to the world in 1 Cor. 1: 18. He asserts, "the cross is foolishness to those who are perishing, but to us who are being saved it is the power of God." This is so because the concern for salvation is at the heart of Paul's theology of the cross. And, further, in a world in which the cross stood for shameful and condemned death, Paul speaks of the cross as the power of God.

The Gospels

The significant extent to which the gospel evangelists have treated the passion of Christ clearly establishes its theological importance. The salvific message of the gospels is based on the historical event of the cross. Along with its description of pain and passion of the cross of Jesus of Nazareth, Martin Luther uses the gospel, for example, the *Magnificat* of Luke 1:46-55, as a source for the theology of the cross.

Further, the gospel account not only of how and why Jesus died on the cross is important, but also, how and why Jesus lived is significant in the portrayal of Jesus by evangelists. We will argue for the decisive role of incarnation in the understanding of the theology of the cross in later sections.

Hebrew Scripture

Though the Hebrew scripture does not contain any obvious text pertaining to the theology of the cross, however, there are some important themes that Luther makes use of in his *theologia crucis*. The theme of the hidden and revealed God is fundamental to Luther's understanding of God in his theology of the cross. Luther uses Isaiah 45:15 and Psalm 18:11 to underscore his perception of the hidden God.[58] Further, the theme of suffering servant is related to a passionate God.[59]

Patristic Period

Tertullian

In his polemic with Marcion's understanding of God's impassibility, Tertullian claims that God feels the passions but not in the way that fallen human beings do. He is not affected negatively by these passions. Tertullian is the first one to use the language of *deus crucifixus* in his book *adversos Marcionos:*

Our knowledge of God comes to us from the prophets and the Christ, not from the philosophers or from Epicurus... But well it is that Christians are allowed to believe that God has even died, and yet is alive forever...As you despise a God of that sort I wonder if you do honestly believe that God was crucified *(nescio an ex fide credos deum crucifium)*.[60]

However, he distinguishes between the humanity and the divinity in Christ.[61] In this distinction, he ascribes suffering to the human nature of Christ and claims that the divine nature can suffer only indirectly. His Christological statement provides a clue when he speaks of the Christ as "one living person, but two Things, possessing the attributes and displaying the activities of each several Thing, without confusion of the Things or division of the Person."[62] Tertullian employs *deus crucifixus* language to establish the reality of Christ's sufferings in order to establish the reality of salvation. Thus, for him the sufferings are crucial in that they demonstrate the reality of the human nature in Christ, which is essential if salvation is to be effective. He concludes that "The powers of the Spirit of God proved him God, the sufferings proved there was the flesh of man."[63]

However, Tertullian's intention in using *deus crucifixus* terminology is not to assert suffering in God or God's way of working in such lowly form. The idea of God dying, as referred to earlier, is not pursued further nor developed with any theological implications. Rather, it is a rhetorical flourish to emphasize God's involvement in human experience through incarnation.[64] He expressly repudiates the idea of the suffering of God in the dispute with patripassian Monarchianism, i.e., the claim that the Father suffered with the Son. He opposes Praxeas for crucifying the Father as he retorts with the assertion that "that which was anointed—died, that is, the flesh…Consequently, neither did the Father suffer with the Son."[65]

Clearly, Tertullian's assumption is that God is impassible by nature. Hence, he asserts that if the Father is incapable of suffering, He is incapable of suffering with another.[66] Engaged in responding to Monarchianism's answer to christological and trinitarian questions, Tertullian also establishes his arguments on christological and trinitarian grounds. His typical patristic tendency of distinguishing the natures and ascribing suffering to the human side, and not to the divine side, helps him to protect God from actual suffering and ignominy of the cross. But the same tendency, works against any revelatory function of the cross. It is surprising to see that he uses Jesus' cry of abandonment on the Cross (Mt. 27:46) to illustrate the claim for divine apathy: God did not heed Jesus' cry, he argues, so as to demonstrate his *apatheia*.[67]

How is it possible for Tertullian to claim suffering in God in the argument against Marcion, but deny it so vehemently in the controversy with Monarchianism? T. D. Barnes points out that the key to this contradictory approach lies in his rhetorical training.[68] Barnes further affirms this attitude by giving an example of how when it suits his purpose, Tertullian stresses the prosperity of the Roman world, and other times, for the same reason, he emphasizes the gloomy hardship of life there.[69] Thus, in the same way, Tertullian uses the language of *Deus crucifixus* against Marcion and just the opposite language against Monarchianism for rhetorical reasons and not for any theological reasons.

Hence, instead of a developed theology of the cross it is a rhetorical flourish to emphasize God's involvement through the incarnation in human experience.

The *Deus crucifixus* terminology is not to assert suffering in God nor to indicate that God works through weakness and suffering but to establish the reality of Christ's sufferings and, therefore, the reality of salvation.

Augustine

For Luther, Augustine as true interpreter of Paul carries obvious importance. Augustine reflects on the humiliation of Christ on the cross. Adolf Hamel points out, "The humiliated Christ has frequently been referred to in the *Enarrationes*. It is an essential part of Augustinian Christology and soteriology."[70] Since Augustine has been considered "the doctor of grace," Luther draws on him heavily. The fact that Luther holds Augustine in highest honor is attested by what Luther has to say in the preface to the complete edition of the German theology. He declares that "no book except the Bible and St. Augustine" have taught him more about God, Jesus Christ, and man.[71]

Furthermore, the humiliated Christ is also a self-revelation of God for Augustine. This is a central claim of Luther's theology of the cross. That God is truly revealed in the pain and suffering of Jesus of Nazareth. However, Luther's understanding is different from Augustine. Lienhard argues:

> Luther, like Augustine, does not see the humiliated Christ only from the point of view of a spirituality of the imitation of Christ, but also in the perspective of theology of revelation, the revelation of God hidden in weakness.[72]

Jaroslav Pelikan points out that Luther like Augustine makes a distinction between Christ as sacrament and example but unlike Augustine, emphasized Christ the gift far more than Christ the example.[73] Behind this, the anthropology for both of them is different. Luther does not describe the person though in a state of grace in Augustinian terms as one capable of keeping the law but as one who is still under sin. Thus, Augustine's partly saint and partly sinner is developed into the doctrine of "simultaneously saint and sinner" by Luther.[74]

On many themes, Luther is very close to Augustine. However, he differed from Augustine both in emphasis and content. Augustine found certainty in the authority of the church, while for Luther this authority with regard to magisterium, councils and dogma conflicted with his exegetical and theological understanding. Augustine saw in the church the prophetic sign of the City of God as the instrument to reform the world. Quite contrary, Luther looked to temporal authority for God's reign to reform the church. Moreover, while, the Bishop of Hippo valued religious life over temporal, Luther in his theology of vocations sacralized the secular work of all the baptized.[75]

Medieval Period

We will consider Anselm for his comprehensive treatise *Cur Deus Homo* and Aquinas for his monumental contribution to the medieval theology. Luther as a medieval man will not remain out of the discussion in this section. However, it must be stated early in this section, we will not enter into the comprehensive discussion of Luther's theology of the cross *per se*, instead, our task here is to simply highlight Luther's tendency to depart from the traditional theological understanding in his explication of the theology of the cross. We will also underline the colossal impact that it was to have in later centuries especially for contexts other than that of the west.

Anselm of Canterbury

The most influential of all medieval treatises on the cross was Anselm's *Cur Deus Homo*.[76] In it the cross is described as satisfaction for sin. God humbled himself for his precious creation because human beings had miserably failed and it was not fitting that God's plan for man should be completely thwarted.[77] The cross is the means by which Christ pays to God on behalf of humankind the satisfaction due to him after human sin. It effects the restoration of the original relationship with God. However, it does not reveal much about the nature of God.

On the question of the impassibility of God Anselm is unequivocal. For him the divine nature is impassible and God can only undergo lowliness in human substance that he assumed. Anselm affirms that "without doubt we maintain that the divine nature is impassible... we do not understand any abasement of the divine substance to have occurred in the incarnation of God."[78] He uses the familiar device of the patristic period, the attribution of the suffering of the passion to the human.

Anselm deals with the hiddenness of God in the passion of Christ. He counters the Augustinian view that God hides in the incarnation and crucifixion to deceive Satan. On the contrary, Anselm argues that God is not a deceiver. For him, the hiddenness was unavoidable, not deliberate. He contends:

For you did not assume a human nature in order to conceal what was known about you, but in order to reveal what was unknown about you...The hiddenness was unavoidable, not deliberate. The reason that the event occurred as it did was not in order to be hidden, but in order to be performed the right way...If this event is called concealed then it is called so only because it is not revealed to everyone.[79]

However, there is no real theological significance of the hiddenness of God for Anselm as there was in Luther's theology of the cross. God hid his strength in the weakness of the cross purely because this was unavoidable in attaining the greater purpose of human salvation. Tomlin concludes that for Anselm God's hiddenness is not deliberate whereas for Luther it most definitely is.[80]

Thomas Aquinas

Aquinas' understanding of the cross is very similar to that of Anselm in that it is thought to be a necessity for satisfaction for sin and the notion that dealing with sin was the prime reason for the incarnation. However, Aquinas differs from Anselm in two important respects. First, God could have chosen ways of salvation other than the cross. Thus, cross is contingent and hence devoid of any significant theological content. Christ's suffering is incidental and not essential because God could have used other means for the same purpose. Second, there is a limited use of the concept of the hiddenness of God in the passion of Christ in Aquinas.[81]

On the question of the relationship between divine nature and Christ's passion, Aquinas stands on the basis of his characteristic Chalcedonian Christology.[82] He contends, "the passion is to be attributed to the divine person, not by reason of Christ's divine nature, which is impassible, but by reason of his human nature."[83]

Whereas for Anselm the death of Christ was necessary for the salvation of humanity, Aquinas, on the other hand, stresses the freedom of God. For Aquinas the suffering of Christ was not necessary but fitting. It was fitting because it demonstrated the love of God for people, provided an example of obedience, humility and other virtues. It was also an incentive to stay away from sin and accorded humanity the dignity of the fact that a man overcame death and Satan.[84] This understanding does not reveal anything about the nature of the economy of God but it is just a means to the greater end of salvation. For Aquinas, Christ suffered by virtue of his intimate union with the human nature. Thus, suffering pertains to the divine nature indirectly. In spite of greater subtlety than Anselm in dealing with this, however, Aquinas does not raise theological implications of considerable consequence for the understanding of God. Nonetheless, Janz finds an agreement between Luther and Aquinas as both emphasized the intimate union of human and divine in Jesus Christ.[85] Despite such agreements the presence and absence of the theology of the cross turns out to be decisive for their important different theological assertions.[86]

The foregoing brief survey demonstrates that there was some interest in the *deus crucifixus* among the patristic and medieval theologians. But, they were largely unaware of its profound theological implications for the understanding of God. It may be said that in patristic and medieval theological tradition, the cross was regarded mostly as contingent rather than necessary; incidental for God's nature and not archytypical or characteristic.[87]

At this stage of our study of the development of the theology of the cross, we find that there is a virtual absence of any theology of the cross in the sense of understanding of God. The obvious question as to what contributed to this should be our next discussion. Thus, the following questions are important to consider. Even with the centrality of the cross, detailed depiction of the passion story in the gospels and Paul's central proclamation of the Crucified God, why did the theological tradition not develop theological implications for the understanding of God? What were the theological, cultural and sociological factors which affected this process of medieval understanding? How was Luther's theology of the cross different from the mainline theological tradition? If Luther's theology of the cross was not influenced by this mainline theological tradition, where do we locate Luther's sources?

Two fundamental theological presuppositions can be pointed out as reasons that precluded any possibility of a theology of the cross being developed in the patristic and medieval periods. These presuppositions were so strong and obvious that they were considered to be two central beliefs of the western theological tradition. First was the concept of the impassibility of God and second belief was the two natures doctrine in Christology.

The reason for *apatheia* is to be found in the gospel's interaction with Greek culture. The idea of divine impassibility (*apatheia*) was a Greek philosophical inheritance in early Christian theology. Philo made *apatheia* a major feature of the nature of God of Israel and virtually all Christian theologians took it for granted.[88] Ngien argues:

> ... the denial of divine passibility occurred because of the influence of Greek metaphysics upon the Church's reading of scripture, and that the platonic principle of divine apathy, in particular, held its grip on what many of the fathers believed may or may not be said of God.[89]

The Greek idea was absorbed so uncritically that any tendency that threatened divine impassibility was looked down upon with suspicion. God was always considered beyond passion, emotion, and suffering. This was again an influence of the Greek philosophy. Greek philosophers like Plato, Aristotle, Parmenides, and the Stoics developed an understanding of God as the Absolute monad, self-sufficient, immutable, impassible and static.[90] Further, whenever any suffering was allowed Christ's two natures were put forward to assert only the human Jesus suffered. However, the Greek idea of God's *apatheia* and Christ's *pathos* are irreconcilable is pointed out by Moltmann:

> The platonic axiom of the essential *apatheia* of God sets up an intellectual barrier against the recognition of the suffering of Christ, for a God who is subject to suffering like all other creatures cannot be 'God'.[91]

During the Reformation of 16th century, the tendency to affirm God's impassibility remained the same except in the case of Luther, the Socinians and some Anabaptists.[92] John Calvin apparently assumed the impassibility of God. His conclusion that "Surely God does not have blood, does not suffer, cannot be touched with hands"[93] makes him stand in the tradition of patristic and medieval understanding of God's impassibility. Luther was the only reformer, according to Mozley, who was open to *deus passibilis*.[94] Luther's doctrine of *communicatio idiomatum* provided the most complete reciprocity between the divine and human natures and mutual sharing of attributes.[95] Galen Tinder states that Luther's notion of *communicatio idiomatum* allows him to assert that in Christ, God himself suffered on the cross.[96] He notes Luther's departure from the traditional understanding and concludes that Luther was the most creative among the reformers. He remarks, "This proved an intolerable thought to those of Luther's age who were imbued with the Greek assumption that God is impassible and free of limitation and imperfection."[97]

For Luther the communication occurs both from the human nature to the person and also in between natures themselves. Thus, the suffering of Christ is predicated both of the person of Christ and of the divine nature. God suffered and died by virtue of hypostatic union *via* the *communicatio idiomatum*.[98] Luther understands that the suffering of Jesus and the suffering of God lie in the unity of the personal identity—Jesus, the God-man *in toto*.[99] Thus, one can say that Luther did not define the person of Christ by *a priori* doctrine of God, namely, the Greek divine idea of *apatheia*. Rather, his understanding of the suffering of Jesus on the cross provided the content to his idea of who God is.

We have already noted the tendencies in Luther that were quite different from the dominant theology of the time. We can further note that Luther's theology of the cross led him to deep and far reaching conclusions in the understanding of God. So profound and decisive were Luther's insights for the understanding of God that they were to impact theologians and theologies for generations. However, the main discussion of the theology of the cross will be taken up in the next section.

Modern Period

We will continue to discuss the theology of the cross in modern time for the sake of, first, continuity and second, to understand how it has been understood more comprehensively than in previous eras. The discussion will also help gauge the significant influence Luther's theology of the cross has had on many of the theologians.

In the non-western world the understanding of the cross is fundamentally grounded in the meaning and purpose of Christian living. It is a notable fact that in modern times, the first person to reflect upon the theology of the cross is an Asian, Kazoh Kitamori.[100] Further, interpreting Luther's realism in the theology of the cross, Douglas John Hall states that liberation theology, feminist theology and other contextual theologies are taking cues from Luther's assertion that the theology of the cross calls the thing what it actually is, in order to challenge the status quo that perpetuates the human misery of injustice and poverty.[101] The theology of the cross has proved to be a constant challenge for theology to talk of God in the category of crucified God who experiences the pain and suffering with people.

Kazoh Kitamori

In Kitamori's attempt to engage Luther, we perceive both the much-needed task of rereading Luther, and the relevance of Luther's theology of the cross in Asian context.[102] Unfortunately, his theology has not received as much attention as it deserves. The main thesis of Kitamori's book, *Theology of Pain,* is that pain is the essence of God.[103] Reflecting upon the suffering and misery of Japanese, especially, after the bombings of Hiroshima and Nagasaki in August of 1945, Kitamori refuses the impassibility of God and claims that the pain of God constitutes the core of the gospel. For him, the pain of God is not simply a pain of sympathy nor empathy for suffering people, but, rather a pain in God's very being as God; it is constitutive of Godhead. Thus, he distinguishes his understanding from the liberal viewpoint that sees God's love as general principle of self-sacrifice. Kitamori's understanding of the pain of God is communitarian as he argues that the agony of people caused by the war is a symbol of God's pain.

Though, acknowledging indebtedness to Luther, Kitamori, however, criticizes him for suggesting that the wrath of God is only a "means" of revealing God's love. He states that Luther was aware of the pain of God, yet, failed to adequately relate this to the hidden God.[104] Nonetheless, for Kitamori, Luther remains authoritative and influential: "As Luther is our leader in matters of faith, so he is our leader in matters of *ethics,*"[105] he comments.

However, C. S. Song criticizes Kitamori's insistence on the pain as the essence of God. He contends that there is too much theology and too little salvation for poor sinners.[106] His concern is that when human suffering is seen as the symbol of God's pain, as in Kitamori's theology, then one can legitimately conclude that in order to remain a symbol of God's pain, man must remain in suffering. Because Kitamori's position is based on God's internal struggle of God's wrath against his love, Song raises the critical question "Does this mean that the Cross is a drama of God's own trial and we humans only its spectators?"[107] However, Song seems to have missed Kitamori's point of a deeply passionate God whose love for the world would not let his wrath decide the fate of humanity even though it means pain and suffering for God-self. With regard to Song's criticism about too little salvation, one can raise the question if the rich necessarily have too much salvation? It is a dangerous tendency to see redemption in terms of the category of poverty and richness.

Moltmann recognizes Kitamori's pain of God as healing human pain and Christ's suffering as God's suffering. However, he proposes to take such suggestions further[108] for much deeper reflection. In spite of criticism, Kitamori's theology of the pain of God serves to underline the perennial nature of the theology of the cross being a contextual theology. His theology has been called "the most consciously Japanese of all current theological tendencies in Japan."[109]

M. M. Thomas

The south Indian theologian, M. M. Thomas, is Christocentric in the interpretation of the cross. The cross of Jesus, for him, is revelation of God's love; revelation of the depth of evil in human life; divine forgiveness; and victory releasing power. "The cross reveals God and his purpose for his whole creation as Love...a heart throbbing for all men with understanding, suffering and forgiving love."[110] The main thesis of his theology is the understanding of salvation in terms of humanization. This theme recur in his many writings. In his famous book *The Acknowledged Christ of the Indian Renaissance,* Thomas states that "Christ in his incarnation, passion and resurrection comes to share man's lot to show what it is to be real person and to help all men everywhere in their struggle for a new humanism."[111] His emphasis on action rather than renunciation, love rather than inwardness, and process rather than being, reveals his status as a theologian of *Karma Marga.*[112]

Aloysius Pieris

Sri Lankan Roman Catholic theologian Aloysius Pieris takes Thomas' way of action still further. Pieris calls for 'double baptism in Asian religiosity and Asian poverty' as he understands the baptism of Jesus in Jordan to be an expression of great humility and the second baptism on the cross as something that completes the struggle with the mammon.[113] He argues that Christians should see the cross as Jesus' identification with those who suffer injustice and oppression; as a symbol of struggle against the mammon and as a result of humble option to side with the poor.

Leonardo Boff and Jon Sobrino

In the context of suffering and marginalization in Latin America, Leonardo Boff and Jon Sobrino have articulated the meaning of the theology of the cross. Both emphasize the primacy of orthopraxis over orthodoxy. It is obvious that the vision of orthopraxis is central to their understanding of Jesus Christ and his cross. Moreover, this emphasis becomes a principle for doing theology in Latin American context. This keeps Jesus and his ministry of solidarity and compassion with the poor and suffering at the center and understands Jesus' involvement with those outcastes and marginalized the driving force. Boff argues in his book *Jesus the Liberator* that the preaching of the kingdom of God involves more than a proclamation of the "forgiveness of sins."[114] As the title of the book suggests, Jesus is understood as the liberator who establishes the Kingdom of God. The kingdom of God stands in sharp contrast to the political and economic injustice in Latin America as it inaugurates a new order that transforms the individuals and their structural work with others in society.

Though there are some similarities between Boff and Luther, their basic understanding of the cross is different in the sense that they emphasize two different aspects of this theology. Both Luther and Boff criticize the Roman Catholic Church for their speculative and philosophical tendency. Both uncompromisingly affirm new life and salvation to be found in Jesus, yet they differ in understanding of what it means to believe in Jesus. Boff primarily understands the cross as an example and hence, he is relentless in his arguments for orthopraxis, while for Luther, the cross remains primarily, though not exclusively, a sacrament that shatters all our human acts and efforts if they are not grounded in the confession of faith in Jesus.

Jon Sobrino's book *Christology at the Crossroads*[115] (especially Chapter VI) gives us the clearest picture of his Trinitarian theology of the cross. For him Jesus' death is not simply a death of a martyr or prophet who dies in continuity with their cause. Jesus died in "discontinuity with his life and his cause."[116] He died abandoned by God. His death, then, cannot be understood as "the consequence of world's sinfulness." He died rather in "theological abandonment." On this basis, Sobrino affirms that the death on the cross establishes the theology of the cross as an ongoing critical theology. The cross becomes the nerve center of a liberative hermeneutics, as such a death serves to question all our conceptions of God. Such forsaken death makes it impossible for resurrection to eradicate it. Thus, the cross must function as a critical tool in community. Sobrino criticizes Anselm's development of the theory of vicarious suffering because he thinks it is merely a noetic explanation. While able to make reparation for sins and able to approximate God, this theory, according to him, fails to deal with how God assumes the reality at hand.[117] Thus, it is unable to question the present reality of sin and evil. He concludes that Anselm's God is apathetic, as God remains unaffected by evil. Salvation in this perspective deals with the forgiveness of sins, "overlooking the much broader conception of salvation as the reign of God and integral salvation."[118]

One may legitimately argue that while the difference between Boff and Sobrino and Luther is sharp and critical, yet, a close study of their context and background and different issues at hand in their theological reflection will enable us to perceive that in emphasizing Christ's centrality they are only talking about the authentic way of Christian living and witnessing. However, the question of order and how works are to be initiated and informed by God's initiative is of decisive importance for Luther's theology of cross.

Jürgen Moltmann

Continuing Luther's *theologia crucis* and expanding its meaning to include its inevitable implication for both human liberation and divine nature, Jürgen Moltmann's book, *The Crucified God*,[119] has become the major contribution in this debate. He understands God as the suffering God in the suffering of Christ. God's being is in the suffering and the suffering is in God's being itself. According to Moltmann, although Luther's theology of the cross emphasized the correlation between theory and practice it remained only in the context of critical and liberating practice in preaching and life. He didn't formulate it as social criticism against feudal society.[120] Nonetheless, Moltmann was developing a theology of the cross in the sense and direction of Luther *theologia crucis*.[121]

Like Luther, Moltmann makes the cross, in all its negativity, the basis and criterion of Christian theology, "the test of everything that deserve to be called Christian."[122] Thus, for Moltmann, the theology of the cross is the only frame of reference to talk about both God in relation to its Trinity and humans in relation to God, one another, and nature.[123]

Conclusion

There are many important developments that we noted in our discussion above. We have seen that the theology of the cross before Luther has been understood as a vicarious suffering of Jesus Christ. The soteriological implications have been an integral part of understanding of the cross across generations, which found new and innovative interpretations in modern times. We also noted that because of the impassibility of God as *a priori* concept of God, theologians before Luther did not understand the theological implications of the theology of the cross. It is clear that before the Reformation, the cross remained a mere means, sometimes even expendable means, to achieve salvation and a mere example to follow to attain God's favor.

With Luther's theology of the cross the passion and the cross was established as God's true revelation which has since been exploited to articulate the pathos of God and its implications both for the understanding of who God is and what authentic Christian living is. Against this background of discontinuity and continuity of the theology of the cross, we will study Luther's *theologia crucis* in depth.

Further, the epistemological implications and contextual nature of the cross were noted for continued relevance of this theology especially beginning with Luther. But above all, in modern times the theology of the cross became a profound way to talk about God. The crucified God, to which Moltmann refers as a 'monstrous phrase,'[124] found the center of sustained theological reflection to understand the depth of what it means to conclude: 'only a suffering God can help.' It is clear that the context of pain and suffering of modern time (in most cases humanly perpetrated), gave rise to a daring conceptualization about the nature of God who broke away from Greek philosophical straight jacket of impassibility to be a God who not only understands and empathizes with those who suffer, but, in fact, suffers with and for the sake of them.

Luther's *theologia crucis,* we noted, provided initial redirection for such bold theological assertions about the nature of God, which was taken further by those who followed him. We will see in Luther's unrelenting insistence on the cross of Jesus Christ as the only place for God's revelation to note both soteriological and epistemological implications. The cross and resurrection are more than the means of salvation; they have become the paradigm of salvation.[125] These emphases will find further sustained reflection in later sections when we discuss the prominent interpretations of the theology of the cross. Presently, however, we turn to Luther's *theologia crucis* proper.

CHAPTER 2

Luther's Theologia Crucis

Background

Before undertaking any elaborate discussion of *theologia crucis*, it will be helpful for us to situate Luther in his immediate context of theology and spirituality. For this, we turn to Luther's context to note both its origin and development. Though Luther found no precedents in the medieval scholastic theology for his theology of the cross, he was not completely without resources. Instead of scholastic theology, which Luther rejected, we will discuss the medieval spirituality to find some clues to understand Luther's theology of the cross in the context of his personal spiritual struggle.

Amidst a life of immense stress and doubt about the certainty of salvation, Luther continued to struggle with the justice and righteousness of God. Even with his extremely austere life as a monk Luther was not sure if he qualified for God's grace sufficiently to be saved. He was alone in living this spiritual dilemma in piercing pain and agonizing spirit, yet he was not without resources of the time. Luther found resources in popular piety.[126] We will underline the influence from two quarters: first, humanism and second, mysticism.

Just like humanists of the time, Luther also insisted upon returning to the original sources. Luther's call to return to the original sources was for understanding the reality of life. Alister McGrath states that the humanist slogan, "back to the sources," indicated for Luther more than a simple return to ancient texts. It also represented "a call to return to the essential realities of human experience as reported in these literary sources."[127] Sharing humanism also meant that Luther distanced himself from scholasticism. However, unlike other humanists who turned to Cicero after rejecting scholasticism, Luther turned to the scripture.[128]

The impact of mysticism on his theology of the cross was obvious. Hence, a brief discussion will show some striking similarities in the direction of the theology of the cross.

Bernard of Clairvaux

Bernard of Clairvaux (1090-1153) influenced Luther significantly in his early years. Commenting on Psalm 118 (119): 45 in his first lecture on the Psalms (1513-5), Luther speaks of Bernard approvingly while speaking a language that was to mark his theology of the cross of the later years:

> He [God] crucifies and kills, so that he may revive and glorify. Thus he does a work that is foreign to him so that he may do his own work (Is. 28:21). As blessed Bernard correctly said, the divine consolation is delicate and is not given to those who grant access to an alien one. Therefore you must be... found entirely in the cross and judgments on the old man if you want to walk at large according to the new man.[129]

Moreover, Bernard's reference to the incarnation and crucified Christ and his emphasis on the sufferings of Christ seem to be in line with Luther's *theogia crucis*. Jaroslav Pelikan underlines Bernard's emphasis:

> "What," he could ask, "is so effective for the healing of the wounds of conscience and for the purification of the intention of the soul as constant meditation on the wounds of Christ?" The "wounds of the savior" were the only refuge of the weak and weary, his passion "the last refuge and the only remedy." The faithful soul could enjoy the presence of Christ and could look forward in the hope to the vision of the glory of God by glorifying in the ignominy of the cross.[130]

The emphasis on the suffering and Christ's passion as the only remedy clearly converge in the thoughts of Bernard and Luther. However, Luther distanced himself from Bernard when his Catholic opponents began to use Bernard in their favor. Lohse argues that this distance was caused partly from a growing awareness that the difference between the two was theological rather than spiritual and on issues like monastic vows, the role of Mary, creation and justification, and the mass.[131] One of the main reasons why many scholars see Bernard of Clairvaux's influence upon Luther is his sermons on the Song of Songs. Luther quotes from this and it clearly shows not only Luther's affirmation of what Bernard wrote but also his indebtedness to him.

Bernard's cross-centered piety recapitulates Augustine's understanding of the cross as both *sacramentum*, which provides forgiveness, and *exemplum*, which is also an example to follow.[132] The cross of Christ is portrayed as highly beneficial and it teaches that the penitent should meditate constantly on this and especially when one is troubled and anxious.[133] It is hard to miss the similarity with Luther while reading sermon 61 which refers to Exodus 33:22-23 where God allows Moses a view of his back. The sermon exhorts to imitate God in the humility and lowliness of Christ and warns against any imitation of God in his glory and majesty.[134] Bernard is emphatic about God's revelation in this lowly form of Christ and says that this provides the precise example for the church and Christians to follow.[135] Thus, Graham Tomlin concludes "it is striking how many of these themes recur in Luther's developing theology of the cross. Luther's preoccupation with the cross in the years 1515-1519 echoes Bernard's cross-centered piety."[136]

Nicholas of Cusa

Nicholas of Cusa (1401-1464) was a German cardinal and Luther came to know about him through the writings of Stapulenis. Nicholas's theme of "simultaneity of opposites" is reflected in modified form in Luther's teaching about *simul justis et peccator* and in the revealing concealment of God in incarnation. However, Gordon Jensen points out that there is a major difference between Cusa and Luther as Cusa does not hold two contradictory forms can exist simultaneously in the same person.[137]

Jacobus Faber Stapulenis

Further, Jacobus Faber Stapulenis (c.1455-1536), a Roman mystic, had spoken of a descent into hell as necessary while following Christ. Other themes such as *via contrarii* of salvation, the emphasis on *humilitas*, and *Deus absconditus sub contrario* were, for him, related to the theme of decent to hell. These themes were "aspects of a general theological motif that Luther was later to refer to as a *theologia crucis*."[138] Another important aspect of Stapulenis' thought that reverberated in Luther was emphasis on the centrality of Christology. Lage points out:

> Stapulensis' exegesis of scripture was dominated by Christological concerns. His purpose was to reveal the paradigmatic figure of Christ, which he held was hidden throughout scripture, in even the most unlikely places. He attempted to

delineate fully the form of Christ for the purpose of devotion and imitation.[139]

However, Luther differed from Stapulensis in how he understood specific themes. He agreed with Stapulensis with regard to the theme of the decent to hell, yet, he insisted that imitation of Christ did not save a person. In other words, for Luther, the decent to hell was not an act of merit.[140] German mystic Johannes Tauler (ca. 1300-1361) provides a hint of *sola gratia*, which became central in Luther's theology.[141] The emphasis on the cross is not only clear but also forceful as Tauler argues for the necessity of confronting the cross of Christ in his sermons. He exhorts people to find the cross in trials and temptations rather than in the full bloom of sentimental emotion. And further, he says that we must always carry the cross and it is by the cross we follow God.[142] However, Luther finds Tauler's idea of synteresis, the *resignatio voluntaris*, etc., incompatible with his understanding of grace.

Johannes von Staupitz

Luther shared the theme of Christology with another mystic named Johannes von Staupitz (1468-1534). During Luther's struggle with an extremely disturbed conscience, Staupitz helped him to see Christ's suffering. By pointing to Christ's suffering, Gordon Rupp suggests, Staupitz laid some of the groundwork for theology of the cross:

> That Staupitz directed him towards the "wounds of Jesus" meant that Luther was turned towards the most tender theme of medieval devotion, and along the road which would lead to his own "Theology of the Cross."[143]

Staupitz advised Luther to face his struggles directly and counseled him to head straight into darkness, relying on scripture and thus, God's promise. Lage points out that mere meditation on the cross of Christ was not adequate for Staupitz; of much more importance was that it must become the center of a Christian life as it was central to the life of Christ.[144] The theme of *Anfechtung* plays an important role for Staupitz. Oberman recognizes this:

> Staupitz did not help the frightened monk by simply giving him the confessional counsel that came to his mind; he spoke out of the fullness of experience. The theology of temptation was his specialty.[145]

Thus, it is quite obvious that there were many themes in the medieval scholastic mysticism that found echoes in the theology of the cross. Such is the prominence of similarities between Luther and mystics that Lage has concluded that the *theologia crucis* of Luther was derived from the penitential affective mysticism of Staupitz and Stapulensis.[146] However, it would be premature to draw such a conclusion especially in the light of crucial differences with radical theological consequences of which the mystics were largely unaware of. Thus, Lienhard contradicts their conclusion by saying "Luther goes beyond the piety and theology of the imitation of Jesus. He returns to the theology of the incarnation of the early church."[147] Further, the failure to capture the theological implications of the incarnation by the mystics is quite pronounced while studying them vis-á-vis Luther's theology of the cross. This means that very little is said about the incarnation as the self-revelation of God. Most of the mystics emphasize a theology of ascent—human attempt to ascend into heavens to be united with God. This is in direct contradiction to an incarnational theology, which stresses that such union is possible only when God comes down to earth to dwell with humans.[148]

Another significant difference between Luther and mystics is that while mystics considered Christ to be primarily an example, Luther's insistence is that Christ the sacrament precedes Christ the example.[149] Luther's concern was theological as he argued that though the imitation of Christ is important, it must not be the basis for justification. Thus, Iserloh notes that Luther confronted two dangers in the development of his theology of the cross. First, Luther had to avoid a speculative form of mysticism that overlooked the incarnation; and second, medieval piety, which focused on the imitation of Christ and neglected it as sacrament.[150]

Martin Luther's *Theologia Crucis*

In this section, we propose to examine the articulation and development of Luther's theology of the cross on the basis of the key texts. However, we must also admit that this exercise is not an exhaustive treatment of the reformer's life and thought. Given the vastness of Luther's own writings and the literature on Luther studies we want to emphasize the limitation. Next, the goal in this dissertation is to study Luther's theology of the cross from the holistic perspective in order to prove it as a viable resource for theological construction in South Asian context.

Despite some definite precedents for Luther's theology of the cross in medieval era, it would not be an exaggeration to state that the theology of the cross brought about the reformation of 16th century Europe. This fact will be verified as we will discuss how Luther's opposition to the practice of indulgences led him to explicate, clarify, defend and justify his theology which he called the theology of the cross, in contrast to the theology of glory. While the theology of the cross seems to have been overshadowed by other prominent themes in Luther research, yet it is hardly debatable that Luther's theology was founded in the theology of the cross. This is why Luther can say "*CRUX sola nostra theologia.*"[151]

As indicated earlier, we have set out to show the resourcefulness of Luther's theology of the cross for contemporary South Asia. Although it would seem out of place to draw similarities between the period of the Reformation of the 16th century and the South Asian context of today, yet it may provide some clues to understand the implications of Luther's theological assertions in his time as well as that of ours.

We must acknowledge that Europe during Luther's time differed quite radically as it did not face the living religions of the world, nonetheless, in this comparison we can actually highlight semblances of apparent similarities. First, we have emphatically emphasized in the earlier chapter, that South Asia presents a situation of plurality of faiths. A further distinction of such a situation is that people of many faiths found in South Asia are, in fact, willing to die for the sake of their faith.[152] In this regard Roland H. Bainton describes a situation during the Reformation not so different from that of contemporary South Asia when he says, "The 16th century was an age of faith... In the Period of reformation men were ready to die and kill for religion, to divide families and to disrupt kingdoms rather than renounce the truth of God."[153] Second, like Martin Luther in his time, many in South Asia are in a deep search for salvation. Third, rituals, religious rites and pilgrimage which are everyday part of South Asian religiosity, also remind us of the religiosity of Luther's day, centered on the similar acts of piety. Fourth, the abuse of religious hierarchy is also not beyond recognition in both situations. While the sale of indulgences ensured easy money for the church before the reformation, so also the church in South Asia is not beyond the tentacles of corruption.[154] The sale of the indulgence and its basis on the penance system of the time underlined a crisis for Luther with regard to the way of salvation, whereas faced with the plurality of faiths and acute poverty, the church in Asia is experiencing no less a crisis of identity and relevance. Fifth, the dominating religious hierarchy is something that religions in South Asia share with 16th century Europe.

In such a world of medieval piety, Martin Luther's theological quest was how to find the certainty of salvation. His entry into the monastery as a monk was "in order to assure himself of his salvation."[155] His deeply troubled conscience did not find rest despite his extreme steps in living the ascetic life of a monk. In the face of the awful presence of the holy and just God, Luther was never sure that he had done enough to earn God's grace. Instead, Luther later admitted that he hated the justice and righteousness of God. While in the monastery Luther subjected himself to rigorous study as well as incessant confession of faith.[156]

Apart from studying Peter Lombard's *Sentences* and Gabriel Biel's *The Canon of Mass*, he also immersed himself in the Biblical text. He encountered an angry God and a judgmental Christ in Biblical narratives. Extremely terrorized, Luther could not even look at the crucifix for it represented judgment and punishment.[157] Unable to confess all his sins before God, he was spiritually paralyzed and plagued by a conscience that incessantly reminded him that he was unable to satisfy the judgmental Christ or wrathful God. His study of the scholastic texts and even his ordination into the priesthood failed to alleviate the affliction of the conscience he described as *Anfechtung*.[158]

However, Luther finally found the evangelical meaning of the phrase "the righteousness of God" and came to realize that the righteous will live by faith alone (Roman 1: 17). Luther was led to this new meaning as he read the scripture Christologically. The evangelical perception of God's way developed in Luther a sharp, perceptive, and critical insight into human nature and the Church's distorted way of relating God's graceful way. As a consequence Luther found the practice of indulgences in the church too contradictory to the meaning of righteousness of God not to condemn. Thus, he criticized the lucrative practice of selling indulgences.

The Context of Penance and Indulgence

Luther's opposition of the practice of the sale of indulgences is significant for several reasons. First, it shows how Luther's theology is changed because of his evangelical discovery. Second, it proves that Luther was a contextual theologian as he responded to the issue of the day that affected people adversely both financially and spiritually. Third, opposition to indulgence, in final analysis, shows his spiritual courage to take on the ultimate authority of the day, i.e., the papacy. Fourth, it reveals Luther's deep sense of responsibility both as pastor and teacher of the church. Fifth, it is in opposing the practice of indulgences that Luther began a process of disputation and theses, in defense of which his basic pattern of *theologia crucis* finds substantial expression. Sixth, in his vehement opposition to it, Luther speaks of a theologian of the cross. Thus, the issue of indulgences deserves more than a passing comment in our dissertation.

The sale of indulgences became the issue against which Luther reacted and unknowingly began the reformation of the church. Indulgences were introduced in the church in the eleventh century in order to raise funds for the crusades. At the beginning, it was a part of Roman sacrament of penance understood in different phases of contrition, confession, absolution and satisfaction. Indulgences removed the burden of the temporal punishments that the church laid upon the penitent for the remission of his or her sins. However, within a very short time this religious practice was abused to serve the most unreligious purposes of the hierarchy of the church of the time. Bernard Lohse provides a glimpse of this abuse:

> The practice of selling indulgences was of immense significance for the financial structure of the church. Indulgences were one of the major sources of income that the papal state required to meet its strong need for money and the finance the many wars in which the papacy was involved. The curia also needed the income from the sale of indulgences to finance its luxurious life style.[159]

Luther's pastoral heart and responsibility, informed by his newly found understanding of the righteousness of God, compelled him to respond to the growing phenomenon of indulgences. This is seen in his publication of *Sermon on Indulgences and Grace* in German[160] in which he advises people against indulgences. Intent on gaining economically the popes issued jubilee indulgences. The succeeding popes shortened the duration for Jubilee and expanded the scope of the indulgence just in order to make more money.[161]

As is obvious, the economy of indulgences spelled a regular means of income and the politics of indulgence reinforced church hierarchy's illegitimate power over laity. Though, the economy and politics of indulgences was critical for inviting Luther's attack, yet, the heart of the problem was spiritual. The crux of the matter was how one is saved. This is right in Luther's alley of dark and disturbing spiritual struggle. However, Luther had seen the light of salvation. His Christocentric understanding of God's gift of salvation in Jesus Christ led him to deny any other way to salvation. So convinced was Luther about the scriptural veracity of this that he denied other proffering of salvation any validity. Thus, indulgences were not acceptable. Grimm interprets Luther's understanding and critique of indulgences in following way: "Therefore, the sale of indulgences was leading people into a false security with respect to salvation."[162] What is at the heart of this debate will lead Luther to a process that will eventually become a roadmap for the development of the theology of the cross.

Luther found the practice of indulgences against the teaching of the scripture. Moreover, he concluded that it rivaled the only way to salvation which was in and through Jesus Christ. Since all other sermons had to be stopped to provide opportunity to the indulgence preachers for the sake of best possible spiritual and financial return, Luther considers in it "a direct competition between the preaching of the gospel as such and the preaching of indulgence."[163] The multi-layered abuse of the means of salvation in the church was especially heart breaking for Luther as he visited Rome with hopeful idealism. Realities at Rome, however, testified to the contrary. Justo Gonzalez states Luther's reaction:

> Luther saw the abuse into which relics and other means of attaining merit had fallen. He had arrived at Rome full of hope and faith; he left with a painful doubt that the means of salvation offered by church were indeed valid—and this is the first indication that we have that he allowed himself to doubt the established doctrine of his time.[164]

Finally, Luther "found and declared the Church's way of salvation to be vain."[165] Luther had a series of crisis that pushed him into a situation of desperation. "It was after his first celebration of the Mass that Luther began to have serious doubts concerning his own righteousness and the monastic life as the surest means for finding salvation."[166] Thus, he began a search with this theological question, the answer to which will impact directly our own study.

Luther's new-found understanding about the truth of the righteousness of God[167] and his sensitivity towards his pastoral role for the people under his jurisdiction compelled him to challenge the indulgence party. However, the indulgences were not part of any simplistic pattern of offering salvation. Yet, Harold J. Grimm argues that though the church had developed a system to distinguish between eternal punishment and temporal punishment so that most uneducated people believed that "they could actually buy their salvation."[168] In the ultimate analysis, the core of the controversy was salvation. James Atkinson correctly concludes that Luther "saw all the scandals and abuses of Christendom as consequences of the rejection of the truth of salvation in Christ alone in favor of a works religion."[169] Soon this opposition led Luther to explicate his evangelical theology in a more comprehensive way. Luther was responding to the practice and system of indulgences in the church. It was the context of Luther's ministry that gave rise to his theological assertions. In this sense, Luther was also a contextual theologian whose work will be applicable in any contextual theological construction.[170]

The issue of salvation is at the heart of the indulgence controversy is attested by what Luther argues for and against in *Ninety-five Theses, 1517*[171] and *Explanation of the Ninety-five Theses, 1518*.[172] Besides these two texts we will also discuss the *Heidelberg Disputation*, 1518; *The Magnificat*; and the *Church Postils*. However, the discussion will not be restricted to these texts; nonetheless, they will offer primary texts to develop Luther's understanding of the theology of the cross.

In the following discussion of Luther's theology of the cross, our intention is to explicate it to underline the thesis that it is in the affirmation of the finality and uniqueness of Jesus Christ as expressed in Luther's theology of the cross that one is truly open to the other and genuinely transformed to serve the neighbor. In order to establish this, we propose to argue that Luther's theology of the cross is a theology of revelation of God for salvation; a theology of God's vulnerability; a theology that renders human beings completely powerless in achieving salvation; theology of the cross is a theology of the incarnation; is a theology of faith; and Luther's theology of the cross is a theology of the proper order of Christ as sacrament and example.

The Ninety-five Theses

These theses, which Luther hung on the door of the castle church on October 31, 1517, were the first occasion in which he confronted the practice of the sale of the indulgence. In opposing the indulgence, Luther speaks of themes and subjects that were to find thorough and sustained reflection in depth, comprehensiveness and crystallization in texts such as *Heidelberg Disputation* and others. In the *Ninety-five Theses*, he argues against indulgences, papal authority, and for the right attitude in life and genuine source of salvation. Though originally intended for scholarly debate,[173] as it was written in Latin and not in German, it was, however, soon translated into German, which helped it spread like wild-fire. The widespread public response to these theses proved that Luther had touched the very basic issues of the contemporary church and the issues troubling the Christian believers.

Interestingly, Luther was both critiquing the laity for purchasing indulgences as well as arguing against any legitimate theological basis for indulgences. Even before publishing the *Ninety-five Theses*, Luther had warned his parishioners against indulgences.[174] Soon Luther recognized a deeper malaise in the sale and purchase of indulgence. The problem was a profound theological one. His theses were the first organized attempt to deal with the problem. As he dealt with the misleading theology of indulgences, it is important to note that this whole exercise is based on Luther's "zeal for truth" and his "desire to bring to light" the truth.[175] This truth is to be recognized in his insistence that salvation is possible not by indulgences but by Jesus Christ and his merits alone.

However, indulgences themselves were not attacked, as seen from thesis 72 and 73 of *Ninety-five Theses*. Yet, Luther's opposition cannot be clearer: "Those who believe that they can be sure of their salvation because they have indulgence letters will be eternally damned, together with their teachers."[176] However, Luther did not deny the validity of the indulgences as yet, as they had grown out of the sacrament of penance; nonetheless, it contained remarks and comments, the logical consequence of which would be nothing less than a new beginning of understanding of all religious issues of the time. However, we should underline at this point that behind Luther's many theses, disputations, writings, sermons, letters, etc., lay his experience of "breakthrough" about the true meaning of the righteousness of God. E. Gordon Rupp and others recognize the dynamic and revolutionary impact of this as it evolved through Luther's writings.[177] It was as if he was able to see practices and principles of faith from the perspective of the righteousness of God so clearly that he could not help contradicting apparent abuses and erring teaching. With every conflict and disputation his opposition became stronger and his theological proposition sharper.

The first thesis in *Ninety-five Theses* declares Luther's foundational understanding about the concept of repentance. He asserts, "When our Lord and Master Jesus Christ said, 'Repent' [Matt. 4:17], he willed the entire life of believers to be one of repentance."[178] His very first thesis of the disputation provides the orientation and attitude not towards the practical problem of indulgences, but more importantly towards life itself. As a result, the comprehensiveness of its scope is established. Grimm says that this "embodies the core of all the others, namely, that penance is not a mechanical act but a permanent inner attitude."[179] It is not hard to see that a life-long attitude of repentance is related to the recognition of one's status in relation to God. Further, this introductory thesis suggests the communal nature of repentance. Luther is calling all believers to repentance. The fact that Luther is calling for repentance underlines the reality of the sinfulness of humanity. And if he calls for a life-long attitude of repentance, it could only mean the life-long pervasiveness of sin in human life. Luther's theology of the cross assumes this biblical reality.[180] Hence, it is important to note the church, i.e., the body of believers, is to have such a posture of repentance throughout her life. In the *Explanations to the Ninety-five Theses,* Luther links the "life of repentance" and the "cross of repentance"[181] for a life-long orientation. Thus the fact of human depravity must be acknowledged if Luther's theology of the cross is to have any meaning and relevance.

Again in his *Explanations of the Ninety-five Theses,* Luther contrasts the pope against the promise of Christ. He argues that "For it is not because the pope grants it that you have anything, but you have it because you believe that you receive it. You have only as much as you believe according to the promise of Christ."[182] Thus, there is no doubt that Luther's concern was with salvation. In denying any efficacy to the indulgences, Luther's main contention in these theses is that salvation cannot be earned by doing works, including purchasing indulgences. Instead, he argues, "The true treasure of the church is most holy gospel of the glory and grace of God."[183] The decisiveness of the element of faith and certainty of the promise of Christ is not to be missed in this. Though not yet completely against the pope, Luther, nevertheless, does not frown from casting aspersions on and implicating the pope and his wealth by challenging him to build the basilica of St. Peter with his own wealth, which is "greater than the wealth of richest Crassus."[184]

The indulgences, though promoted and protected by the papal church, remain for Luther merely a means to fleece the poor and hence meets with his strong denunciation and ridicule. As much as these theses repudiate the practice of indulgence for religious, economic, and hierarchical reasons, they, above all, prove Luther's application of his evangelical discovery that there is nothing one can do with regard to salvation, which is sheer gift of God. Thus, Luther denounces the security of the indulgence, "It is vain to trust in salvation by indulgence letters, even though the indulgence commissary, or even the pope, were to offer his soul as security."[185] Further, Luther exposes the doctrine of the hawkers of indulgences as human doctrine and hence, utterly against the doctrine of God. Theses 27 and 28 declare:

27. They preach only human doctrines who say that as soon as the money clinks into the money chest, the soul flies out of purgatory.[186]

28. It is certain that when money clinks in the money chest, greed and avarice can be increased; but when the church intercedes, the result is in the hands of God alone.[187]

Disgusted at the indulgence party's obsession with money and its misuse for a life of self-indulgence, Luther is challenging their concept of God. God is neither about extracting money from the believers nor is God about transacting grace. Quite opposite to this, Luther contrasts the certainty of increased greed and avarice due to money with the humble trust in God. He declares the 'indulgence party' to be the "enemies of Christ" because of the practice of giving preference to the preaching of indulgences over against "the preaching of the Word of God."[188] Such strong language of Luther is to be understood in the light of general reference to the Turks as the enemies of Christ and his cross.[189] Luther's denouncing declaration is a sure sign of his deep anguish and indignation at the 'commercialization' over as central an issue as salvation.

The *Ninety-five Theses* contains the most important theme of the theology of the cross namely, Christ and his benefits.[190] It is true that Luther is arguing mostly against the legitimacy of the indulgence and papal authority in these theses, the basis of his opposition, however, is Christ and his benefits understood according to the theology of the cross. His theology of the cross is further explicated in *Explanations of the Ninety-five Theses,* in which Luther contrasts this with the theology of the glory. After arguing how "the righteousness of Christ and his merit justifies and remits sins,"[191] Luther brings it to a climax in the sharp contrast between the theology of the cross and theology of glory:

> ..., so that whoever does not take up his cross and follow him, is not worthy of him [Matt. 10:38], even if he were filled with all kinds of indulgence. From this you can now see how, ever since the scholastic theology—the deceiving theology (for that is the meaning of the word in Greek)—began, the theology of the cross has been abrogated, and everything has been completely turned up-side-down. A theologian of the cross (that is, one who speaks of the crucified and hidden God), teaches that punishments, crosses, and death are the most precious treasury of all and the most sacred relics which the Lord of this theology himself has consecrated and blessed, not alone by the touch of his most holy and divine will, and he has left these relics here to be kissed, sought after, and embraced.[192]

The Christ as the sole treasure is further pitched against what a theologian of the glory does in the name of a false God:

> ... the theologian of glory still receives money for his treasury, while the theologian of the cross, on the other hand, offers the merits of Christ freely. Yet people do not consider the theologian of the cross worthy of consideration, but finally even persecute him. But who will be the judge of these two, in order that we may know which one to listen to? Behold Isaiah says, chapter 66 [:4], "I will choose what they ridicule." And in Cor. 1 [:27] states, "God chose what is weak in the world to shame the strong, etc."[193]

In comparison, it is clear that the theologian of the cross seeks punishment, cross, and suffering whereas the theologian of glory avoids them. On the one hand, the theologian of the glory is interested in making money, and on the other, the theologian of the cross offers the merits of Christ freely.

Clearly, by the time he wrote *Explanations of the Ninety-five Theses* (1518), Luther had expounded his theology of the cross in *Heidelberg Disputations* (1518), which by necessity of the logic of its theology enabled Luther to continue to denounce indulgences to replace it with the only security for the soul of people, i.e., the merit of Christ perceived in his suffering and death. Hence, Carl W. Folkmer says in the introduction to the *Explanations of the Ninety-five Theses* that "In explaining his theses Luther now applied his newly developed 'theology of the cross,' already enunciated in *The Heidelberg Disputation,* and challenged the authority of the church."[194] Though, it should be noted that at this time Luther still believed that "everything the pope does must be endured."[195] Many themes of the *Ninety-five Theses* were to be given much sustained and systematic treatment in the *Heidelberg Disputation.*

The Heidelberg Disputation (1518)

Now, we turn to the *Heidelberg Disputation* (1518),[196] which is generally considered to be a fundamental text for the theology of the cross. One reason is that it is in this document that Luther uses the term *theologia crucis* and "theologian of the cross" a couple of times —of the few times he used it in his entire life.[197] However, the second reason for the significance of the theses of *Heidelberg Disputation* is that as a corollary to what preceded, namely Luther's critique of the indulgences, and church authority, it provided Luther with an opportunity to present his evangelical faith.

As *Heidelberg Disputation* was written to clarify Luther's stand on the controversy over *Ninety-five Theses*, it is not a simple attack but was more of a programmatic vision of Luther's evangelical theology. And hence, it occupies a more significant place than the *Ninety-five Theses*.[198] However, it must also be remembered that the *Heidelberg Disputation* was occasioned by the controversy started by the *Ninety-five Theses*. Hence, instead of separating them, these two texts should be read in consultation with each other.

Following the turn of events, this was Luther's chance to explain, expound, and clarify his theology as forcefully and persuasively as possible, both for those who seemed to follow Luther and also against those who opposed him. Further, this was also, in some sense, a climactic writing in a series of his writings during 1518, which bore the marks of theology of the cross.[199] Thus, it is a document, though written in a highly polemical context, remains a product of "sustained reflection on the theme" and hence, invites a serious and systematic response.[200]

On 26 April 1518, Luther presided over the opening disputation of the Chapter of the Augustinian Order at Heidelberg. Luther had prepared a series of theses for the disputation, which took place at the invitation of Johannes von Staupitz. In the course of these theses, the main elements of Luther's emerging *theologia crucis* became clear.

The context of the *Heidelberg Disputation* should provide us some clue as to what Luther was trying to do. Unlike the *Ninety-five Theses* Luther here had an opportunity to explain his fundamental evangelical theology in much more organized and programmatic way. At the same time, as a faithful teacher of the church, Luther was responding to the prevailing religious ethos in the light of the word of God. He found many beliefs and practices in the church that were not only inconsistent with the scripture they were downright opposite to it. Such malaise in the church was being bred by the scholastic theology of the time, which had given rise to popular cults, saint worship, pilgrimages, penances, pardons, indulgences, paid masses, trinkets, shrines, images, etc. They were not only many practices of contemporary religiosity but were understood as different means to attain God's favor and thus were means to salvation. Therefore, they were issues of grave concern for Luther. With his theology of the cross Luther knocked down these pseudo and spurious ways to salvation. On biblical and theological grounds he refused anything in scholastic theology any validity whatsoever for salvific significance. Instead, he asserted that the theology of the cross is the only way to God and hence to salvation. The two ways of the theology of glory, one moralism and the other, rationalism, as the way of works and the way of knowledge, respectively, were rejected.[201] In the face of many ways to God, Luther's theology of the cross relentlessly stood as the only way to God.

Not unlike the first thesis of the *Ninety-five Theses*, the first thesis in the *Heidelberg Disputation* is critical to understand what is at stake here. The first thesis reads:

> 1. The law of God, the most salutary doctrine of life, cannot advance man on his way to righteousness, but rather hinders him.[202]

The all-important theme to be recognized at the beginning of this disputation is the way to righteousness. This is the key phrase for the understanding of the whole disputation. We claim this for two reasons. First, as pointed out earlier, the *Heidelberg Disputation* was called in the light of the theological issue of the efficacy of the indulgences. In other words, Luther's vehement opposition to the practice of indulgences as a means of salvation and his potentially devastating critique of papal authority led to the *Heidelberg Disputation* in which Luther was asked to defend himself. Although the problem of indulgences was no longer the focus of this disputation, it remained a part of the controversy. Instead of one particular problem of the contemporary church, now it was the foundation of the theological system of the church that was at stake. Thus, what Luther is defending in the *Heidelberg Disputation* is no less an issue than that of salvation.

Second, the human way of righteousness is a sure way of unrighteousness, thus a way of powerlessness. Whereas the first thesis in the *Ninety-five Theses* states the reality of sinfulness by calling for a life-long attitude of repentance; now, the first thesis of the *Heidelberg Disputation* speaks of the total powerlessness of the human way to righteousness. One establishes the reality of sin and the other, human being's utter helplessness to do anything about it. The issue for Luther was "how do human beings come to know God?"[203] Before establishing his thesis of the legitimate way to righteousness, Luther debunks the prevailing theology of man's capacity. However, the question persists as to how and why did man need to know who God is? Ironically, 'well-intentioned' religious rituals and requirements did not help Luther as he scrambled for the assurance of God. Instead, he discovered in them only human doctrine that kept people from God's promise of free gift of salvation. Luther's search led him to find the saving God in the scripture. With a new understanding of the phrase the "righteousness of God," Luther finds the meaning of scripture enlightened. He witnesses again and again to the testimony of the scripture concerning the absolute powerlessness of human beings in front of God with regard to salvation.[204]

The truth revealed in the theology of the cross can only be grasped from a position of profound awareness of powerlessness.[205] This is based on the fact that God revealed on the cross can only be known from the cross of the believer. Such a cross leads one to a sense of despair about one's capacities and thus prepares one to hear the promise of Christ. Thus, experience is important to realize one's desperation that enables one to acknowledge one's powerlessness before God. Moreover, "Luther's criticism of scholastic theology flows directly from this: that it does not know what the experience of weakness and powerlessness is like."[206] The important assumption of the theology of the cross is clarified in the first thesis on the basis of which Luther argues for the foundational inevitability of theology of the cross.

It is important to remember that Luther purposefully speaks of "the most salutary doctrine of life," namely, "the law of God," only to deny its ability to do any good to human beings. As long as the human being and righteousness are understood together, the force of Luther's conviction declares the law of God not only to be useless but actually an impediment. His own extremely mortifying efforts and rigid discipline as a way to righteousness is contrasted with his evangelical discovery of the meaning of the phrase "righteousness of God." In the proof of this thesis, Luther speaks of Romans 3:21: "But the righteousness of God has been manifested apart from the law to show that the righteousness of God is manifested in Jesus Christ."[207]

It is interesting to underline that Luther followed Staupitz's direction of the topics to be dealt with in the disputation. Yet, Luther's need to discredit the way of righteousness led him to use the same order creatively for developing his theology of the cross. In this connection, one might raise the question about the continuation of controversial subjects of the *Ninety-five Theses* in the *Heidelberg Disputation*. Staupitz presumed that he was avoiding the controversial topics in the *Heidelberg Disputation* when he suggested that Luther avoid controversial topic "but to prepare theses concerning sin, free will, and grace."[208] However, to the great surprise of the unsuspecting Staupitz, who wanted to avoid any further controversy involving Luther, the so-called "non-controversial" topics of sin, free will, and grace turned out to be the key issues involved in the question of salvation: a question over which Luther would denounce the pope and the authority of the church, and he would not give in even if it meant the division of the Roman Catholic Church. Hence, Nestingen concludes the safe strategy of Staupitz to be "a magnificent failure."[209] In reading the *Heidelberg Disputation* we would like to highlight some of the main emphases.

Theology of the Cross as Theology of Revelation for Salvation

Some scholars with little or no regard for the theses preceding theses 19 and 20 fail to underline the important aspect of soteriology towards which the whole disputation is oriented. Thesis 18 declares the complete powerlessness of the human for the grace of Christ: "It is certain that man must utterly despair of his own ability before he is prepared to receive the grace of Christ."[210]

For a desperate person a revelation of where he or she can find God is urgent. It is to this question Luther responds in theses 19 and 20. In his characteristic paradoxical style, Luther, in contrast to the theologian of the glory, asserts that a theologian of the cross "comprehends the visible and manifest things of God seen through suffering and the cross."[211] He declares any knowledge of God, however deep and profound, inadequate if it remains without the truth of the cross. "Now it is not sufficient for anyone, and it does him no good to recognize God in his glory and majesty, unless he recognizes him in the humility and shame of the cross."[212] Thus, for Luther, God is supremely revealed on the cross of Jesus Christ. And this revelation of God on the cross is for the purpose of the salvation of the world. Thus, the theology of the cross is about God's revelation in Jesus of Nazareth. Paul Althaus says that the "true theology and knowledge of God are to be found in the crucified God."[213] Such revelation of God is for the sake of salvation of the world.[214] Hence, Luther's theology of the cross is not only a theology of revelation but it is a theology of revelation for salvation.

Jesus Christ is the only basis upon whose sole saving authority Luther is able to scuttle what would in normal circumstance be "the most salutary doctrine of life" (Thesis 1). Thus, we agree with Nestingen when he concludes that Christ is "the implied or stated subject of all verbs" who holds the unity of the *Heidelberg Disputation* together.[215] Not only as the subject and the unifying element of the *Heidelberg Disputation* is Christ significant, but the whole thrust of the *Heidelberg Disputation* depends on the fact that he is the only saving God who is to be found in pain, death and suffering of the cross. We should remember that the false promise of salvation sold by the indulgences had first prompted Luther to this protest. The principle of evangelical discovery which Luther applied first to the indulgence controversy, now finds wider application with more profound consequences, this time not only for the exchequer of the papacy but for radical division between false and true theologians. The true and false theologians are aligned with the theology of the cross and the theology of glory, respectively.

In the unequivocal soteriological assertion of the theology of the cross and the downright denunciation of all speculation manifested in different forms and content as the way to salvation, an inbuilt exclusiveness can neither be denied nor avoided. This will inevitably lead to the uniqueness of Jesus Christ. This is not good news for many.[216] While discussing Luther's theology of the cross one cannot gloss over this inescapable truth. Thus, we are faced with two options in this regard. One is to ignore this exclusiveness of the theology of the cross for the sake of convenience by compromising the very truth upheld by Luther's gallant efforts. The second option will be to truthfully interpret Luther's theology of the cross in its exclusiveness and attempt an understanding that will create legitimate space for a life of Christian faith grounded in the crucified God. Of course, in pursuing the second option, we will show that it is not only possible and desirable but, in fact, mandatory for the Christian to live a life of openness to the other and a life of critical intervention on behalf of the other. This is to be explored and located in the design and pattern of God's revelation.

Vulnerability of God [217]

This pattern of the revelation of God on the cross of Jesus Christ for the sake of salvation is revelation on the basis of weakness and vulnerability. The crucified God is the vulnerable God. God's revelation on the cross is a revelation of God's vulnerability. Against the God of speculation who is strong, in control, all powerful, and perfect, Luther speaks of God in terms of the one who is suffering the worst pain and ignominy and who is dying a despicable and shameful public death. In being born of a virgin in a stable;[218] chased by King Herod;[219] homeless[220] and being in deep anguish during the prayer in Gethsemane; in his helplessness in front of the Roman authority more than once; in bearing the brunt of people's ridicule; and being whipped, carrying the cross and finally being nailed on the cross[221] Christ shows nothing but God's vulnerability. Even the resurrected Christ is not beyond the vulnerability as he still carries the wounds in his palms and invites those who doubt to once again reenact his vulnerability by putting fingers[222] in his wounds. And though raised from the dead, he joins the company of people as an ignorant traveler.[223] Thus, Luther's theology of the cross is a theology of God's vulnerability. The truth of the exclusiveness of the theology of the cross, then, finds its content in the power of the vulnerability of God.

In sharp contrast to the impassibility of God, Luther claims God to be fully revealed in the passion of Christ. His God is no more an untouched God of the scholastics; not merely the unmoved mover of Aristotle, but rather a God who chooses the shame and humiliating suffering to reveal the God-self to the world. Still deeper and profound are the theological implications when Luther asserts that God is not only revealed in the ignominy of the cross but he is *only* known in and through suffering. The theme of the pathos of God was to be a major category for theologians, especially, in the theologies of the developing world. The centrality of Jesus' humanity is an important aspect of Luther's theology of the cross that opens up new vistas for theological innovation and creativity.

Now we turn to theses 19 and 20, for they seem to be accorded much value and are subjected to oft-repeated reference in the debate of theology of the cross. The reference to theologian of the cross and theologian of the glory occur in theses 19 and 20, which has prompted many scholars to jump to them as the basis of Luther's theology of the cross. However, we would contend that jumping to theses 19 and 20 in order to unearth Luther's theology of the cross does an injustice to the integrity of the total message and argumentation. This betrays a somewhat shallow attempt to explicate Luther's theology of the cross without fully recognizing the overall thrust in the terms of the *Heidelberg Disputation*. There are many scholars who have made this fatal mistake.[224] Such a selective approach is less helpful because it risks ignoring the context and issues raised in the theses preceded by celebrated theses 19 through 22 for the theology of the cross.

> 19. That person does not deserve to be called a theologian who looks upon the invisible things of God as though they were clearly perceptible in those things which have actually happened (Rom. 1:20).[225]
>
> 20. He deserves to be called a theologian, however, who comprehends the visible and manifest things of God seen through suffering and the cross.[226]

There is no doubt that these two theses are pregnant with fundamental theological insights for the understanding of the true theologian and all important revelatory values of the suffering and the cross. Further, not only is the true theologian's definition derivable in and through them, but upon them depends the two conflicting understanding of the theologies which, in turn, decisively shapes one's own theological vision. However, these theses, we should remember, fall in their place according to an order, suggested by Staupitz, namely, sin, free will, and grace, and also, they follow eighteen other theses that provide a hermeneutical context too important to ignore. Thus, starting from the law of God as a hindrance for human righteousness, Luther continues to discredit "works of man" as mortal sins and affirms free will as a means only for more mortal sins. Luther speaks of the total and necessary desperation of humans to qualify for the grace of Christ on the basis of human work. It is only in the soteriological context that these theses must be interpreted. Gerhard Førde emphasizes the danger of ignoring this when he says:

> Unfortunately what usually happens then is that these theses (19 to 24) are taken out of their context in the *Heidelberg Disputation* and treated as though they were to stand by themselves as a more or less discrete theological program or treatise on the knowledge of God according to the theology of the cross and such matters.[227]

Førde is correct in taking exception to this approach with regard to the theses. We agree that it is only in the context of comprehensive argumentation of the disputation can one derive the full meaning that Luther intended. Hence, Luther deals with the life of grace in the later part of the disputation not because it is of less value but, first, he is following Staupitz's order of themes and second, his own deep awareness of the urgent need for the demolition of scholastic theology before building his own. As such, he speaks of the Christian life of grace in theses 25 through 28. In thesis 27, Luther says that "Actually one should call the work of Christ an acting work and our work an accomplished work, and thus an accomplished work pleasing to God by the grace of an acting work."[228] We, further, believe the soteriological emphasis of the *Heidelberg Disputation* was warranted by the deep-seated malaise of scholastic theology. Once Luther was beyond the compelling challenge on account of serious theological issues at stake in controversies, he reflected on Christian life, which showed what it means to live a life truly powerless yet profoundly conscious of redemption. This will be abundantly clear when we take up the discussion of Luther's *Church Postils*.

On the other hand, without undermining Førde's argument for due attention to the preceding theses, it can also be argued that the reverse is also true. That is to say that Luther's thought and arguments find crescendos in theses 22 to 24.[229] Such a conclusion is maintained because of the fact that Staupitz requested Luther to address the issues of sin, free will, and grace in the *Heidelberg Disputation*.[230] That Luther will reach the climax of his argument in theses 22 to 24 is understandable because of the centrality of grace in the light of his evangelical discovery. However, without considering theses 25-28, the place of the ultimate intention of the *Heidelberg Disputation* will be undermined if not ignored. Vercruysse concludes that first twenty-four theses are held together by a common purpose,[231] while making such a judgment he fails to understand that the last four theses are as determinative and conclusive as any before them. Nestingen criticizes Vercruysse for not including the last four theses as part of common unity.[232]

We have been arguing that Luther's disputation is primarily soteriological both in the light of his personal struggle and also for the abuses of the means of salvation in the contemporary church. More importantly, this is so because of the nature of reality in terms of human sinfulness and God's free gift of salvation in Jesus Christ. Against the economy driven soteriological practices of the church and the deeply established theological tenet of *synergesis*, Luther argues for a particular way to salvation.[233] Thus, Luther's theology of the cross establishes Jesus as the way of salvation.

Some theologians have tended to interpret the cross of these theses as the cross of the Christian (only in terms of example), which, though within the scope of legitimate theological interpretation, however, may rob Luther of his original intention. By no means do we intend to undermine this important insight especially while dealing with the challenge of contextual theological construction in the context of South Asia. In fact, we propose to discuss this critical hermeneutic adequately later on while contextualizing Luther in South Asia. Nonetheless, our interpretation of theses 19 to 22 will remain flawed if we fail to underline the fact that the cross primarily refers to the cross of Jesus Christ and not some non-specific generic act. One reason why it is tempting to completely ignore Christ is that this section does not mention Jesus Christ. Hence, the whole *Heidelberg Disputation* should be understood and interpreted in totality of its intention in order to account for its soteriological dimension. Once again, remembering Nestingen's conclusion that Jesus Christ is the subject of all the verbs[234] in the disputations will serve us well.

The soteriological accent, though foundational and essential, is first and foremost part of the theology of the cross. In these two theses, we must emphasize, lie significant epistemological clues to interpret Luther's *theologia crucis*. Our earlier emphasis on the soteriology of the *Heidelberg Disputation* seemingly over against the epistemology of it is to recognize and stress the foundational importance of the order of the two in Luther's thought. However, along with the soteriological insight of the theses, we must not ignore the epistemological wisdom. Especially in the theses 19 and 20, a fundamental epistemological principle is developed, without which theology of the cross as understood by Luther will remain not only lopsided but also distorted. Thus, Tomlin argues against Ole Modalsli's one-sided soteriological emphasis of the *Heidelberg Disputation*. His contention is that at "the heart of theses are two parallel insights, one soteriological, and the other epistemological."[235] To deny the epistemological significance of the theology of the cross is to deprive it of its continuing relevance for an authentic Christian living. Recognizing the relevance of the epistemological dimension of Luther's theology of the cross, Heino Kadai also declares it to be the backbone of the *theologia crucis*.[236] The significance of this observation lies in the fact that such an orientation of the theology of the cross imparts timeless relevance and resourcefulness for theological construction.

However, Luther attacks the legal basis of epistemology to introduce a valid and legitimate epistemological starting point in the cross of Christ.[237] Contrary to all expectations, God's presence is not to be sought in glory and majesty, but in the shame, ignominy and the dereliction of the cross. Therefore, for Luther "*crux sola nostra theologia*" (cross alone is our theology) is both the constitution and the justification of how and what one would know about reality.

It is clear that Luther is speaking of the true and false theologians in theses 19 and 20. Based on the ability or inability of theologians to perceive the divine presence in the shameful suffering and agonizing death on the cross, Luther speaks of two kinds of theologies authored by two kinds of theologians. They are not only different but, in fact, diametrically opposed to each other. He calls the theology of the scholastics "theology of glory" which is contrasted with his own "theology of the cross".

There is an implied question in this thesis about who is a theologian, to which thesis 20 provides an answer. Those who comprehend manifest things of God in suffering and the cross are worthy to be called theologians. Luther explains Jesus' human nature, weakness, and foolishness, which are avenues in and through which knowledge of God is attained. God's presence in his humanity, weakness and foolishness[238] is totally opposed to where theologians of glory locate God. Yet, this is the fact of God. Since God has chosen to reveal himself in the suffering and the cross of Jesus Christ, the possibility of the knowledge of God through his works in the creation is rendered null and void. Luther asserts that "Now it is not sufficient for anyone, and it does him no good to recognize God in his glory and majesty, unless he recognizes him in the humility and shame of the cross."[239] It is clear from this comment that Luther is not denying God's presence in other places; what he is insisting is that it is of no avail to recognize God any place other than the cross. Again, his concern is salvation, for which one has to know God in the crucified Jesus.

Thesis 19 rejects as false theologians those who seek invisible things of God such as "virtue, godliness, wisdom, justice, goodness, and so forth" in created things. In other words, the revelation of God is not in the beautiful and glorious things. God's revelation is to be found in the humility, weakness and suffering of the cross.[240] Luther's opposition to the scholastic theology of speculation based on Aristotelian philosophy is sharp and severe because they deny unashamedly the reality of God on the cross. Luther contrasts the theology of the cross with the theology of glory and says that all religious speculation is a theology of glory.[241] Heino Kadai claims between a false and a true way to the knowledge of God, the way of speculation, reason and philosophical reflection are false ways.[242]

Obviously, the theologians of glory have gotten it wrong, as the revelation of God is the other way round.[243] God's presence in the unlikely place of the cross demands an attitude and approach that itself is foolishness and a stumbling block to the world. God's wisdom, justice and power are manifested for those who, against the reasonableness of reason and sensibility of commonsense, choose to find them in the Crucified God. Faith is the only appropriate attitude of this epistemology. In the framework of this epistemology of the theology of the cross a reversal takes place. Thus, what seems to be foolish, weak and unwanted, is, in reality, valuable and desirable. This will mean that the shameful death of Christ on the cross is truly God's revelation and human works of goodness, wisdom and philosophy, that have high value in a worldly sense, are, in fact, worthless and misleading.

Luther not only denies the theologians of glory the status of theologian but disdainfully dismisses them as "enemies of the cross of Christ".[244] Another problem with those who look at God in glory and majesty is that they inevitably seek to establish their own glory and majesty at the expense of others and especially those who are poor and marginalized.[245] The pre-reformation church, run by corrupt officials installed and inspired by a theology of glory, offers an overwhelming number of such examples.

Luther understands the radical incompatibility between the theology of the cross and the theology of glory so that he is not even ready to grant any nuanced interpretation of scholastic theology. Vercruysse criticizes Luther for lack of nuances and claims that "His attack is even so unshaded that the exposition as such, will hardly convince anyone who knows the scholastic treatment of man's knowledge of God."[246] This criticism proves our point that Luther will not allow any tendency, however small and insignificant, to replace what solely and utterly belongs to Jesus Christ. Moreover, between the theology of the cross and the theology of glory it is not even about the tendency but it is about the origin and the very first point of starting that is totally misplaced. After criticizing Luther, Vercryusse himself explains the reason, "Because of its starting point itself is wrong, the whole pursuit is aimless and vain."[247]

The insight of the epistemological value of the theology of the cross is established on the basis of thesis 21 of the *Heidelberg Disputation*: "A theology of glory calls evil good and good evil. A theology of the cross calls the thing what it actually is."[248] Contrary to many interpretations, the reference is to the sinfulness of humanity. Whereas in the conceit of human ability, the theologian of glory calls good what is, in fact, imbued with the sin, the theologian of the cross lives in constant awareness of his sinfulness and powerlessness before God. Thus, the theology of the cross "affirms that God deals with sinners, not on the basis of their achievement or work but rather on the basis of their sin."[249]

However, this also speaks of the theology of the cross as having the courage to name the evil of the world: the diabolic design of injustice, unquenchable thirst for self-indulgence, corruption of power for domination, and exploitation of the other. It is to indicate this, John Hall says, that Luther wanted "a gospel that drove men into the world, not away from it...as it [theology of the cross] is the permission and command to enter into that experience with hope."[250] Loewenich succinctly expresses Luther's ethical implications based on the epistemology of the theology of the cross at the personal level:

> For Luther the cross of Christ and the cross of the Christian belong together. For him the cross of Christ is not isolated historical fact to which the life of the Christian stands only in a casual relationship, but in the cross of Christ the relationship between God and man has become evident.[251]

Such epistemology is the power of naked truthfulness of the theology of the cross, which acquires added potency when applied in a context of injustice and unjustly choked humanity. Just as it accorded insight and courage to Luther to oppose the abuses in the church, it also promises true insight even today into the reality to call the thing what it actually is and veritable might to commit in faith for the change needed. Such commitment was obvious when Luther opposed indulgences in Wittenberg, which was probably one of the ways Frederick the Wise supported Martin Luther at the university. By worldly standards, Luther was a fool who was cutting off the tree branch on which he was sitting.[252] Yet he did not refrain from doing so.

Theology of Incarnation

In his proof of the thesis 20, Luther gives the example of Philip as a theologian of Glory because he wanted to see the Father apart from Jesus.[253] It is evident that any attempt to bypass Jesus of Nazareth is a sure means to fall into the unacceptable category of theology of glory. Luther's words are unmistakable, "For this reason true theology and recognition of God are in the crucified Christ."[254]

Luther's example of Philip is critical for our purpose as it critiques those who understand and interpret the cross as merely the event on that fateful Friday. On the other hand, it also establishes that Luther's understanding of the theology of the cross is comprehensive to include the whole of incarnation. This is in line with how Luther interprets Jesus Christ. His defining Christological orientation is to be kept in mind throughout our discussion. The point in the Philip example is that Jesus is the true revelation of God even before his death and resurrection. Consequently, Jesus' earthly ministry, his proclamation of the kingdom and claim to be the way, the truth and the life, will bear upon the discussion especially on how Christian life is to be conceived in a South Asian context. Luther's firm conviction about Jesus of Nazareth even before his death has profound theological implications for the incarnation. This validates Luther's theology of the cross as the theology of the incarnation. We will ask if Jesus' death validates atonement and whether his life among people will play any role in this validation. For now, we conclude that the cross and suffering refer to Jesus' passion and death both soteriologically and hermeneutically.

Hidden and Revealed God

The assertion that the revelation of God is in the suffering of the cross is indirect and hidden. It is hidden, as anyone, just by the help of their sensory motor, cannot know this revelation. Moreover, it is indirect, as the God who is revealed in the cross is not recognized as God. Luther's claim that those who do not know Christ also do not know God hidden in suffering[255] becomes the reason for completely discrediting the theologians of glory. Luther finds the basis for the hidden God concept in the scripture. Speaking of Exodus 33:23, Luther cites the example of Moses who was able to see only the rear parts of God. The reason is clear: if humans were to see God's face, they would die.

A true theologian, for Luther, knows about God as he is hidden in the humanity of Christ. Thesis 20 says, "He deserves to be called a theologian, however, who comprehends the visible and manifest things of God seen through suffering and the cross."[256] Luther emphasizes how one comes to the knowledge of God. According to him, God's invisible nature is opposed to his visible nature and conversely, works of creation are not the true source of knowledge of God, rather the true source of the knowledge of God is Christ suffering. Luther purports the reasons:

> Because men misused the knowledge of God through works, God wished again to be recognized in suffering, and to condemn wisdom concerning visible things, so that who did not honor God as manifested in his works should honor him as he is hidden in his suffering.[257]

It is true that the God who is revealed in the helpless suffering and the ignominy of the cross of Christ is not immediately recognizable as God. Once again, human natural faculty remains helpless. However, against all natural tendencies, the revelation of God is to be recognized in the sufferings and the cross of Christ rather than in human moral activity or the created order. The cross shatters human illusions concerning the capacity of human reason. True theology and knowledge of God are found in Christ crucified.

This leads us to the theme of the revealed (crucified) God and hidden God which is a major feature of the theology of the cross of Martin Luther. God is decisively revealed in the cross of Jesus Christ; however, because of the appalling spectacle of Christ dying on the cross with condemnation and rejection, a Christian is forced to concede that God does not appear to be revealed there at all. This insight is fundamental to a correct appreciation of the significance of Luther's theology of the cross. The God who is revealed is the God who is hidden in his revelation. For Luther finding God elsewhere is idle speculation. The theologian is forced, perhaps against his will, to come to terms with the mystery and riddle of the crucified and hidden God. Luther's basis is Isaiah: 'Truly you are a hidden God' (Isaiah 45:15).

Theology of Faith

Forceful and passionate, however, are the arguments of Luther for the perspective of a theologian of the cross, yet, it would mean nothing to those without the advantage of an eye of faith. Since, apparently, the revelation on the cross is full of pain, shame, suffering and helpless death, it is difficult to accept such a phenomenon as anything salutary for salvation. For a student of history, this was how a criminal was executed in the worst form ever invented by humans. Still, for many, this was simply how the life of Jesus who was from Nazareth came to a violent end. However, only those with an eye of faith are able to discern this as revelation of God, whereas for those without faith, it remains hidden and concealed. The friends of the cross know that beneath the humility and shame of the cross lie concealed the power and the glory of God, but to others this insight is denied.[258] Thus, faith is at the heart of Luther's *theologia crucis*. Since the cross reveals God, which is a hidden revelation, thus it is a paradox. In fact, the decisiveness of faith plays a critical part in resolving this apparent paradox in his theology.

For Luther, the theologian of the cross is he who, through faith, discerns the presence of the hidden God in his revelation in Christ even in his suffering and death. Giving both the reason for faith and the power of faith, Luther states:

> For through faith Christ is in us, indeed, one with us. Christ is just and fulfilled all the commands of God, wherefore we also fulfill everything through him since he was made ours through faith.[259]

The very nature of God's revelation requires faith. And conversely, because faith can only be meaningful in the context of concealment, Luther is able to use faith in the discussion of the revealed and hidden God. Loewenich, once again, speaks of the decisiveness of faith in this discussion:

> It is precisely for the sake of faith that Luther must here undertake the apparently rigid metaphysical separation between the hidden God and the revealed God. The difference between the lines are summarized in this way: In the

former the idea of the hidden God means that revelation in principle is possible only in concealment; in the latter it means that also in the revealed God secrets remain. Both lines intersect in the concept of faith.[260]

Thus, faith is nothing less than what gives meaning to the content and method of the theology of the cross.

Magnificat

We will now consider Luther's *Magnificat* to understand how God occupies the first place in his theology of the cross.[261] There are some interesting facts about the *Magnificat*. Firstly, we are interested in looking into Luther's interpretation of a woman's song. This is Mary's song, which Luther chooses for devotional writing for an individual. Secondly, Luther wrote on the *Magnificat* for the young John Frederick about Godly rule by choosing the humbly-born Mary's example. Thirdly, the worldly affairs seem to be in the center of Luther's thought, which we want to analyze to see how it relates to the theology of the cross. Fourthly, unlike the *Heidelberg Disputation*, the *Magnificat* is written without any controversy.[262] Thus, we think it has relevance for a context other than disputation. Fifthly, Mary's song reiterates the appropriate order of attitude and action in relationship with God. Luther deals with the theme of knowing God, loving God and praising God in the *Magnificat* and while he does not use the term *theologia crucis* in the *Magnificat*, "the entire commentary is based in his theology of the cross."[263] In God's option for Mary, the lowly and despised maiden, Luther speaks of the theme of reversals.

Luther's main concern is raised when he states that "therefore all rulers should fear God more than others do; learning to know *him* and his works and walking diligently."[264] For Luther, this purpose can best be achieved by the example of Mary's song in the whole of scripture because she sings "about the fear of God, what sort of Lord he is, and especially what his dealings are with those of low and high degree."[265] There is another important reason for considering Mary. Mary's exemplary humility and her response first and foremost to the Lord's regard speak of the true attitude of Christians. The point is that Luther sees the Lord at work, which is recognized by Mary. Thus, Luther's purpose is to make this prerequisite for a young prince's authority, and the selection of Mary's song as an appropriate model, all underline the relevant dimensions of the theology of the cross.

The theology of the cross as the least expected place for God's presence is reiterated here. How true is this even with regard to Mary's situation, as Luther said, "when all seemed most unlikely—comes Christ, and is born of the despised stump, of the poor and lowly maiden!"[266] A young girl of no royal standing nor dignity is chosen by God to be *theotokos* (the carrier of God). A "poor, despised, and lowly maiden," Mary served God in her low estate. Even when she was favored, instead of either glorying on her virginity and humility, or focusing on her low estate, she gloried in what God "regarded". Luther makes this point very clear when he says that Mary confesses God's regard for her as the foremost work of God "which is indeed the greatest of his works."[267] Even here, Luther is not away from his main thrust of the theology of the cross as he discloses that whenever there is God's regard there is nothing "but grace and salvation."[268]

The theology of the cross is about the right order. This right order is at the heart of Mary's song, which Luther highlights. In distinguishing between gifts and grace and his regard, Luther analyzes as to why Mary puts his regard in the first and highest place:

> In giving us the gifts he gives only what is his, but in his grace and his regard of us he gives his very self. In the gifts we touch his hand; but in his gracious regard we receive his heart, mind, and will.[269]

Again the right order is of paramount importance for Luther as he exegetes Mary's song:

> And, truly, she sets things in their proper order when she calls God her Lord before calling him her Savior and when she calls him her Savior before recounting his works. Thereby she teaches us to love and praise God for himself alone, and in the right order, and not selfishly to seek anything at his hands.[270]

As noted earlier, the aspect of faith as fundamental to the theology of the cross is once again brought to the fore in this discussion. It is interesting to note that he associates faith with peace. It should be understood in the context of preparing a prince for his responsibility. Not only does a religious life depend on faith but a ruler's life must be adorned with living faith.[271] In his characteristic contrasting style, Luther concludes that "works breed nothing but discrimination, sin, and discord, while faith alone makes men pious, united, and peaceable."[272] For Luther, peace primarily relates to one's relationship with God as he argues that one is made pious and righteous neither by work nor by outward things but solely by faith. A living faith realizes God's will toward him and firmly believes that he will do great things for you. Having faith in this way is to be transformed by it.

The *Magnificat* is the supreme exercise in knowing God. It does not only know God but knows 'him aright. Luther says that he, who knows that God regards the lowly, knows God aright. It is important to note "From such knowledge flows love and trust in God, by which we yield ourselves to him and gladly obey him."[273] Thus, it is no surprise that George H. Tavard rightly says that "Mary follows what Luther had called the theology of the Cross in article 21 of the *Heidelberg Disputation*."[274]

This is especially significant for those with power and authority. Quoting Jeremiah chapter 9, Luther allows one to glory in this "that he understands and knows me, that I am the Lord who practice kindness, justice, and righteousness in the earth."[275] He continues to argue that God is to be found in kindness, justice and righteousness and not wisdom, might, and riches. The fact that God practices these things on earth suggests that God is found in the life and practice of kindness, justice, and righteousness. The reference to Jesus' earthly life and his inauguration of God's kingdom of kindness, justice and righteousness is obvious. Such knowledge of God is not contrary to the primary emphasis of faith of the theology of the cross, but is a necessary corollary of living faith in Jesus Christ. Given as works of God, however, they remain important for a cruciform life.

Discovery of the New Meaning of the Righteousness of God

We have been assuming and arguing the pivotal role played by Luther's discovery of the meaning of the righteousness of God which led him to develop a critical attitude towards the faith practice and theology of the time. That ultimately led him to the theology of the cross. After studying Luther's discovery of the righteousness of God as the breakthrough, McGrath concludes that:

The formulation of the *theologia crucis* occurred over a period of several years, and was catalysed by Luther's initial difficulties concerning the question of what was meant by the 'righteousness of God'. As a consequence of Luther's 'new' answer to this question, the entire substance of his theology had to be reworked, leading eventually to the theology of the cross.... the leading features of the theology of the cross are present in Luther's discovery of the true meaning of *iustitia Dei*.... Luther's discovery of the righteousness of God is but one step in the process leading to the theology of the cross—but it is nevertheless the decisive catalytic step.[276]

In his second commentary on Psalms (1519-1521), Luther wrote two thought provoking lines which are indicative of his theology: *CRUX sola est nostra theologia*.[277] The centrality of the cross in his theological reflection cannot be mistaken when he adds, *Crux probat omnia*.[278] Even Luther's early lectures on Psalms reveal his struggle with the concept of the righteousness of God (*iustitia Dei*). There are a great many disagreements and controversies over the date and content of Luther's understanding of the righteousness of God. The lectures on Psalms provide very clear evidence of a gradual process of development of this understanding.[279]

As we have mentioned earlier, Luther's struggle to find a righteous God relates to his uncertainty about the righteousness of God and its relation to justification or salvation. In reading Paul, Luther does not interpret Paul's phrase of the righteousness of God as distributive righteousness by which God judges people but rather the righteousness by which God gives.[280] In other words, if righteousness means rendering good for good and evil for evil, how can God justify sinful man? How can a righteous God return good for evil? How can the righteous God be good news for sinful man?[281] Before Luther arrived at what he later called "passive righteousness,"[282] which is referred to as "causative"[283] (God makes people righteous with this righteousness) by Bernard Lohse, he had to struggle with the prevailing exegetical tradition of a Latin-speaking church; the *via moderna;* Ciceronian and legal concept of righteousness; and meritorious justification, etc.

During the final stages of the first lecture on Psalms, Luther maintains that man's preparation or disposition for the reception of grace is itself a work of grace.[284] The exact time of Luther's discovery is not far from dispute.[285] Although, it would be impossible to argue convincingly that, by now, Luther has successfully parted ways with the interpretation of his time, yet, it can safely be concluded that by the end of the lecture on Psalms, Luther comes to reject the presuppositions of the soteriology of *via moderna*. Certainly, it must have taken place before 1517 because Luther clearly distinguishes the difference between man's righteousness and God's righteousness[286] in his first publication *The Seven Penitential Psalms*.[287] Luther's own comment is indicative of its theological value.[288]

Upon arriving at the new meaning of the righteousness of God, Luther insisted on 'grace alone' and 'faith alone.' This has led some to criticize Luther for undue concentration on the Pauline corpus[289] at the expense of the gospel accounts. Implied is the criticism of Luther's undue emphasis on faith over against work/action/involvement of the Christian.

Church Postils

In considering Luther's *Church Postil*, this criticism, we will argue, is ill founded. As the collection of sermons, the *Church Postils* are an important source for Luther's understanding of the theology of the cross because of its "remarkable objectivity."[290] Moreover, Luther regarded *Church Postils* "The best of all books."[291] The other reason for its significance is that unlike Luther's many other important writings, it was not written in response to theological controversy. Rather, it was a response to the pastoral need of preaching of the time.[292]

Meditating upon Christ sufferings, Luther speaks of seventeen ways to contemplate and not to contemplate Christ's suffering in his sermon for Good Friday.[293] His emphasis that Christ's passion must be understood as sacrament, yet should not be ignored as example,[294] is holistic in nature and comprehensive in its scope for faith and witness. Luther provides the definition of Christian faith when he says:

> That alone can be called Christian faith, which believes without wavering that Christ is the Saviour not only to Peter and to the saints but also to you. Your salvation does not depend on the fact that you believe Christ to be the Saviour of the godly, but that he is a Saviour to you and has become your own.[295]

The personal and existential nature of this faith leads Luther to denounce impersonal and generic faith in Christ. He condemns a faith about Christ as something that even devils and evil men have, in fact, for him it is denial of Christian faith because it makes "heathen and Turks out of Christians."[296] Luther's insistence on the personal nature of faith is actually bound with ethical implications for the other. He argues that such personal faith will work love for "Christ and joy in him, and the good works will naturally follow."[297]

In the light of Luther's vehement opposition to works and their theological validity, it may be argued that Luther is against all forms and understandings of works in this theology. Such a conclusion would be far from being true as Luther insists on validity of works in their proper place:

> We receive Christ not only as a gift by faith, but also as an example of love toward our neighbor, whom we are to serve as Christ serves us. Faith brings and gives Christ to you with all your possessions. Love gives you to your neighbor with all your possessions. These two things constitute a true and complete Christian life; then follow suffering and persecution for such faith and love, and out of these grows hope in patience.[298]

Luther refuses to name the good works because it would limit Christian involvement or it might even be manipulated. As he argued for unwavering faith in Christ for salvation so does he preach equally passionately on the complete giving of oneself in the service of the other. Luther's radical stance is much pronounced in the context of neighbor:

> Thus it is not your good work that you give alms or that you pray, but that you offer yourself to your neighbor and serve him, wherever he needs you and every way you can, be it with alms, prayer, work, fasting, counsel, comfort, instruction, admonition, punishment, apologizing, clothing, food, and lastly with suffering and dying for him.[299]

He even provides an understanding of what is good, to underline the same aspect of centrality of the other in one's Christian faith. It is clear from Luther's assertion that no one but the neighbor/person is the goal of all works. Against those who advocate good works for God and dead saints, Luther argues that they have no need of such good works. He also indicates that those who have Christ need no works done to them as they have everything in Christ.[300] He, then, concludes that something is "good only when it is useful to others and not to yourself."[301] His definition of good works establishes the centrality of the other: "If you find a work in you by which you benefit God or his saints or yourself and not your neighbor, know that such a work is not good."[302] Therefore, it is abundantly clear that Luther does not disregard the work or the life of praxis. Recognizing the inevitable power of the work to puff up humans with pride, Luther insists on a right order to faith and work.

Since faith and work are both essential for Luther, they must be seen as two significant loci of the theology of the cross. However, there is an order in Luther's theology of the cross, which is essential and indispensable for the true knowledge of God. The order of faith and works cannot, by any means, be reversed without demolishing the very foundation of what Luther's theology of the cross stands for. The challenge, then, is not one against the other but to understand both faith and works in terms of Jesus' life and death, both as sacrament and example.

Conclusion

The preceding discussion of the theology of the cross of Luther has abundantly demonstrated that the fundamental truth about it is that it is a theology of God's revelation for salvation. We know God's true identity only in God's saving relationship in the suffering and the cross of Jesus Christ. Thus, the Christological centrality of the theology of the cross is obvious. The soteriological claim of Luther's theology of the cross will be seen as narrow and exclusivistic in nature. Which is true, yet affirming God in the uniqueness and finality of Jesus Christ within the framework of the theology of the cross truly opens one to live an authentic Christian life in witness and service. Because the theology of the cross emphasizes God's vulnerability, one finds authentic Christian existence in terms of a crucified or vulnerable God. Naturally, this will lead to the discussion on the pluralistic approach and theology of religion in today's context of South Asia, which will be undertaken in a later chapter.

Luther's theology of the cross speaks emphatically about human sinfulness and hence, concludes the absolute powerlessness of the human being. Luther's theology of the cross argues that God can be known only through the experience of profound powerlessness before God.[303] Luther could not have emphasized more the fact that Christ is the righteousness of God, which we appropriate in faith. Despite all of the human unpreparedness and even inability to acknowledge the presence of God in pain and suffering, God has so deliberately revealed himself on the cross. The utterly disturbed and restless conscience of Luther ultimately finds rest and theological repose in the discovery of God's righteousness in Jesus Christ.

Contrary to many scholars who take into account merely the passion of Christ while considering the theology of the cross, we have maintained that Luther's theology of the cross is a theology of the incarnation; hence, this encompasses the whole life of Jesus Christ. As many have underlined the practical nature of the theology of the cross any attempt to constrict it will only result in distortion and one-sided emphasis. Thus, without Jesus of Nazareth the theology of the cross will be devoid of both historic foundation and theological history.

It is in this regard, we have highlighted Christ to be both sacrament and example. The order of sacrament and example is as critically significant as Luther's theology of the cross itself because it so consciously, as we have seen, destroys any human effort towards salvation and right relationship with God. Førde points out this aspect in his discussion of the theology of the cross in the *Heidelberg Disputation*.[304] However, these two aspects are very closely related to each other. We will discuss these aspects in more detail in conjunction with the theology of Aloysius Pieris and M. M. Thomas. In this regard, the two insights of the theology of the cross, namely soteriological and epistemological, as pointed out will be indispensable for a holistic understanding of the relevance of it. Both are inseparable, as for Luther both must be understood from the same standpoint of the cross.[305]

The focus that quite often escapes experts' approach and appreciation is that Luther's theology of the cross is, in fact, the theology of vulnerability, marginality and helplessness. Abundantly obvious in the shameful and helpless death of Jesus Christ is the reality of acute marginality and utter helplessness. In the final analysis the theology of the cross is not about the center, the power and the beautiful but rather it proves to be a theology of a theologian who is on the margin devoid of any power and beauty for the world to be attracted.

Again, one should always remember that the center and focus even in vulnerability is God and God's regard, as we have seen in the *Magnificat*. Here, we also noted that the life of faith and knowledge of God go hand in hand. And the true knowledge of God is that God is found in the practice of kindness, justice and righteousness. Thus, faith and the practice of these godly values are not opposed. Further, we also underlined in the discussion on the *Magnificat* that God's regard for the lowly and despised is the right way to know God, which also refers to the theme of reversals.

The *Church Postils* provided us the clearest picture of how Luther understands the life of faith with regard to neighbors. In acknowledging the crucified God and trusting his promise of justification and salvation, we are made free to act on behalf of the other. It is this freedom to act that is significant for Luther as this will always turn a person of faith in Jesus Christ to the other and his/her needs without the risk of pride. Against the constraint and imposition of works for either validation of Christian life or for attaining God's favor, a life of grateful response is mandated in Luther's theology of the cross. A life of grateful response constantly remembers its powerlessness and God's power of vulnerability in the generosity of the free gift of salvation in Jesus Christ. Thus, the Christian life of witness and proclamation is to be lived in the vulnerability of life experience, which will produce radical service for the neighbor. However, the freedom to act on behalf of the other and grateful response to God's gracious justification remain grounded in perpetual acknowledgement and proclamation of both our sinfulness and God's saving grace expressed in the cross.

How is such unglamorous and ego-defying theology ever to be embraced? Certainly, it can neither be understood nor embraced if we approach it without the gift of faith from God. Thus, the centrality of faith is recognized in the theology of the cross. We will continue to unravel the meaning and message of such an understanding of the theology of the cross in the context of South Asia.

CHAPTER 3

The Present Debate on the Theology of the Cross

In this chapter we turn to a critical engagement with scholars who have interpreted Luther's theology of the cross. Such engagement will help expand and solidify the debate for the concentrated discussion on theology of the cross in the South Asian context. We will attempt to defend and reiterate our conclusions by critically reading the following theologians.

Walter von Loewenich

With his seminal work, *Luther's Theology of the Cross,*[306] Walter von Loewenich's name is forever associated with the theology of the cross, conclusions of which have influenced all the research and every publication since. He was the first scholar to contradict an earlier claim that Luther's theology of the cross is medieval and a monkish remnant.[307] In order to discredit the previous interpretation as misplaced and unfounded, he examines Luther's *Heidelberg Disputations* (1518), *Bondage of the Will* (1525) and later *Lectures on Isaiah* (1527-1530) and concludes that Luther's theology of the cross is central to his theology. Loewenich's conclusion is remarkable: "... the theology of the cross is a principle of Luther's entire theology, and it may not be confined to a special period in his theological development."[308] He further declares "for Luther the cross is not only the subject of theology; it is the distinctive mark of all theology."[309] Perhaps the fact that the theology of the cross took shape in the very early years of the Reformation led some to conclude inaccurately that it was a medieval and monkish remnant of Luther. Contrary to this evaluation, we hold that it remained for Luther an indispensable point of view to understand and evaluate everything in life, especially *coram Deo*.

Walter von Loewenich lists the five essential aspects of Luther's theology of the cross.[310]

1. The theology of the cross as a theology of revelation stands in sharp antithesis to speculation.
2. God's revelation is indirect, concealed revelation.
3. Hence God's revelation is recognized not in works but in suffering, and the double meaning of these terms is to be noted.
4. This knowledge of God who is hidden in his revelation is a matter of faith.
5. The manner in which God is known is reflected in the practical thought of suffering.

This very helpful summary of the characteristics of Luther's theology of the cross has been followed by many scholars.[311] In our discussion of the same, as is evident in the preceding discussion, we have concluded many similar emphases of Luther's theology of the cross. However, the list is also somewhat artificial and arbitrary as it leaves out important assertions of Luther's theology of the cross; nonetheless, its helpfulness can hardly be denied.

Graham Tomlin criticizes Loewenich's list as he argues that "it fails to place these elements in relation to one another, to give them any sense of sequence, whether logical and chronological."[312] However, we think even a cursory look at this will make it clear that there is a definite sequence. It also provides some sense for the centrality of the epistemological framework and the dimension of faith. The major drawback of the list, however, lies in the fact that it fails to address the question of soteriology.[313] We agree with Tomlin that Luther's theology of the cross took shape precisely while he was wrestling with the question of how to be certain of his salvation. Any list of characteristics of theology of the cross, then, should incorporate the foundational import of salvific orientation.

A comment about the content of the list is necessary before we supply our version of the summary. Loewenich's first point about Luther's theology of the cross being revelation of God is both correct and a critical observation. This is also the basis for all the rest. In a way, points two to five explain the nature, content and requirement of the first most important conclusion of Loewenich. However, in the light of Tomlin's criticism of this list, we will suggest that Luther's theology of the cross is a revelation of God in Jesus Christ for the salvation of the world. Though far from being comprehensive this, at least, has Luther's main thrust incorporated in it.

One reason why Loewenich seems to have not emphasized the soteriological aspect is that he interprets Luther's theology of the cross in terms of its epistemology. His emphasis on the epistemological value of the theology of the cross is evident in the sheer number of times he underlines this. A few of them will be adequate to substantiate this: "... in Luther's theology of the cross we are not dealing with paraphrases of the monkish ideal of humility, but with a distinctive principle of theological knowledge...."[314] "It has its place not only in the doctrine of vicarious atonement, but it constitutes an integrating element for all Christian knowledge."[315] "What is involved here is the question about the knowledge of God."[316] At the end of his book he summarized his project saying: "The goal of my investigation was to show that the theology of the cross was theoretical principle of knowledge for Luther."[317]

There is no doubt about the centrality of epistemology in his interpretation which, one must not forget, is a very important aspect of Luther's theology of the cross. However, Loewenich's approach results in one-sided interpretation of the theology of the cross as presented in the *Heidelberg Disputation* of 1518. This is the reason why Lowenich concentrates on theses 19 and 20. We have critiqued such an approach earlier as it does not take into account the complete context of the arguments. Not that this cannot be done but it will seriously distort the way Luther intended his contentions. Nonetheless, with his concentration on the epistemology of the theology of the cross, Loewenich raises the very important issue of life under the cross.[318]

Loewenich is correct in asserting that a person living according to the theology of the cross will live a life under the cross. Drawn into the life of the cross of Christ, a person invariably finds his life transformed and lived under the cross. For Loewenich the cross of Christ and the cross of the Christian belong together. He makes this understanding of the cross a basis for life under the cross. He argues:

> The cross of Christ and the cross of the Christian belong together. The meaning of the cross does not disclose itself in contemplative thought but only in suffering experience. The theologian of the cross does not confront the cross as a spectator, but he is himself drawn into this event. He knows that God can be found only in cross and suffering.[319]

He further defines the content of suffering when he says that first, "Christians must become like their Master in all things. They must therefore take Christ's disgrace upon themselves. The Christian life is one of lowliness."[320] Second, the "Christian life is a discipleship of suffering" because suffering is "the surest way to God" and "in suffering God meets us."[321] Third, "the true meaning of Christ's suffering can be discovered only in the act of experiencing, acting, and suffering."[322] Fourth, Loewenich says that "To be conformed to Christ means nothing else but experiencing the fact of the cross also in our lives."[323]

In all these statements, Loewenich argues for an ethical implication[324] that suggests an active participation on behalf of the Christian. His epistemological emphasis calls for much stronger argument for a life of suffering as that of Christ. However, there are a few difficulties in his presentation. Loewenich has been very emphatic about the hiddenness of God in this book. The hiddenness of God is one of the three categories along with faith and life under the cross that he explicates for his understanding of the cross. His stress on hiddenness is perceptible as he understands all three of them in terms of hiddenness. He argues that God, faith, and Christian life all are hidden yet connected in the most intimate way.[325] Though the concept of the hidden God is fundamental to the understanding of Luther's theology of the cross, yet, Loewenich's explication of the same is not in proportion to his five characteristics of the theology of the cross (explained earlier). In that list, Loewenich seems to interpret the same in terms of revelation.

Loewenich's overemphasis on the hiddenness of God leads him to interpret thesis 20 of the *Heidelberg Disputation* in a manner which seems to be far from what Luther intended. Loewenich states that "For it is precisely as the God of revelation that God is the hidden God."[326] It is difficult to agree with what Loewenich concludes "...God can reveal himself only in concealment, 'in the humility and the shame of the cross'."[327] Lowell Green rightly criticizes Loewenich for reading hiddenness into the text which does not really speak of hiddenness.[328] Luther simply says, "Now it is not sufficient for anyone, nor does it do him any good, to recognize God in his glory and majesty, unless he [first] recognizes him in the humility and shame of the cross."[329] Green further finds Loewenich mistaken in his understanding of the meaning of the whole passage when he says that God is hidden in his revelation. Because, for Luther, God is concealed to those without faith and hence, God is not hidden in his revelation to those who perceive that revelation in faith, otherwise "it would be revealing of nothing at all."[330]

Loewenich seems to be wrestling with the tension and conflict of Luther's theology of the cross with regard to the passivity of faith and activity of faithful response. Hence, in the course of expounding Christian life as discipleship of suffering, he asserts the meaning of bearing Christ's cross, which is very different from his earlier emphasis in the preceding pages:

> The cross of Christ is nothing else than forsaking everything and clinging with the heart's faith to Christ alone, or forsaking everything and believing that this is what it means to bear the cross of Christ.[331]

This contradicts the main emphasis of a life of Christian discipleship of suffering. Moreover, Loewenich quotes from many different sources of Luther's writings that make it difficult to comprehend in terms of the sustained thought of the reformer. But on the other hand, on the basis of his extensive research of Luther's texts, he is convinced that Luther's theology of the cross is a theological principle that is not restricted to any one period of his life.

Paul Althaus

Paul Althaus has followed Loewenich quite closely with regard to Luther's theology of the cross. Writing just three years after Loewenich he is clearly influenced by him and at times betrays his dependency on Lowenich. Althaus deals with Luther's theology of the cross in his book *The Theology of Martin Luther*.[332] Similar to Lowenich, Althaus also considers theses 19 and 20 of *Heidelberg Disputation* as the heart of the theology of the cross. Thus, both of them place great emphasis on the comparison and contradistinction between the theology of the cross and theology of glory. Both Loewenich and Althaus underline the epistemological character of the theology of the cross.

By bringing Jesus' suffering and human suffering together, Althaus imparts a mandatory character to the way we know and its inevitable concern for ethics. His opinion is unambiguous. "For Luther, concern for the true knowledge of God and concern for the right ethical attitude are not separate and distinct but ultimately one and the same. The theology of glory and the theology of the cross each has implications for both [epistemology and ethics]."³³³ In speaking of Christ's suffering and man's suffering, Althaus expresses the inbuilt vulnerability in the incarnation of Jesus Christ and in the lives that have decided to follow such a vulnerable God on the cross. This insight is both helpful and critical in maintaining what we call the uniqueness and finality of Jesus Christ and the continued relevance of such affirmation in its ever deepening reality of vulnerability that ought to be a living experience of a Christian. Echoing von Loewenich, Althaus asserts:

> Luther uses "works" not only in the sense of God's works but also in the sense of man's works; and "suffering" refers not only to Christ's suffering but also to man's suffering. Luther makes the transition from the one to the other as though it were self evident.³³⁴

However, we should distinguish between God's works and man's works as works of God always in relation to *coram Deo,* whereas the works of man, though related to the works of God, have legitimacy only with regard to one's neighbor. Likewise, the suffering of Christ generates meaning only as long as it is first understood as a proper place to know God that invariably leads to what Luther asserts: "From such knowledge flows love and trust in God, by which we yield ourselves to *him* and gladly obey *him*."³³⁵ Nonetheless, the important insight of the theology of the cross which Loewenich and Althaus insist upon should not be lost sight of, i.e., that true meaning of Christ's suffering is discovered when one experiences suffering. Their epistemology of the theology of the cross is rightly asserted to be embodied in "practical suffering."³³⁶

Luther's theology of the cross is diametrically opposed to activism for its own sake without the foundation of faith in the crucified God. Thus, Althaus concludes that "Luther recognizes the inner relationship and even the identity of religious intellectualism and moralism. He shows that both are in opposition to the cross. These are the two deepest insights of his theology."³³⁷ Against any pretensions of the scholastic theologians' metaphysical speculation and its basis in works righteousness, Althaus reiterates Luther's understanding of God's revelation as both revealed and yet hidden. All Luther scholars including von Loewenich and Althaus recognize the valuable theological insights of both the freedom and mystery of God in it.

However, Althaus detects a shift in Luther's concept of the hidden God by the time of *The Bondage of the Will.* The concept has undergone radical change in meaning in comparison to the meaning found in *Heidelberg Disputation* (1517).[338] Luther's concern for the hidden will in his later writings become more rigid and, in fact, threatens the gracious promise revealed in Jesus Christ. The biblical testimony of balanced tension as found in Paul for the sake of God's freedom is tilted towards the unintelligible supremacy of the hidden God. In expressing legitimate theological concern over Luther's full-blown doctrine of the hidden God's double will with undue emphasis on the inscrutability of the will of the hidden God, Althaus asks:

> whether Luther's doctrine of the hidden God as it is presented in *The Bondage of the Will* does not abrogate the rest of his theology as we have come to know it.... Is it not immeasurably dangerous, even deadly, to man's trust in the word of promise? It actually asserts that God, according to his secret will, to a great extent disagrees with his word offering grace to all men.[339]

Nevertheless, Althaus acknowledges its usefulness in safeguarding the sovereignty of God against all human attempts to control. McGrath also finds Luther's doctrine of the hidden God stretched and self-defeating, especially in Luther's insistence on the particular manner in which God is hidden. But, before putting Luther's hidden God to critical scrutiny, McGrath undertakes a helpful analysis of what exactly Luther means while using this term.[340] He discredits the general tendency of Luther scholars "to impose a far greater precision on the term *Deus absconditus* than Luther intended."[341] While noting many different meanings and uses of the term, McGrath concludes that there are two main senses in which Luther employs this term apart from the general meaning of hiddeness.[342] First, *Deus absconditus* is hidden *in* his revelation. God's strength is revealed in weakness and his wisdom in apparent folly. The important aspect to note in this understanding is that the hiddenness of divine revelation means that hidden God and revealed God are identical.[343] Thus, it is the eye of faith that discerns the revealed God. McGrath opines:

> In the one unitary event of revelation in the cross, God's wrath and mercy are revealed simultaneously—but only faith is able to recognize the *opus proprium* as it lies hidden under the *opus alienum*; only faith discerns the merciful intention which underlies the revealed wrath.[344]

The second aspect of the hidden God is that this God is hidden *behind* his revelation. Employed as a polemical device to discredit

Erasmus' apparently legitimate exegesis of the scripture,[345] Luther's understanding of the hiddenness of God both changes and becomes difficult in *de servo arbitrio*. For Luther, the God who is forever hidden behind his revelation is beyond the comprehension of human beings. There is tension between the revealed and hidden God that can be understood on the basis of Luther's hints, to be in total antithesis. Though an explanation can be given on the basis of noetic and ontic understanding of the same, yet Luther is "forced to concede that behind the merciful God who is revealed in the cross of Christ there may well be a hidden God whose intentions are diametrically opposite."[346]

This problem reached an impasse by 1525 as Luther asserts that God wills many things which he does not disclose in his Word.[347] His further assertions verify the contradiction between the revealed and hidden God with dreaded theological implications. One can reach a very disturbing conclusion after reading that God "does not will the death of a sinner, according to his word; but he wills it according that inscrutable will of his."[348] The implications suggest that Luther has abandoned his earlier principle of deriving theology on the basis of the cross and the cross is no more the final word of God on anything. If the validity of what we know of the revealed God is trumped by the inscrutable will of the hidden God then it ultimately renders all theologies irrelevant and worthless. The controversy and polemics, which so often brought out the best in Luther, seem to have trapped him in a theological quagmire. McGrath concludes:

> His dilemma is his own creation, and his failure to resolve it in *de servo arbitrio* is an indictment of his abandonment of his own principle: *Crux sola est nostra theologia!*[349]

It seems in the highly polemical context Luther overstated his position in order to defend the foundational theological statement about the reality of lack of free will in the matter of salvation. Thus, Brian Gerrish also concludes that Luther's chief concern was to "affirm the sole agency of God in bringing about [human] salvation."[350] In one sense, Luther's pastoral concern for the purity of the doctrine is what drives Luther's stand, as Paul Althaus comments:

> Finally, we remind ourselves again that Luther declares that the hidden God and his secret activity must be discussed *for the sake of the elect!* In the final analysis, Luther does not establish a theoretical doctrine of double predestination as Calvin does. In spite of all appearances to the contrary,

his theology at this point is completely untheoretical and pastoral. His idea of the hidden God finally intends only to purify Christians' faith from all secret claims and all self-security by proclaiming the freedom of God's grace.[351]

However, Luther's early understanding of the hiddenness of God is excellently expressed in his sermon of 24th February 1517. He remarks that "Man hides his own things, in order to conceal them; God hides his own things, in order to reveal them."[352] God works in a paradoxical way, which is supremely evident on the cross. God's strength is hidden in apparent weakness and his wisdom is found in apparent folly. Thus, McGrath states that "there is radical discontinuity between the *empirically perceived situation* and the *situation as discerned by faith.*"[353]

Despite all its power to the contrary, reason is unable to recognize God's revelation in such abominable condemnation. Based upon the empirically discernible, reason deduces that God cannot possibly be revealed in the cross of Jesus Christ. On the cross, reason can only see a man dying a helpless and condemned death. It is, as McGrath concludes, because the perceived situation does not correspond to the preconceived situation.[354] We will recall that the theologian of glory expects God to be revealed in strength, power and glory and such prefixed parameters do not allow him to understand and see God in helpless suffering and the ignominious death on the cross. This discussion on the hiddenness of God is important for understanding the complex thought pattern of Luther and at the same time his clear presentation of it in the early thoughts under consideration in this dissertation.

Gerhard Førde

Recognizing the increasing attention to the theology of the cross in recent theological reflection and at the same time, finding that the central issue of being a theologian is being left out, Gerhard Førde explicates the subject of the theology of the cross in *On Being a Theologian of the Cross: Reflections on Luther's Heidelberg Disputations, 1518.*[355] Førde explains the purpose of his book, which is actually a sharp critique of the way in which theology of the cross is being reflected in many parts of the world, by stating:

> In the absence of clear understanding, the theology of the cross tends to become sentimentalized, especially in an age that is so concerned about victimization. Jesus is spoken

of as the one who "identifies with us in our suffering," or the one who "enters in to solidarity with us" in our misery. "The suffering of God," or the "vulnerability of God," and such platitudes become the stock-in-trade of preachers and theologians who want to stroke the psyche of today's religionists. But this results in rather blatant and suffocating sentimentality. God is supposed to be more attractive to us because he identifies with us in pain and suffering. "Misery loves company" becomes the unspoken motif of such theology.[356]

It is clear that Førde's observation stands as a critique even of our own conclusion that the theology of the cross is, in fact, the theology of God's vulnerability. Hence, in order not only to defend our conclusion about God's vulnerability but, even more importantly, to maintain our thesis that Luther's theology of the cross is still relevant and a major resource for doing theology in the South Asian context, we will have to undertake a more detailed discussion of Førde's claims and conclusions in this book. We must point out that Førde does not deny that the theology of the cross speaks about suffering. His assertion that it is "certainly true that in Christ, God enters into our suffering and death"[357] should not be forgotten while interpreting him. Førde's third reason for writing this treatise explains one major reason for his criticism. He detects a serious erosion or slippage in the language of theology as sentimentality takes the central role, to cause a shift in focus, which ultimately results in out of place language.[358] Far from being theoretical about this, Førde quickly gives illustration for this. He rightly points out that in many contemporary theological conversations we are no longer sinners but rather victims. This furthers the slip of language, where we are victims and thus require therapy rather than sinners requiring evangelical language.[359] Recalling Luther's assertion in thesis 21 of *Heidelberg Disputation* that a theologian of the cross "says what a thing is," Førde underlines the significance of language in Luther's theology of the cross. He claims "language and its proper use in matters theological is a fundamental concern of the theologian of the cross."[360] His main concern is the tendency to impose the secondary meaning over the primary meaning of the text. In referring to the so-called activism of theological tendencies, Førde argues that the theology of the cross is about the end of all work. He is right in his interpretation of Luther's Heidelberg disputation as primarily dealing with a denial of any worth whatsoever to works, free will, law with regard to the question of righteousness *coram Deo*. There is hardly anything debatable in that a person is totally helpless and completely dependent on the grace of God for his salvation through faith in Jesus Christ.

Yet, there needs to be some explanation about how the theology of the cross speaks meaningfully to the present day readers in a context radically different from both Luther's Germany and Førde's North America. Here, our intention is not to deny what Førde says but to interpret him to enlarge the scope of the theology of the cross. This exercise will also refer back to Luther himself as his own interpreter. Førde is helpful because he understands the cross in terms of incarnation. We quote him to understand the full implications for our arguments:

> The word "cross" here and in the entire treatise that follows is, of course, shorthand for the entire narrative of the crucified and risen Jesus. As such it includes the OT preparation (many of the foundational passages for the theology of the cross come from the OT!), the crucifixion *and* resurrection of Jesus, and his exaltation.[361]

Against the idea of the theology of the cross being concerned only with crucifixion, he rightly argues for an understanding that includes the life and work of Jesus of Nazareth. On the other hand, this also raises some profound theological questions for the understanding of the theology of the cross of Martin Luther. Certainly for Luther, Jesus died for the sins of the world; could we also in the same breath ask whether he also lived for the sins of the world? It is not a hypothetical question but, we think, a question largely ignored in the discussion of the theology of the cross. Luther himself raises this in some sense as he rebukes Philip who wanted to find God somewhere else than Jesus himself. As a result, Jesus, in fact, declares Philip to be a theologian of glory.[362] This will suggest that Jesus was a revelation of God even before the event of crucifixion. How do we understand God's revelation in Jesus before his passion and death on the cross? How does this element shape the theology of the cross?

Førde argues rightly that "it is not possible to have a theology of the cross without resurrection."[363] However, we must ask, is the theology of the cross that comprises of the whole life of Jesus possible without the incarnated life of Jesus of Nazareth? As resurrection is an integral part of the theology of the cross of Luther so also Jesus' words and actions prior to his passion ought to be considered an integral part of the same. If Jesus tells Philip that God is to be found in him and not any other place, then the question, on what ground can we understand the passion and death to be more important than any other time, becomes critical. Attributing greater importance to one period than the other will lead to a Christological problem of the humanity and divinity of Christ.

One helpful way to understand the theology of the cross is to understand it in the totality of Luther's thoughts. Indeed, Førde is right in his interpretation of the *Heidelberg Disputation* as a perennial criticism against human pretensions of work and scholastic theologians' lies of wisdom. True to its purpose, the *Heidelberg Disputation* mercilessly makes a case for the absolute helplessness of human beings without first being grasped by God's grace. Though the *Heidelberg Disputation* most definitely rules out any work as the origin for righteous standing before God, yet human response to God's gracious initiative is only natural as God's astounding grace fills the heart of the recipient of such grace full of joy and gratitude.

At the same time, Førde acknowledges that the resurrection, assumed in this disputation, should not undermine the fact that Jesus' life (words and works) is equally validly presumed in the same discourse. While resurrection imparts an eternal and ultimate character to the theology of the cross, the life of Jesus before his crucifixion and resurrection endows the same with penultimate and temporal responsibility for the one smitten by God's grace. On the one hand, the theology of the cross, in the light of the resurrection, names the proper relation with God, and on the other, in the light of Jesus' ministry of inaugurating, preaching and practicing of the Kingdom of God, names the proper relation with the neighbor. We must maintain Luther's dialectic of *sacramentum* and *exemplum,* for in this is realized the promise of his theology of the cross for South Asia. In his legitimate critique of those who exclusively emphasize the *exemplum* aspect, Førde seems to run the risk of compromising this dialectic.

Though a sinner is acted upon by the grace of God and made righteous, nonetheless he remains a sinner according to Luther's principle *simul iustus et peccator.* Thus, the process of being declared righteous on the basis of faith and thus continuously propelled not only to acknowledge this as the work of God but also act for the sake of one's neighbor is the constant predicament of a Christian. In this sense, the theology of the cross has a legitimate place for epistemological elements.

Luther's own example of his life in not sitting idly after being acted upon by God in Jesus has something to say in this regard. Luther's courage in condemning both the misleading speculation of the theologians of glory and the hypocrisy of the papacy even at the risk of his life is no less a model of the life of the theologian of the cross. For Luther, being acted upon was not enough, not in the sense that his salvation was incomplete, but in the sense that he could do no other under the impact of God's grace. There is a relationship between soteriological understanding and its epistemological implication. Though this connection is not a requisite corollary, yet it is naturally related. The relation is one of loyalty to faithfulness rather than of logical necessity. This is not without either Luther's comment or Førde's interpretation. To give just one example from Luther's *Heidelberg Disputation*:

> Since Christ lives in us through faith so he arouses us to do good works through that living faith in his work,.... If we look at them we are moved to imitate them. For this reason that Apostle says, "Therefore be imitators of God, as beloved children" [Eph. 5:1]. Thus, deeds of mercy are aroused by the works through which he has saved us, as St. Gregory says: "Every act of Christ is instruction for us, indeed, a stimulant."[364]

We could not agree more with Førde when he paraphrases Luther and says that "The impetus to good works comes entirely from being moved, aroused, and motivated by the completed work of the Christ, who dwells in the believer through faith."[365] Also his assertion about how the power to do good originates speaks of both the cause and effect of what we call a continuum, of course without logical necessity. He says that "The point is precisely that the power to do good comes only out of this wild claim that everything has *already* been done."[366] Thus, the issue is about the order and not about choosing between the two. This important aspect will be discussed in relation to the theologies of the Asian theologians in later chapters.

However, we want to assert that Luther's own act of disputation in opposing the established and institutionalized church was more than confession; it was a deliberate struggle against the forces of the theology of glory. His evangelical theology in this regard became something which we can recognize as vital as a spiritual source for courage and conviction. In defense of our conclusion that in the theology of the cross we witness God's radical vulnerability, we recognize the total helplessness of humans but we also acknowledge the fact that Christ died in total helplessness and abandonment on the cross. That God's power is manifested in the weakness of the cross is a fact of Christian life. True Christian power is to be found in a life of vulnerability. Thus, such a crucified God for Paul and Luther was no less than a stumbling block and foolishness to the world (I Cor. 1:23).[367] Yet, the crucified God is not without power and wisdom. The apostle Paul recognizes this power and wisdom in Christ crucified (1 Cor. 1:24). Such power is the power of vulnerability and such wisdom, the wisdom of the one who lays down his life on his own (John 10:18). Therefore, the followers of the crucified God (vulnerable God) can have no other power than the power of vulnerability. Yet another important insight to avoid a lopsided emphasis on just one aspect of theology of the cross, namely, one's passivity as seen in Førde's arguments, is to realize that the sinner is crucified in order that a new person may arise. The death of sinners will bear the mark of crucifixion of Jesus forever,[368] verification of which again is not to be found in the sinner but in the risen body of Christ with the enduring mark of wounds (John 20:27). If the mark of the wounds of Christ's body is real, then the mark of the cross is also not just symbolic and hence, the reality of the cross in the justified sinner is no less real.

Regin Prenter

Regin Prenter, the Danish Lutheran theologian, argued for this understanding. Against the medieval mysticism in which the cross was chosen for pietistic purposes, Prenter argues that the cross that nullifies all human works is not chosen but "God lays his cross upon us for our salvation."[369] He further clarifies his stand:

> Luther, however, did not consider the cross of Christ primarily as the supreme example of humility which we are called upon to imitate, instead it was that act by which Christ endured the actual punishment for our sin. For this reason his cross is identical with ours, because he bore our punishment upon the cross.[370]

By no means is Prenter against what Førde says about the criticality of the passive reception of Christ's righteousness by the power of the gift of faith. In total agreement with Førde, he actually sees Luther's theology of the cross identical with the Lutheran doctrine of justification through faith alone.[371] Prenter differs from Førde in his insistence on the form of the proclamation of the cross of Jesus Christ. His three facts about the theology of the cross are descriptive:

> 1) its content is the historical cross of Christ; 2) its proclamation of the cross of Christ is always in combination with the work of the individual crosses of men, and 3) it points to the crucifixion of all human sin and self-justification.[372]

The tension between the interpretation of Førde and Prenter is about the second point in Prenter's summary of the theology of the cross. While Førde and Ebeling emphasize radical discontinuity between human and divine initiative, Prenter insists on necessary continuity between the cross and Christ and the Christian. For those with a radical discontinuity position, the cross first and foremost, is an eternal judgment against all human endeavors and pretensions of works. However, for those siding with Prenter's position, the cross is both judgment and a pattern for the justified Christian.

It is understandable that in the historical context of profound theological issues that shaped the doctrine and practice of faith in 16th century Germany, and the limitation of the framework of the *Heidelberg Disputation*, Førde seems to have laid emphasis on the aspect of radical discontinuity between humanity and God. Prenter's concern is to avoid cheap grace as well as the existentialist theology of Bultmann.[373] His main concern is to avoid a medieval theology of the cross without the word and also a post-reformation theology of the word without the cross.[374]

We will pursue this pertinent debate as it will help us understand the two aspects of Luther's theology of the cross—Christ as a sacrament and as an example. What can we detect in Førde's insistence on the passive acceptance of Christ as a sacrament who died for our sins and his righteousness as not only what we need but freely available as a gift for a believing heart to stand before God justified? It is not true that he ignores the life of faith completely; nonetheless, this is relegated to the end of his discussion of the *Heidelberg Disputation*. One reason may be that Luther himself speaks of this at the end of the *Heidelberg Disputation*, which naturally leads Førde to take up this at the end since he discusses the disputations numerically. More importantly, the enormous stake for which Luther rallied the power of the evangelical theology, namely, the free gift of the power of the gospel of Jesus Christ over against human invention and contribution, is too high a stake to even let the work, infused and aroused by faith in Jesus Christ, take a prominent place. Certainly, it is understandable in the context of the 16th century *Heidelberg Disputation*. And the legitimacy of such emphasis should not be lost sight of because the constant danger of falling victim to the theology of the glory is never abolished. There cannot be any valid theological argument against the primacy of God's grace as a fundamental point of departure for an authentic Christian life of trust in the gracious promise of God in Jesus Christ against the *anfechtung* of life.

However, one can also make a case that Luther's arguments against human works, the scholastic theology of speculation and *synergesis*, etc., all lead us to understand life *coram Deo* as well as *coram hominibus*. We think that the inevitable relation between "an acting work" and "an accomplished work" of thesis 27 of the *Heidelberg Disputation*[375] is fundamental to the progression of Luther's thought as well as its basic scheme. The Christ's acting work and our accomplished work is to be seen and grasped as continuity in one respect, that is, in respect of neighbor. For Luther, it is as if after providing solid and true foundation to the Christian life, he is arguing for the inevitability of 'accomplished work' in the life thus founded by the grasp of the grace of Christ. Hence, Luther concludes about such a person:

> ...love of God which lives in man loves sinners, evil persons, fools, and weaklings in order to make them righteous, good, wise, and strong. Rather than seeking its own good, the love of God flows forth and bestows good.[376]

Prenter regards such a newly created attitude towards the cross of Christian life as a prerequisite that protects us from a theology of the cross without the individual cross of daily living under the cross. While commenting on post-reformation Lutheran theology he states that it quickly accustomed itself to the separation of the cross and the word of the cross. The preaching became devoid of the cross of the individual and had nothing to do with the actual crucifying of the old Adam. As a consequence, a theology of the word without the cross was established.[377] His critique is sharp and consequential:

> The word about the cross became an "objective doctrine," it lost its character as a word which not only teaches something about the cross, but actually works as the cross in connection with the cross in our lives. Faith became the intellectual affirmation of this objective doctrine of the word; it also lost its character as a cross, that is, it no longer meant the real destruction of all individual righteousness.[378]

Prenter further clarifies his assumption and asserts that if faith is without the willingness to carry one's cross then, it means that "the crucifixion is not taken seriously as that event by which Christ bore the punishment for our sins."[379] Such an assertion is problematic as this will make the effectiveness of Christ's cross dependent on one's willingness to carry the cross. The theology of the cross stands against any condition, let alone human condition, for being operative and effectual. Luther's theology of the cross is objective in the sense that it does not need human help for the indispensability of grace and Christ's righteousness. On the other hand, it is subjective as the reality of grace and Christ's righteousness is to be appropriated by faith alone.

However, for Prenter the theology of the cross is not only about the cross of the individual. We should not take his interpretation of the theology of the cross as purely existential. On the contrary, he criticizes the existentialist theology of Rudolf Bultmann as a theology of the cross without the word.[380] Bultmann's existentialist understanding of faith is rightly rejected because it negates the historical content of the faith and, in the ultimate analysis, denies any theological value to the historicity of the saving events of crucifixion. The vicarious suffering of Christ is condemned as mythological and for Bultmann, it is a "hotchpotch of sacrificial and juridical analogies, which have ceased to be tenable."[381] The cross is only meaningful when it enables people to choose a particular existence of the crucified one as their own existence possibility. Thus, discipleship of imitating Jesus and his sacrifice is the only way to understand the value of the Christ event. Prenter declares this existentialist theological interpretation as "the modern version of a theology of the cross without the word."[382] And hence, it is utterly unacceptable, for Prenter points out that in Bultmann's theology of the cross "the cross as a form of personal existence has become sufficient, and the cross as a historical vicarious act is no longer regarded as essential."[383] Luther would call such self-centeredness a perfect example of humanity turned in upon itself.

In the light of Prenter's scathing critique of Bultmann, it is a little intriguing that he would establish logical necessity between Christ's cross and our own cross in his earlier argument against a theology of the cross without the cross. Clearly, his profound concern is to uphold the truth of the theology of the cross in maintaining that both Christ's word of gracious righteousness and the cross of one's own life are to be understood in inseparable relationship. His struggle is manifestly a search for adequate metaphor and language. In his deep concern for the theological validity of both aspects, he cannot stop himself from making a radical statement at the end of his treatise as his position on the subject. He says that "The deep truth of Luther's theology of the cross is that it views the cross on Golgotha and the cross which is laid upon us as one and the same."[384]

Unfortunately, such an equation of Christ's cross with our individual cross will entail the theological problem of the meaning and effectiveness of Christ's cross in its own terms. Any claim for a human cross as a part of the cross of Christ, no matter how insignificant it is both in terms of reality and understanding, will eventually prove Jesus Christ less than a savior of the world. As there is no prerequisite for the grace of God except the gift of faith, so also there cannot be any requirement for this grace to be effective after one is justified. In his justification a person is freed from all requirements. This is freedom from all attempts to justify ourselves and also freedom from any logical necessity of responsibility towards one's neighbor. Such is the radical nature of the theology of the cross. This will seem for all practical purposes, the grand risk of following Luther's theology of the cross. Indeed, it is a risk and a profound one, as one's absolutely unconditional, utter, and thorough dependence only on the righteousness of Christ for salvation is taken to be a fact of Christian life. Moreover, dismantling a justified person of all responsibility toward the neighbor is only to assert that the salvation is still complete and that it is God's business. Truly, this is good news simply experienced by faith. In such depth, the theology of the cross is both *a risk of freedom* and *a freedom to risk*.

Yet Luther's theology of the cross does not end there. The acting work of Christ, which is complete and total, moves and finds manifestation in the accomplished work of the justified sinner as we have already seen in thesis 27 of the *Heidelberg Disputation*. Luther's assertion in thesis 28 is that "the love of God does not find, but creates, what is pleasing to it."[385] Creation out of nothing is both an affirmation of the radical discontinuity and the only means of continuity. It is impossible to overemphasize the discontinuity between human works and God's work of salvation, yet, it is in this act of God by which the old Adam is put to death that the new Adam is brought to life. One helpful way to understand this is to remember that when Luther is speaking of salvation he is speaking in the context of *coram Deo* and likewise, when he speaks of love of God creating something new in the person, he is speaking *coram hominibus.* The first approach is confessional and the second liberational.

In the present debate of the theology of the cross the second approach has become the theological loci for critical and constructive theological endeavors especially in the third world context. However, it is not restricted to only developing situations where the issue of poverty and injustice has most definitely reached an alarming level to threaten the lives of millions by starvation and scarcity. We discussed two of these writers who have taken a liberational approach to the theology of the cross in our survey at the beginning of this chapter. In this section, we propose to discuss Moltmann much more critically to understand his contribution and viability in the light of our thesis of this project, namely, that it is in the affirmation of the uniqueness and finality of Jesus Christ that we become truly free and strong to witness in love and vulnerability.

Jürgen Moltmann

Jürgen Moltmann cannot be left out of any discussion of the theology of the cross as he has influenced this debate beyond his western context. Moltmann's book *The Crucified God*[386] has become a standard against which many have tested their own take on the theology of the cross. Moltmann followed the footsteps of Kazoh Kitamori in writing about the theology of the cross, in that he reflected about God in the context of the darkness of the tragedy of Auschwitz.

Though Moltmann borrowed the term from Luther[387] his theology of the cross is quite different from that of Luther. Moltmann argues that the theology of the cross has inevitable implications for both human liberation and divine nature. He understands God as the suffering God in the suffering of Christ. Also for him, God's being is in the suffering and the suffering is in God's being itself.[388] In his opinion Luther's theology of the cross emphasized the correlation between theory and practice, however, it was restricted to the religious world of the time. Luther failed to formulate it as a social criticism against feudal society.[389] However, Moltmann, like Luther, makes the theology of the cross the basis and criterion of Christian theology, "the test of everything that deserves to be called Christian."[390]

For him, Jesus' abandonment on the cross entails radical implications for the concept of God because Jesus, even in this event, is the second person of the Trinity. Thus, Jesus is abandoned by the

Father. This is what has been termed "radical kenotic Christology."[391] His pattern of argument is that since the Father rejects the Son he becomes utterly destitute on the cross. Thus, this event brings him in solidarity with all the destitute and the rejected of the world. Jesus acquires the status of destitute by abandoning his "divine identity" at the cross.[392] Thus, Moltmann sees that in this way Jesus identifies with all the forsaken, poor, godless and homeless of the world.

The Jesus who relinquishes his divine identity to become destitute is strange to Luther; on the contrary, Luther maintains that God is revealed supremely in the cross of Jesus Christ. However, both agree that Jesus suffered on the cross: for Moltmann, in Jesus' suffering God's divinity was humiliated, and for Luther, as God's revelation Jesus' suffering represented God's suffering. Moltmann's understanding is radical as he asserts that in the abandonment of the cross the Father suffers 'Sonlessness' as the Son suffers 'Fatherlessness.' On the basis of trinitarian understanding, Moltmann expands the theological meaning of the theology of the cross to talk about the concept of God.

Even Moltmann's frequent use of the basic terms of Luther's theology of the cross such as faith and trust are used with quite differing meanings. He employs them to denote an understanding of the responsibility one has towards the world which is in line with the emphasis of his theological reflection, namely, political theology.[393] For him the call to follow Jesus is not a call to believe in *him*,[394] but as the "commandment of the eschatological moment."[395] The clarion call to engage in the activity of bringing the eschatological moment, the completion of God and his creation to pass, is the ultimate meaning of following Jesus.[396] This is further substantiated by Moltmann's argument that "More radical Christian faith can only mean committing oneself without reserve to the 'crucified God.'"[397]

Though both Luther and Moltmann speak of the suffering God, their understanding and appropriation of this God for one's life is quite different. For Moltmann the acceptance of Jesus can be understood "only as an act of identification with the crucified God,"[398] whereas Luther will not allow any act, no matter how radical, to come between the crucified God and a helpless yet needful human. Moltmann argues for an *act* for identification whereas Luther denies any act for identification, yet acknowledges acts or works flowing from faith confession. For Luther, identification is God's gracious work alone.

The fundamental distinction between them lies in their perception of God. Their distinctive concept of God leads them to interpret the event of the cross differently. To Luther, as to traditional Christianity, God is being. Not so, however, for Moltmann. Moltmann considers God as an event and thus in the process of being completed.[399] Moltmann confesses his panentheistic tendency.[400] Moltmann and Luther remain irreconcilable. However, Luther's understanding of God is not static in any event. Luther's understanding is based on the biblical account that would undermine Eckhardt's strict category. However, Eckhardt underlines the distinction between the two, as he asserts that for Moltmann:

> The Trinity is still being perfected at this point in time, and since Moltmann is pantheistic, he holds that God will be perfected only when creation is perfected. Therefore, the cross is for Luther an activity which has nothing to do with God's internal perfecting, since he is already perfect and complete. But for Moltmann, the cross is the key element in God's process of being perfected.[401]

It is true that the cross does not perfect God; nonetheless, it shows who God is in a real and concrete way for Luther. God is revealed on the cross. This is the most revolutionary concept that has clear ramifications for living a life of faith. Even though Luther's theology of the cross does not allow a progressive understanding of God as is the case with Moltmann, yet, his concern for Christian life by no means takes a back seat in the framework of the theology of the cross. However, as pointed out earlier, this cannot be determinative as to who we are *coram Deo*. Burnell Eckhardt is right in his conclusion:

> Because of these differing interpretations, Luther's theology of the cross is a system which shapes his interpretation of reality, while Moltmann's is one which seeks to shape reality itself.[402]

The basis for the distinction between Luther and Moltmann further seems to lie in what Moltmann intends to do in his book *The Crucified God*. After concluding that Luther's theology of the cross remained confined to the religious world, Moltmann states:

> The task therefore remained of developing the theology of cross in the direction of an understanding of the world and of history....A thorough going theology of the cross must apprehend the crucified God in all the three areas in which the ancient world used the term theology, and in which even today men are inescapably religious; in mythical theology, in the form of demythologization; in political theology, in

the form of liberation and in philosophical theology, in the form of understanding the universe as creation.[403]

It is clear the focus and scope of his theology of the cross is quite different than that of Luther. However, in his Trinitarian understanding of the theology of the cross, Moltmann states that "The content of the doctrine of the Trinity is the real cross of Christ himself. The form of the Christ is the Trinity."[404] As a result of this dialectic, Moltmann understands God as 'event.' He says that " 'God' is not another nature or heavenly person or a moral authority, but in fact an 'event.'"[405] Thus, even though he maintains theology of the cross to be dialectical theology,[406] it is to be understood in terms of inner Trinitarian framework and not in terms of Luther's dialectic of Christ as *sacramentum* and *exemplum*. Based on this, he argues for involvement and solidarity with those poor, marginalized and disenfranchised. It is clear that Moltmann's concern is the nature of the triune God as he underlines that "suffering would be history in the midst of God himself."[407] Not concerned about the paradox of Luther's theology of the cross, he asserts that his concern is not "to set up paradoxes, but to ask whether the experiences of the passion and the suffering of God lead into the inner mystery of God himself in which God himself confronts us."[408] God's mystery is not what Luther is concerned with in his theology of the cross. Luther is concerned with what is revealed in Jesus on the cross, namely, God's righteousness revealed for the salvation of the world. Thus, Burnell Eckhardt concludes that in sharp contradiction to Luther, Moltmann rejects the foundational meaning of the cross for atonement.[409] Such a conclusion seems to be not without basis as far as the emphasis of the book *The Crucified God* is concerned; however, in his expressed intention of widening the scope of the 'thoroughgoing theology of the cross,' Moltmann emphasizes the need to develop it "as social criticism, in association with practical actions to set free both the wretched and their rulers."[410] Moltmann, however, is not against the atonement as he believes that vicarious atonement is necessary.[411] In his Trinitarian theology of the cross discussed in *The Crucified God*, vicarious suffering of Christ is presupposed as a very important aspect. Even the confession of Jesus is given emphasis in terms of eschatological meaning.[412] On the other hand, Luther's theology of the cross would not let go of the dialectic of Christ as *sacramentum* and *exemplum* that, first of all, requires confession of faith. However, Moltmann's understanding of the political theology of the cross is significant in providing a relevant content to the present day implication of doing theology of the cross.

However, strictly judging in the framework of Luther's theology of the cross, Moltmann's assertion will seem to be speculative; hence, a part of theology of glory. In this concept of God he seems to have fallen victim to what the theology of the cross stands against, namely speculation about God.[413] Indeed, Moltmann's conceptual development of God based on the event of the cross transcends the strict paradigm of Luther's theology of the cross according to which God is to be found only in Jesus of Nazareth and nowhere else.[414] Both Moltmann and Luther speak of the concept of God on the basis of the cross. For Moltmann the cry of dereliction is the basis, whereas Luther considers the whole event of the cross. Though the radical conclusion of Moltamann revolutionizes the understanding of God, the revelation of God in Luther is no less radical. Even the forsakenness of Jesus, the basis for Moltmann's conclusion, may need a somewhat different understanding in the light of the complete account of the cross event. This includes among other things, Jesus' promise to the second thief, "Truly I tell you, today you will be with me in paradise"[415] and his relationship of trust with the Father as he speaks the last word, "Father, into your hands I commend my spirit."[416]

At this point we should also consider Carl Braaten's critique of Moltmann's theology of the cross.[417] Braaten's critque is significant because it can equally be leveled against Luther's theology of the cross as Luther is also dependent on Paul's interpretation of the cross. His basis of criticism is that the theology of the cross is based on Paul's writings and hence inadequate as he argues "Paul is not the whole canon. His theology cannot even determine the sole norm of what is Christian."[418] He is right in recognizing Paul as the main source for the theology of the cross, yet, he seems to have ignored the fact that the most of the gospel narratives are dedicated to the description of the passion story of Jesus Christ. His criticism also betrays his restricted understanding of the theology of the cross as confined to the event of the cross and not something that is truly a theology about the incarnate life of Jesus Christ. While Braaten highlights the theology of the cross to be a sporadic theme in the history of theology, he miserably fails to take into account the contribution of the doctrine of the impassibility of God developed and taken for granted since patristic times. Moreover, it does not establish the fact that what has been ignored is necessarily a matter of periphery. Braaten's historical inquiry seems to have blunted his theological sensibility to the centrality of the cross.

Given Moltmann's minimal regard for the salvific aspect of the theology of the cross, which was the central character of Luther's theology, his theology of the cross will be what Prenter calls the theology of the cross without the word. While reading Moltmann's *Crucified God* one may get an impression that Luther disregarded works completely which is, however, far from being true. Luther is against works when they are understood as being meritorious. Against the challenges of speculative theology that promoted work as essential part of one's salvation, Luther argued that works have no place as far as obtaining God's grace is concerned. No doubt Luther stressed faith because that was warranted by the opposition and the theologically unsound doctrine taught by the church of the time.

Does this mean that works should be our emphasis in our present time as we are living in the 21st century? Many who, like, Moltmann, insist on works, especially fighting for the destitute think this to be the case. No, says the theology of the cross, because the human tendency is always to put work before God. This will defeat the whole purpose of the theology of the cross as this will prove God a liar and incompetent in two senses. First, humans beings are not helpless and powerless. The need for God's grace is not mandatory but optional and God's revelation on the cross has only exemplary validity. Second, God's promise that faith in Jesus Christ is sufficient for salvation will not only be disregarded but be proved utterly unnecessary. One cannot help wonder, then, what would be the basis of one's relation with the neighbor or the destitute in Moltmann's parlance? Moltmann will say the basis is Jesus' solidarity with all on the margins of society by his abandoned death on the cross. What would Moltmann say to a statement that one should rather follow Gandhi's example of self-sacrifice than Jesus' example of sacrifice as Gandhi is historically more appropriable because of the proximity in time and context for South Asian? We will continue this discussion in the following chapters to argue that one need not deny the finality and uniqueness of Jesus Christ to find an adequate paradigm to live an authentic Christian life of proclamation and witness.

The theology of the cross will always oppose this perennial tendency of humanity to put work before faith in Jesus Christ. Nonetheless, we should not conclude that Luther is against work. He says:

> It is impossible for it [faith] not to be doing good works incessantly. It does not ask whether good works are to be done, but before the question is asked, it has already done them, and it is constantly doing them.[419]

We will discuss this aspect of Luther's theology further when we interact with Asian theologians in later chapters.

Conclusion

The preceding discussion made it clear that there are different interpretations of the theology of the cross of Luther. In many cases, Luther's profound influence was noted to underline his continued relevance. The two major emphases in all interpretation were clear: first, Christ as the sacrament and second, Christ as the example. Both emphases have valid theological reasons that must not be compromised if the theology of the cross is to be held true to its essence. At the same time, the soteriological and epistemological basis of the revelation on the cross is not to be undermined for the theology of the cross to be holistic. It is in keeping these two aspects in creative balance and tension that Luther's theology of the cross promises to be resourceful for contextual theology for South Asia. We will speak of this in later chapters while discussing Luther's theology of the cross vis-á- vis plurality of faith and poverty of South Asia. However, many theologians in their effort to underline one aspect of this theology seem to have ignored the other aspect.

We believe that Regin Prenter's thesis that the theology of the cross must always be a theology of the cross with the word and at the same time, a theology of the cross with the cross, maintains the dialectical relation of Christ as *sacramentum* and *exemplum*. Thus, it will mean the cross is both to be confessed in proclamation and followed in praxis. There is no question about the indispensability of these aspects in Luther's theology of the cross. However, the question as to how they should be understood as two sides of a coin without making any mandatory demand is yet be clearly delineated. We have, nonetheless, provided some direction and analysis towards this.

The theme of Christ as *sacramentum* and *exemplum* will further be discussed. We will use Luther's idea of holding tightly the *simul justis et peccator* to argue that just as a person is always both saint and sinner, so also, Christ is both sacrament and example at the same time. However, as we have maintained the order of the two, to begin with, is most critical for theological reasons. Finally, we will propose the Way as a possible metaphor to bridge the gap between Christ the *sacramentum* and *exemplum*. But now we should turn to Asian theologians M. M. Thomas and Aloysius Pieris to understand their theology of the cross.

CHAPTER 4

South Asian Theologians and the Theology of the Cross

In this chapter, we will discuss the theology of South Indian theologian M. M. Thomas and Sri Lankan theologian Aloysius Pieris. Our focus is their understanding of the cross, which plays a critical role in their theological construction. Although their theologies are wide in scope, our discussion of their theology of the cross will provide a basic orientation to their theology, which will enable us to engage in critical interaction with Luther's theology of the cross in later chapters.

M. M. Thomas

Madathilparambil Mammen Thomas[420] (1916-1997) is an Indian ecumenical theologian, well known around the world. He was born in the Southern state of Kerala and was educated in Trivandrum and at the University of Madras. As a member of the *Mar Thoma* Church,[421] he was involved in Youth activities of the church. His involvement in Christian youth and student movements led him to Student Christian Movement (SCM) and World Student Christian Federation (WSCF), which provided him worldwide exposure. Deeply interested in social issues and Christian commitment, he organized many ecumenical study conferences on the issues of Asia. As a self-taught theologian and social analyst, Thomas was in the very center of the ecumenical movement, first in the WSCF, and then World Council of Churches(WCC). In 1968, he reached the very helm of ecumenical activity when he was elected the moderator of the Central Committee of WCC, a post that he held till 1975. Thomas also served as the director of the Christian Institute for the Study of Religion and Society (CISRS), Bangalore, India from 1962 to 1975.

His significance as a theologian and ethicist can be seen in the fact that a number of studies have been conducted on his theological and ethical thought. A glimpse of his stature as theologian is to be seen in what Prof. Hendrik Berkhof had to say on the occasion of conferring of the honorary Doctorate in Theology by the theological faculty of the University of Leiden, Holland. Prof. Berkhof recorded his ecumenical contribution and recognized him as a great bridge-builder.[422] His influence has been far and wide both by virtue of the many important positions that he held and also through lectures, addresses and publications. He has published extensively both in his mother tongue, Malayalam, and English.[423] However, our task in this section is to discuss Thomas' theology in terms of the Asian reality of plurality of religions and poverty of the masses.[424]

Interpretation of the Cross

Faced with the reality of revolutionary times manifested in anti-colonialist nationalist struggles and nation building in the context of multi-religiosity and the mass poverty of Indian sub-continent, Thomas finds transforming power in the cross and recognizes the universal lordship of Jesus Christ for authentic Christian witness. Accordingly, he speaks of the humanizing power of the gospel. The core of the gospel, for Thomas, is that in the life, death and resurrection of Jesus of Nazareth God acted to save the world.[425] In his theological venture Thomas is primarily concerned about a search for a relevant interpretation of the gospel of salvation vis-á-vis the struggle for fuller humanity. In his book *Salvation and Humanization,* Thomas says that the true understanding of salvation can only be perceived from the dialectic between faith in the Christ-event and the collective struggle for fuller humanity.

Thus, based on his theological perception of the cross, he enlarges the traditional understanding of salvation only as spiritual relationship with God. For him, salvation involves the eschatological promise of God's reign with its characteristic new creation of justice, righteousness, and peace. Thus, salvation is understood in terms of qualitative change in the transformation of socio-political structures. The close relationship between salvation and humanization is evident when he concludes, "The mission of salvation and the task of humanization are integrally related to each other, even if they cannot be considered identical."[426] Thomas believes all polarization between salvation in history and salvation beyond history is fruitless.[427] The basis of this belief is that "the gospel is for nations as well as for individuals."[428]

A professed Christocentric theologian influenced by Barth, Thomas' theological and ethical thoughts are both deeply impacted and shaped by the cross of Christ. In discussing Thomas, we will argue that the cross is foundational for his basic theological project of "struggle for fuller humanity": A goal which informed his Christology, ethics, theology of religions, and other aspects of his theology.

Cross as Revelation

Like Luther, the cross is a revelation for Thomas. However, unlike Luther, it is not a revelation of the God-self but the supreme revelation of love. Thomas' unique understanding of the cross as heart is to be noted for its deep theological implication for his theology of humanization.[429] He asserts:

> The cross reveals God and his purpose for his whole creation as Love. It gives the assurance that the universe has a center not chaos, not even a cold calculating Mind, but a Cross—i.e. a heart throbbing for all men with understanding, suffering and forgiving love.[430]

Acutely aware of the signs of the time and critically reflecting on the meaning of the cross, he finds a new possibility for life owing to what God has done on the cross of Jesus Christ. Thus, his Christological emphasis remained a point of reference for doing theology in revolutionary times recognized in liberal humanism, nationalist movements, religious movements, etc.

Thomas further identifies the cross as the release of power with the concept of the kingdom inaugurated in the incarnation of Jesus. Thus, he says "the cross is the Kingdom of God moving with power into the history of mankind, taking control of the powers of this world, bringing to men the righteousness of God in which every man becomes a brother for whom Christ died."[431] It is significant to note that here Thomas speaks of the cross in terms of the Kingdom of God which has become a reality in history. The kingdom of God, then, is the purpose of the cross, which is symbolized in peace, freedom, and justice. In Thomas' words, the kingdom of God represents a situation where fuller and richer life is continuously realized.

In his search for fuller humanity, Thomas affirms the potential for positive contribution of the contemporary revolutions in liberal humanism, religious movements, and ideologies. However, in relating his theology of the cross to liberal humanism and its belief in "easy optimism about human nature and historical progress," Thomas notes that it is unable to recognize "the fact of evil in the higher self of man" and "the powerlessness of moral idealism."[432] He gives the example of the Pharisees who were the guardians of morality, and *Pax Romana* that was the symbol of peace and justice, to assert that "these expressions of man's best in religion, morality, nationalism, and state that reveal themselves at the cross as inherently incapable of transcending self-centeredness."[433] In his encounter with Gandhism and Marxism, Thomas discovered the basic problem of ideologies as one of the powerlessness of moral idealism and self-righteousness leading to ideological fanaticism. In order to counter this and enable them not to betray human goals, Thomas found the application of the message of the cross as offering divine forgiveness to be most relevant. Thus, the divine forgiveness revealed on the cross of Jesus Christ, according to Thomas, is indispensable for revolutions to be true to what they portend, namely, humanizing forces.

Similarly, Thomas notes that what makes Marxism an absolute dogma is the tendency to claim ultimate loyalty for relative scientific truths. At this point an ideology is turned into faith and then it becomes "an expression of human self-righteousness and the doctrine of justification by works."[434] Only a commitment to a transcendent realm of grace can keep ideologies of humanism in their truly secular character without clamoring for absolute claims. Therefore, the answer to this ideological problem, for him, is a theological one. Thus, he observes:

> It is here that the forgiving Grace of God mediated through the Crucified and Risen Jesus Christ justifying every man without works but releasing him for works of love is relevant to the redemption, involving a redefinition of the politics and ideology of Marxism-Leninism and to make it truly a secular humanism.[435]

When the cross is accepted as the source of divine forgiveness it is possible for Christians and others to carry out their political witness with the "glad acceptance of the world of sin and death, and the commitment to a path of overcoming this world through the way of self-giving love."[436]

In agreement with his theological project of humanization, Thomas views sin predominantly in terms of its corporate dimensions. Both sin and salvation have corporate dimensions:

> Sin has its corporate expression in the dehumanizing spiritual forces of corporate life, the demons of principalities and powers, and the victory of Christ should mean victory over

them and salvation in Christ must find its manifestation in power over these forces as power for humanization of our structures of collective existence.⁴³⁷

Sin is understood primarily in the structural injustice in society. The structures such as casteism, capitalism, patriarchy, and others perpetuate the unjust and oppressive social, economic, and political systems that are rooted in human sinfulness. Hence, the context of mass poverty in the South Asian context is the result primarily of oppressive socio-economic structures manifested in caste, class and patriarchy. He declares that the "corporate sin has a momentum unknown to personal sins."⁴³⁸

Historical Cross and Eternal Cross

Thomas' understanding of the cross has two hermeneutical dimensions, which provide the basic theological framework for the self-understanding of Christian faith and mission in regard to their integral relation with the two prominent realities of his context, namely, secular humanism and renascent Hinduism. On the one hand, he vigorously defended the historicity of the Christ event⁴³⁹ because, for him, the historical cross is the basis for the eternal dimension. On the other hand, the cross of Jesus Christ is perceived in its eternal dimension. His deep commitment to the project of humanization draws its theological rationale from the eternal dimension of the cross as it is articulated in terms of its meaning for contemporary time. Thomas argues:

> The Cross is the identification of God with the suffering of the poor and the oppressed, of the refugee and the disinherited, of the Negro and the outcaste, and is therefore a source of hope for their liberation and their future.⁴⁴⁰

Such divine solidarity made concrete on the cross of Jesus Christ with those yet to achieve fuller humanity remains a source of hope as well as a pattern of existence. However, Heilke Wolters contends that the divine forgiveness is more consistent with the entire framework of Thomas' theological reflections than the cross, understood as divine solidarity.⁴⁴¹ Divine solidarity for him, raises the problem of the theological meaning of hope in the absence of victory. Wolters is correct in emphasizing the paramount value of the divine forgiveness in the thought of Thomas. Nonetheless, while dealing with renascent Hinduism and other movements of humanism, Thomas applies the category of solidarity of the cross more, not only in frequency but also with inescapable theological implications. Moreover, Wolters' contention is self-defeating as the very thesis of his book on Thomas' theology is about the centrality of prophetic participation, which underlines the deep and profound reality of solidarity with suffering humanity in Thomas' theology. The cross as a mandate for prophetic participation is to be perceived in Thomas' emphasis on humanization, to which we will turn presently.

Salvation and Humanization

The concept of humanization is clearly the central category of Thomas' work. In many of his writings Thomas argues for an end that is to be summarized in the concept of humanization. However, Thomas does not provide a precise definition. In *Towards a Theology of Contemporary Ecumenism,* he speaks of it in terms of its goals:

> If abundance and peace are not to be accompanied by cries of distress among the people, it requires a high quality of community life, with justice for the poor built into the laws of society, and the submerged and suppressed groups of the traditional society (e.g. the outcastes, the tribal, and the women of India) being given due participation in the structures of power and the processes of decision-making. Elimination of pockets of poverty and distress and indignity among the people is the goal for realizing community. People seeking a richer and fuller realization of the potentialities of their humanity through building a new society with health and plenty, peace and justice—this secular pursuit of happiness is the context within which I must speak of spiritual salvation.[442]

It is clear that humanization is creating an environment conducive to realize human potential to the maximum. Although Thomas is not explicit about the relation between the theology of the cross and the process of humanization, it is not difficult to conclude that his understanding of the cross as power breaking forth to inaugurate the Kingdom of God is a theology of humanization.

Thomas' focus on humanization found centrality and indispensability owing to his own struggles over how to affirm that "the self-emptying and self-sacrificing love of Christ Jesus was itself the disclosure of the nature of divinity's Love."[443] His attempt to resolve this in the light of Indian tradition failed as both Joshua Marshman, a missionary, and Ram Mohan Roy, a Hindu social reformer, were unable to help him.⁴⁴⁴ On the one hand, the evangelical Baptist Missionary Marshman could not adequately appropriate the depth of Christ's self-emptying love and on the other hand, despite Thomas' admiration for Ram Mohan Roy's social passion, he found Roy lacking in his understanding of the meaning of love.⁴⁴⁵ Thomas recognizes a deeper and more adequate appreciation of his search in Keshub Chandra Sen's idea of Christ emptying himself of self and demonstrating his oneness with God through "an active unity of will and communion through obedience to God and his righteousness."⁴⁴⁶ It is interesting to see that Thomas links Sen's conception of Christ's 'divine humanity' with the idea of Christ's 'inhumanization' of divinity, found in Russian orthodox theologians.⁴⁴⁷ This, in turn, leads Thomas to his own term 'humanization'. The concept of humanization is of foundational value in Thomas' theology⁴⁴⁸ as it suggests his Christological understanding in terms of Christ's offer as well as it speaks of the missional implications of Christian faith. It remains significant throughout his life for its defining relationship with salvation.

Hielke Wolters rightly points out a dialectical relationship between salvation and humanization in Thomas' theology. Wolters states that Thomas' thinking developed out of "his ardent search for a relevant interpretation of the gospel of salvation vis-á-vis the struggle for fuller humanity."⁴⁴⁹ For this search, he often used A. G. Hogg's phrase "challenging relevance"⁴⁵⁰ to speak of the gospel's integral aspect of humanization.

His theology of the cross pertaining to the struggle for fuller humanity is to be seen when Thomas argues, "that salvation is the spiritual inwardness of true humanization, and that humanization is inherent in the message of salvation in Christ."⁴⁵¹ He speaks of two important events, which may be designated as the move for humanization. First, on the basis of his interpretation of the mission history, Thomas further bolsters his argument by saying that it was "the promise of humanization inherent in the gospel of salvation that led to the influx of the oppressed into the church."⁴⁵² Many historians have underlined this aspect of the gospel. Especially in South India many mass conversion in the 18th and 19th centuries were attributed, among other things, to the masses' desire to escape the stigma and indignity of lower caste within the Hindu fold. Secondly, in the concept of humanization, Thomas finds continuity rather than discontinuity with the indigenous Christological thoughts of Indian tradition. For him, Indian Christian theologians Keshub Chandra Sen, Chenchiah, Chakkerai and Paul Devanandan and their characteristic understanding of Jesus Christ as the Divine Man, the New Adam, the bearer of New Humanity, New Creation, etc., only provided creative impetus to understand salvation in terms of humanization. Thomas contends "the final destiny of man is ultimately an incorporation into Christ's glorified humanity. That is, salvation itself could be defined as humanization in a total and eschatological sense."[453]

Thus, concerned with humanization, Thomas recognizes in the secular revolutions the quest for humanity, which is basic to the socio-cultural and political struggle in Asia.[454] This begins with discerning Christ's presence in the human quest and with full participation in the struggle for fuller humanity. Thomas says:

> It is within the context of modern man's quest for the human and the search for the spiritual foundations of that quest that Christ's salvation becomes challengingly relevant to the modern human situation.[455]

Thomas' insistence on the decisive significance of the context of revolutions and its potential has led Sugand Sumithra to conclude his study of Thomas' theology as 'Revolution as Revelation.'[456] Dr. D. Wolf criticizes Thomas for equating God's revelation with Asian revolutions, to which Thomas replies that this kingship of Christ manifested in revolutions emphasizes the person of the crucified and risen Christ. Thus, the core of the Christian message,[457] as fundamental and decisive as it is for him, renders the basis for his unusual positive evaluation of the revolution. Further, the meaning of salvation perceived in terms of human efforts towards humanization has attracted criticism from Tübingen missiologist Peter Beyerhaus. Beyerhaus accuses Thomas of replacing theology with anthropology. Thomas is quick to respond with his characteristic Christological assertion:

> ...the ultimate framework of reference for Christian thought is neither God nor man in abstract ... but Jesus Christ who is God-Man...to use Karl Barth's expression, the humanity of God... Therefore, properly speaking, Christian missionary thinking cannot be either theology or anthropology except as either of them related to Christology.[458]

Given such emphasis on humanization it will not be hard to perceive Thomas' insistence on participation. The efforts towards humanization are to be understood through participation in revolutions of the time, namely, movement of secularization, technological and cultural revolutions and nation building. Thus, Hielke Wolters has rightly designated his theology as the theology of prophetic participation.[459]

Theology of Religions[460]

In fact, the issue of plurality of religions is addressed by Thomas' concept of humanization.[461] Thomas is unambiguous about the validity and significance of humanization among religions:

> It is my conviction that the relation between salvation and humanization, i.e. between the ultimate destiny of man and his historical destiny...is also debated within all the religions...my thesis, therefore, is that it is the theme of humanization which provides the most relevant point of entry for any Christian dialogue with these movements on salvation in Christ at spiritual and theological depth."[462]

Thomas outlines his framework of theology of religions by considering the questions as to why and how Christians must understand religious plurality.[463] According to him, the history of isolation of religions has moved into what he calls a "dialogical existence."[464] Thus, there is no alternative to dialogue among religions and he speaks of three levels of dialogue.[465] We should remember that Thomas is primarily thinking of Hinduism in his theology of religions. However, all three levels of dialogue remain important. Thomas' own special interest is in the first type of dialogue, which aims at creating an open culture based on common humanity.[466] In this emphasis one cannot miss Thomas' deep commitment to humanization.

Apart from the approach based on the attempt at humanization, Thomas puts forth Christ-centered syncretism as the final solution to the problem of religions. While dealing with other religions Thomas remains Christocentric. He argues:

> Can we not, at a time when all religions are in the ferment of change, speak of the Cross of Christ as in some measure breaking down the walls of partition between peoples of all religions and ideologies as it did the wall of participation between Jew and Gentile? Is it not legitimate to welcome a Christ-centered process of inter-religious and inter-cultural penetration through dialogue? If you will permit the use of the word 'syncretism' to denote all processes of inter-penetration between cultures and religions, the only answer to

a wrong syncretism which means the uncritical superficial normless mixing of basically incompatible religious conceptions and cultural attitudes is Christ-centred syncretism which grapples with and evaluates all concepts and attitudes critically in the light of Jesus and converts them into vehicles for communicating the truth of the gospel and for expressing its meaning for life.[467]

Apparently, Thomas is grappling with the issue of pluralism and finds the Cross of Christ capable of transcending religions and ideologies. This idea is systematically developed in his book *Man and the Universe* as he concludes that Christ-centered syncretism is a viable approach to the plurality of religions. However, he is critical of theologians such as Harnack, Bultmann and Russell Chandran (an Indian theologian) who used the term syncretism to denote "the process whereby one religion utilizes and assimilates elements of other religions and cultures to communicate or embody its message." He also disagrees with Kraemer and Visser T. Hooft's concept of syncretism as "the illegitimate mingling of different religious elements." However, Thomas agrees with Pannenberg's connotation of syncretism as "the processes of reciprocity and integration in the relationship between cults, myths, individual gods and whole religions."[468] Thus, Thomas rightly anticipates a mutually enriching process of interaction among religions. The theology of religions has to do with the fact that theological exploration for M. M. Thomas is a life-long struggle to come to grips with faith. He does this by seeking to relate the truth of the person and meaning of Jesus Christ to the reality of other religions in India, on the one hand, and secular ideologies, on the other.

In his creative construction of Christology, though, not without precedence, Thomas presents the concept of "conversion of religions," parallel to the conversion of individuals. He concludes "If Jesus Christ transcends the Christian religion as its judge and redeemer, it opens up the possibility of Christ reforming all religions and in-forming himself in them."[469] By his own confession, Thomas has been a theologian with much emphasis on Christology. Though we have noted that the concept of humanization could be termed the single most representative term for the theology of Thomas; however, the true humanism, for Thomas, is to be found only in the divine humanity of Christ. He often speaks of "Jesus Christ and his New Creation"[470] to refer to the divine humanity of Jesus Christ. Deeply convinced and committed to the fact and principle of incarnation, Thomas vigorously defends the humanity of Jesus Christ. Thus, Thomas speaks of P. Chenchiah approvingly for his rejection of the conception of God as the absolute both in the theology of Sankara (Hinduism) and Hendrick Kraemer's understanding in *Christian Message in a Non-Christian World*. For Thomas, such emphasis on absolute God not only removes God away from people but it can also isolate people from each other. Instead, he emphasizes God's proximity to the people in Jesus and often refers to Jesus in Bonhoeffer's phrase "the man for others."

Against the tendency of Neo-Hinduism to deny the theological significance of the historicity of Christ event, Thomas asserts the foundational importance of the historicity of Jesus:

> Probably most important task of a theology of mission is to restate the significance of the historicity of the person of Jesus within the essential core of the Christian gospel that historical human existence can acquire a positive relation to our eternal salvation.[471]

Thus, the integral relation between incarnation and salvation is of foundational import for essential theological assertions. This is seen in his understanding of the incarnation itself. Incarnation is not just a temporary travel to the earth for the purpose of fulfilling his mission merely in the pattern of *avatara*.[472] Convinced about human existence as determined by matter and spirit, he depends on the Pauline meaning of *sarx* to include the whole existence.[473] Hence, Thomas speaks of "inhominization" in addition to incarnation.[474]

As is evident in our discussion, Thomas' primary concern in his theology has been Christian response to what God has done in Jesus Christ. Sumithra recognizes the action-reflection methodology in Thomas' theological reflection.[475] Thomas' consistent emphasis and persistent arguments for participation, solidarity and humanization only confirm Sumithra's evaluation.[476] While consistently contending for Christian responsibility in society, Thomas, nonetheless, holds to the all-sufficiency of the divine redemption in Jesus Christ. However, he is acutely aware of the strong critique of the western Orthodox and neo-orthodox for putting undue insistence on the doctrine of justification to the extent that it creates apathy and holds Christians blindfolded to the human struggle for humanization as an integral part of the divine plan of salvation. Hielke Wolters gives voice to Thomas' concern when he states, "The doctrine of justification has overshadowed the doctrine of sanctification to such an extent that reconciliation between God and the human being has lost its effectiveness in the Christian life."[477]

Being aware of such static interpretation of justification, Thomas consciously attempts to interpret the doctrine of justification by faith in dynamic terms. Thus, he understands justification by faith as a release of spiritual power and frequently uses phrases like the power of the cross, the power of forgiveness, etc. Justification is the release of the person from struggle for self-justification. Thomas states:

> The release from anxiety from the search for means of self-justification is a release for self-giving love of God and neighbor, which the Cross itself reveals as the destiny of man.[478]

Hence, Hielke Wolters concludes, "The dynamism in Thomas' interpretation of the cross in terms of forgiveness is that the cross becomes a way of life. That is to say, justification is not prior to sanctification. It is the momentum of sanctification."[479] Thus, it is beyond contention that Thomas is influenced both by the Christian tradition of the past and the present reality of the context for his Christological assertions.

Conclusion

In recognizing both the astounding condition of dehumanization and rich religious traditions of Asia, Thomas is able to provide deep relevance and comprehensive contextuality to the theological task, especially in the Indian sub-continent. Different from many theologians of his time, Thomas takes deep interest in the positive contribution and further potential of secular humanism for the theological task of humanization as he interprets it in the light of the cross. Thus, Charles West speaks of him as "an elder statesman wrestling afresh with the problems of Christian faith and cultural pluralism, with salvation and humanization."[480] His innovative theological construction has inspired and challenged many to engage in contextual theology.

Grounded on the perennial relevance of the gospel, he explores the present day theological construction in the intersection of Christian faith with other faiths (especially Hinduism) and secular ideologies such as Marxism and Gandhism. His understanding of Christ's New Humanity based on the resurrection of Christ led him to assert the presence of Christ's transforming power in secular movements and religious traditions. Thus, Thomas helped create an atmosphere of cooperation rather than competition among religions and also opened up new vistas in the secular movements for fresh possibilities for theological construction.

Rightly concerned with the question of the relevance of the gospel in present day context, Thomas emphasizes the human response to the Christ event. Consequently, he insists on the decisive relationship of the incarnation and its subsequent implications for social, political and economic life of humanity. Samuel Ryan, an Indian theologian, recognizes this relationship when he opines:

> He [Thomas] encountered the sacred at the center of the secular and the secular in the heart of the sacred. Thomas knew that the two belonged together and needed each other....The sacred, to be truly meaningful, must be earthly and incarnate. It will have to do with the whole human reality and entire gamut of history.[481]

In paying serious attention to the context of revolutions of the time and recognizing the human quest in them, Thomas' methodological approach reveals similarity to Paul Tillich's "method of correlation," according to which the "Christian message provides answers to the questions implied in human existence."[482] This explains Thomas' preference for the contemporary expression of Hinduism to classical Hinduism, which most Indian theologians before him have considered to be of critical importance for Indian Christian theology.

In his unrelenting stress on humanization, Thomas is consistent with the ecumenical understanding of mission not as Christianization or verbal proclamation of the good news of Jesus Christ but rather continuing Jesus' *works* of compassion, solidarity, and justice for the poor and the marginalized. Thomas understood well that in pursuing this understanding of mission, which took a systematic shape in his concept of humanization, a chord of concord could be struck with all other religions and ideologies of his time.

Though influenced by the western theological tradition of Barth,[483] he is deeply rooted in Indian reality as he attempts to develop his own theological expression in critical conversation with the theological tradition in India. Both his critical interaction and theological position are to be noted in his publication *The Acknowledged Christ of Indian Renaissance,* which he wrote in response to Raimundo Panikkar's book *Unknown Christ of Hinduism* (1964).

Like Luther, he speaks of the cross in terms of revelation. However, his perception of this revelation is quite different from the understanding of Luther as Thomas' action-reflection methodology originates in the cross as opposed to Luther's assertion of the end of all human activity for the salvation in the encounter of the cross. Luther's theology is based on God's action first and human response second, which maintains the order throughout. Thomas' emphasis on action is well accounted by Robin Boyd when he comments on Thomas' theology:

> Thomas has drawn together many different strands, from the east and west, from past and present, and woven them into an attractive and convincing way of action—a Christian *karma marga* (way of action).[484]

In developing a theology in response to the context in critical interaction with the tradition, Thomas hopes to continue Hogg's tradition of the gospel of Jesus Christ as "challenging relevance": To make the gospel meaningful and relevant for "greater human dignity, enhanced human creativity and mature human living."[485] Further, in order to avoid the danger of theological apathy and divinely contented inactivity of Christians, Thomas explicates the action of justification and human action of response, as one and the same. Although his concern is worthy and well-intentioned, however, in doing this he seems to have equated human action with divine action, which creates serious theological problems of making God's work dependent on human action. In the framework of Luther's theology of the cross, this will prove to be utterly against the understanding of human response as, and only as, the second action.

Another aspect of his theology that lacks depth and comprehensiveness is his superficial treatment of the truly oppressed communities of his country, namely, Dalit and tribal communities. Notwithstanding his reference to these communities as having been wronged and marginalized for centuries, Thomas is unable to speak powerfully on their behalf, about the injustice often inflicted upon them by those who profess to represent them. In the world scene, without any doubt, Thomas remains a strong voice of Indian Christians and "a great bridge-builder" in the words of Prof. Berkhof,[486] however, in the more immediate and local level of Indian Christianity, he seems to be an elite voice representing only a small group of privileged Christians. By his only referential treatment of the categories and perspectives of the Dalit and tribals, he seems to have failed to represent the majority of the Christians. Involved in this attitude towards the Dalit and the tribals is the serious issue of religious apartheid of Hinduism, which has profound implications for theological construction in that context. Arvind P. Nirmal, a Dalit theologian, argues against what Thomas' theology represents and says that Christian Dalit theology needs to break radically with the traditional Indian Christian theology because it has been in dialogue primarily with Brahmanic Hinduism. Recognizing the elitist element and a tendency of adopting oppressive religious symbols and systems of Brahmanical Hinduism, Nirmal declares that the Christian Dalit theology needs to challenge Indian Christian theology.[487] In his passionate and timely analysis of injustice and pleas for justice for the oppressed in the society, Thomas hardly discriminates between layered and specific structure and nature of oppression of people such as Dalit, tribals, fisher folk, etc. Perhaps, Thomas' own so called elite background, as a "St. Thomas Christian," became a sociological and cultural wall that he could transcend only in scant theory.

Nonetheless, Thomas' contribution to Indian Christian theology and the world ecumenical theology has been of critical significance for both its innovativeness and also for wider ecumenism.

Aloysius Pieris

Well known for his unflinching insistence on an Asian theology of liberation, Aloysius Pieris represents a voice of those who have demonstrated radical commitment to the church's witness in the light of Asian realities. He is a Roman Catholic theologian (a Sri Lankan Jesuit Priest), whose credentials are self-evident in academic degrees from Asia and Europe in Pali, Sanskrit, Philosophy, Theology and Prepolyphonic music. As the first Christian to receive a Ph.D. in Buddhist Philosophy from the University of Columbo (Sri Lanka), Pieris is uniquely qualified to speak of liberative elements of both Christianity and Buddhism.[488] Profoundly immersed in the Buddhist context of Sri Lanka, Pieris' theology exudes both creative radicalism and emendatory criticism of the church in Asia. In his very illustrious career he has dealt with different aspects of Asian liberation theology in his writings. However, we will limit our discussion to his understanding of the theology of the cross and Christological assertions within his theological framework. The central concern that is at the heart of Pieris' theology is how to make the church *in* Asia,[489] a church *of* Asia by taking into serious consideration 'the twin poles' of Asian reality, namely, pervasive poverty and profound religiosity. Thus, his sole focus is on how and why the church must witness to be a church that is truly a church *of* Asia.

The Understanding of the Cross: the Calvary of Asian Poverty

Aloysius Pieris has expressed his understanding of the cross-event by his signature phrase "the Calvary of Asian poverty." In this phrase is compressed Pieris' deep sense of theological validity for doing theology amidst crippling poverty for its liberative implications for subdued and subjugated humanity. Like Latin American liberation theologians, Pieris is writing, "almost exclusively in response to the questions posed by the situations in which he is involved."[490] As a result, the alarming extent of poverty in Asia and the omnipresent Asian poor occupy the central place in his theological reflection. While similar to Luther and M. M. Thomas in his understanding of the revelation of God on the cross, Pieris, however, interprets this revelation to conclude with radically different assertions. The revelation on the cross, for him, not only validates the integral relationship between Jesus and the poor but most certainly mandates it:

> Here, we are announcing an *entirely new concept* of God, revealed on the Cross. There, God has discarded the mask of the *Actus Purus,* the Immovable Mover, Unchanging Deity, Impassible Power…; instead, this God has foolishly and scandalously (1 Cor. 1:23) expressed the true Divine Self as Love that gets hurt and even breaks down before human ingratitude, a God who weeps, sweats and bleeds, sharing the pain and the fear and the despair of Her co-victims on earth, a God who does not live on others but dies that others may have life in abundance, a God who opts not just to be human but to associate with the socially degraded persons in the manner of living and dying.[491]

Thus, the integral relationship between God, Jesus and an option for the poor is definitive of how he understands the cross. Deeply convinced about such a central and defining understanding of God, Pieris argues for radical actions on behalf of the poor and with the poor.

It is to be noted that in Pieris' theological construction poverty is not merely a sociological category, but it is an indispensable theological paradigm for liberation. The two categories of the poor are distinguished, first, as victims of mammon⁴⁹² (nonetheless, they are considered by Pieris 'THE VICARS OF CHRIST') and the second group of the poor is the renouncers of mammon (who are called true "FOLLOWERS OF JESUS").⁴⁹³ However, instead of an attitude of pity and mercy for the poor, Pieris, based on Jesus' own admission, proclaims them to be the eschatological judge of nations (Mt. 25:36ff). And as powerless, the poor are called to partner with God in "confounding the powerful," and as those subjected to 'imposed poverty', they qualify to be elected as God's covenant partners."⁴⁹⁴ Further, for Pieris, the theological importance of the poor is beyond doubt, for he insists, "the poor must be seen as *those through whom God shapes our salvation history*.⁴⁹⁵ Thus, "the poor" is not simply a sociological category but they are a group invested with supreme potential for liberation.

Pieris immerses deep into Asian religiosity to draw out liberative characteristics of voluntary poverty to refer to the second group of the poor. In their renunciation of wealth and worldly desires, such people act as renouncers of mammon to bring about liberation. A self-conscious and deliberate option for poverty is a most certain and potent way to fight poverty. Pieris primarily recognizes this in monasticism, *Sangha*⁴⁹⁶ of Buddhism, Hindu Ashrams and Catholic monasteries, etc. As such, he claims Asian religions to be liberative. Further, according to Pieris, only those who have voluntarily made themselves poor for the sake of the gospel qualify to preach the gospel and such poverty, for him, is "evangelical". Again, far from mere sociological consideration, Pieris insists on the scriptural foundation for the poor "as inheritors and the proclaimers of God's reign.⁴⁹⁷ Thus, the action of the poor is his transforming goal and liberation, his ultimate objective. In a recent essay the same cardinal perception of the cross of Christ is expressed. Pieris contends:

> The cross, in the language of liberation, is the political conflict in which God vanquishes mammon, love defeats power, life rises from death, and the victim turns victor. It is the symbol of the good news of liberation, of which the main addressees and the sole announcers are today's victims of political conflicts.⁴⁹⁸

In his theological framework, Pieris establishes the indispensable relationship between Jesus Christ and the poor of both kinds. Against Barthian discontinuity, he argues a radical continuity between God and the poor. Thus, responding to poverty is not merely Christian responsibility for Pieris, it is the very core of who the Christian/church is. His relentless effort in making precisely this point is obvious in his declaration of Jesus as a living norm. He concludes:

> Our radical option for God's reign (love of God) which is simultaneously a radical option for the poor (love of neighbour) is the sum and substance of the Law and the Prophets, made flesh as a living norm in Jesus, the Christ.[499]

Further, the same is quintessentially expressed when Pieris says that "God's language of liberation which Jesus is."[500]

Contrary to his contemporary M.M. Thomas, Pieris concludes that Jesus' mission, inaugurated in his baptism in the Jordan, was consummated on the cross.[501] However, Pieris is not unlike Thomas in his understanding of the cross as the basis of *all Christian discipleship*.[502] Resolute and committed as a proponent of the Asian theology of liberation, Pieris recognizes liberation theology as having restored the theology of the cross:

> Liberation theology has restored the theology of the cross to the post-Vatican II church. Contemplation and action receive their authenticity not from each other, but from the cross that stands whenever altars are built to mammon on the graves of God's poor. True spirituality, then, is founded on self-transcendence—self-abnegation that grows into self-fulfillment (Matt. 16:25), in and through the *Other*; who hides in one's own self waiting to be sought through prayer, but also this same Other who hides in others as the victim-judge of human injustice (Matt. 25:35-36) waiting to be served through action. Both Abrahamic and Mosaic models of spirituality converge in indicating that Christ can be encountered as God-Man on the cross where God's search and human concern constitute one salvific process—that is to say, one liberational enterprise.[503]

In the light of overwhelming poverty, he is convinced that the accent should be "on the hard gospel demand for *renunciation*, 'denying oneself,' the 'taking up the cross,' as the *condito sine qua non* of true discipleship."[504] True to the spirituality of his order (Society of Jesus), he draws on Ignatius of Loyola's synthesis of *contemplativus simul in actione* (a contemplative in action) to argue for self-abnegation "as an authentic criterion of any genuine spirituality."[505] Moreover, the same emphasis of self-abnegation is reiterated as Pieris refuses to understand the mission mandate of Matthew 28 in any other way except in terms of the cross, in which he recognizes the cross to be more than mere price:

> The Baptism of the cross, therefore, is not only the price he paid for *preaching* the good news, but the basis of all Christian *discipleship (Mk. 8:34). Thus, the threefold missionary mandate to preach...baptize and make disciples*—understood in the past as the juridical extension of one local church's power over other localities through a rite of initiation, must be redeemed of this narrow ecclesiocentric interpretation by tracing it back to the cross: the final proof of authentic *preaching*, the only true *Baptism* that gives meaning to the sacrament that goes by that name, and the criterion of true Christian *discipleship*.[506]

Pieris is persistent in arguing for the cross as an example for Christians to emulate to discover the authentic meaning of their faith. The emphasis is on human response rather than God's action, which is consistent with the liberation theology of Latin America. However, he is critical of liberation theology for its tendency to replace the religious reality of Asia with the mentality of the west.[507]

However, "The Calvary of Asian poverty" or understanding of the cross remains one-sided and to a large extent distorted without any reference to that which Pieris, in another signature phrase calls "the Jordan of Asian religions." Presently, we will turn to the discussion of "the Jordan of Asian religions," which will underline the fact that both phrases namely, "the Calvary of Asian poverty" and "the Jordan of Asian religions," pregnant as they are with meaning and symbolism, truly remain the two theologically valid tools for imagining the reality of liberation. Thus, his thoughts on the Jordan of Asian religions can only further help explicate his theology of the cross. As indicated before, Pieris responds to what he calls 'the twin poles' of Asian reality, which in his theology has turned out to be what David Tombs refers as 'the two poles of Pieris' theology.'[508]

Jordan of Asian Religions

Pieris believes that Jesus' prophetic ministry finds its destiny when Jesus opts to accept the baptism of John the Baptizer and follow his spirituality. Jesus thought it fit to begin his messianic mission by becoming himself a follower of John the baptizer. In order to underline the significance of Jesus' option for John the Baptist's spirituality, Pieris presents Jesus as having to make a deliberate choice for prophetic asceticism. Thus, the traditional religiosity such as zealot movement (narrow ideology), sectarian Puritanism of the Essenes, Pharisaic spirituality of self righteousness, Sadducees, etc., are rejected by Jesus. In this prophetic asceticism, Jesus discovers an authentic spirituality and an appropriate point of departure for his own prophetic ministry.[509] More importantly, this act of baptism, for Pieris, is a definite and conscious act of identification with the 'religious poor.'[510] In his symbolic language of the "Jordan of Asian religions," Pieris expresses both the radical option of Jesus for prophetic asceticism in his baptism as well as the inevitability of Asian religions as resources for liberation.[511]

At the same time, Pieris recognizes Jesus' baptism to be an act of humility. It was due to this act of humility that God certified Jesus' credibility in the presence of the poor: 'Hear Ye Him'. It was a prophetic moment as his messianic self-understanding and missionary credentials before the people were bestowed on him. Acutely aware of the need for the church *of* Asia, he is convinced that it is only in the acceptance of the Asian religions that the church can truly be an appropriate legitimate voice for the people. Modeled after Jesus' own option for the prophetic asceticism in humility, Christians are invited to discern the similar liberative resources in Asian religions about which he is most certain.[512]

Again, arguing for the same humility as that of Jesus, manifested in his baptism at the hands of John, Pieris wonders if the Asian church would ever be humble to "seek to be baptized rather than baptize."[513] What Pieris means by this is that the church in Asia needs to immerse itself in "the baptismal waters of Asian religions" because, he argues, "It is only in the Jordan of Asian religiosity that she will be acknowledged as a voice of being heard by all: 'Hear ye him'."[514] Similar to the confluence of two spiritualities[515] in Jesus' baptism, any immersion in the Jordan of Asian religions will be a baptism in the twofold traditions of the monks and peasants of Asia, because Pieris believes that both traditions of the monk and peasants representing cosmic religiosity are liberative.

It is obvious that Pieris' focus is liberation. Any attempt that shifts this focus distorts the nature of doing theology. Hence, in his approach to other religions, Pieris criticizes the fulfillment theory of the ancient fathers and Vatican II. He argues that it relegates other religions to a pre-Christian category of spirituality to be fulfilled through the church's mission. He further says that on this basis some argue to baptize the religiosity and culture rather than the prophetic imperatives to immerse oneself in the baptismal waters of Asian religions that predate Christianity.[516] Pieris is correct in saying that other religions are not to be conquered but understood as genuine partners in the task of liberation. For Pieris, this is an essential precondition for Christian faith in order to acquire authenticity and acceptance in Asian context.

Symbol of Jesus' Baptism

The events in the river Jordan and on Calvary, according to Pieris, represent Jesus' "baptismal immersion" in Asian reality for self-understanding and self-revelation.[517] Pieris remarks about Jesus that "his first prophetic gesture at the Jordan and his last prophetic gesture on Calvary, both of which are designated in the gospels as 'baptism.'"[518] Thus, he argues that since both events are described by evangelists as "baptism" (MT. 3:13-15; Mk 10:35; Lk. 12:50) *"Each was a self-effacing act which revealed his prophetic authority."*[519] Baptism is understood as a universal call to live for others to the point of self-immolation.[520]

It is in the interpretation of these two baptisms that not only the content and core value of Jesus' earthly ministry is determined but also Pieris' understanding of the Asian theology of liberation is articulated. Further, that both baptismal events relate to one mission of liberation is apparent when he says, "Jordan was only the beginning of Calvary."[521] His theology of the cross is what Asian theology of liberation demands from all those who follow Jesus, whose mission, according to Pieris, was "a mission of the poor and a mission to the poor, a mission by the poor and mission for the poor."[522]

Pieris says that the struggle of Jesus that begins immediately after his baptism, is against mammon with all its principalities and powers. Jesus' poverty[523] was more than a passive solidarity with the religious poor of Israel and his action and pronouncements[524] more than mere negative protests. In fact, Pieris declares, "It was a calculated strategy against mammon whom he declared to be God's rival."[525] Pieris invests immense energy and imparts powers to his theological arguments in order to equip the church to demolish mammon that stands against the liberation of the people and hence, against the Kingdom of God.

It is obvious that Jesus' baptism in the Jordan transcends mere symbolism to establish a virtual pattern of life in which seeking, finding and affirming of what the Asian religions have to offer for the liberation of humanity is a veritable norm of Christian living and witness. His acute awareness of both plurality of religions and mass poverty give reason and boldness to his critique of the Vatican II.

Religious Dialogue

Reacting against the Vatican II, he asserts that the Asian theology of liberation goes beyond the theological vision sponsored by Vatican II. The council, in his opinion, resulted in "liberal theology that spoke mainly to the challenges of faith encountered by western culture."[526] He contends that Asian theology required a more radical liberation theology that arises out of Christian immersion in the lives of the poor and the religious traditions to which they belong.[527] The Asian context, states Peiris, is 'a blend of profound religiousness' (which could be Asia's greatest wealth) and overwhelming poverty. An authentic Asian theology must be built around these two realities. In a sense he was not saying anything new as Asian Christians before him had called for inter-religious cooperation to promote social justice. Yet he went beyond earlier calls, by viewing liberation as the *raison d'etre* of both Christian theology and inter-religious dialogue.[528]

Religious dialogue is clearly a fertile way to enhance his core understanding of human religious existence for liberation. His deep commitment to Buddhism arises out of the context in which the church finds itself and hence he says that Christians must take Buddhism seriously, describing it as "the air which the church here continually breathes."[529] Thus, it is precisely because liberation is the *raison d'etre* of inter-religious dialogue, for him, it is a costly option. It is a dangerous commitment that upsets various religious and political interests.[530]

> Thus, the personal struggle *to be poor* (the anti-idolatrous spirituality shared by all religions) is the common platform for inter-religious dialogue, whereas the political struggle *for the poor* as a condition of personal salvation constitutes a unique Christian contribution to the dialogue.[531]

Liberation is so central and decisive for inter-religious dialogue that he declares assertively that those who renounce mammon are the disciples of Jesus irrespective of his or her religious profession.[532] Conversely, those who practice the Beatitudes are to a great extent the disciples of Buddha too.[533] His concern for religions is a concern for liberation.⁵³⁴ Thus, Christian insight into dialogue, for Pieris, is "agapeic involvement in the struggle of the poor [which] must take the shape of the cross."⁵³⁵

Two Biblical Axioms

Pieris is forthright and passionate in his commitment to the liberation of Asian society on the basis of what Jesus opted and sacrificed his life for between his baptism of "prophetic asceticism" in Jordan and baptism of the cross at the Calvary. However, this is to be grounded in the recognition of the two fundamental axioms:

> No liberation theology can claim to be rooted in the word of God if it does not hold together the two biblical axioms mentioned above: (1) the irreconcilable antagonism between *God and* mammon, and (2) the irrevocable covenant between *God and the poor* (i.e., a defense pact against their common enemy: mammon).⁵³⁶

Pieris once again finds common ground between biblical axioms and non-Semitic religions of Asia. He observes that the first axiom is "a universal dogma that defines the very core of practically all religions of Asia."⁵³⁷ The order of monks in Buddhism and Hinduism and other Asian religions substantiates this fact. Thus, the institution of the monkhood and other equivalents that voluntarily reject wealth accumulation remain the "universal symbol of *opted poverty* [which] can never be dispensed with in any liberational action or reflection"⁵³⁸ and which "constitute the *starting point* of a liberation theology in Asia."⁵³⁹ The first axiom acquires an added accent for the church as Jesus spelled out the implications of it (the God-mammon conflict) in the *beautitudinal spirituality,* which he preached and practiced.⁵⁴⁰ These axioms are the foundation of his vision for liberation.

However, the second axiom, namely, the irrevocable covenant between God and the poor, Pieris claims, is revealed only in the Bible and is *totally absent in the non-Semitic religions,*⁵⁴¹ which invariably leads to a new understanding of the poor. In this new perception, the poor are not only a sociological and dialectical category but, more importantly, are a "dynamic group who are not the passive victims of history but those through whom God shapes his history,"⁵⁴² even "salvation history."⁵⁴³

As an example of what we might call doing the theology of the cross in an Asian context in the light of the debate of the theology of the cross, according to Pieris, is to be found in basic human communities.[544] With its Christian and non-Christian membership these communities give testimony to the first axiom namely, "the God-mammon antimony." Underlining a life of struggle against mammon in these communities, Pieris sees the possibility that they would become "founders of the not-yet-discovered liberation theology of Asia, for they are the seeds of the not-yet-developed local churches of Asia."[545] Thus, his hope of a mammon free community will truly reflect what it means to live in Asia as well as the meaning of true church *of* Asia.

Conclusion

Within the two paradigms that have become his signature phrases, namely, "the Jordan of Asian religion" and "the Calvary of Asian poverty", Pieris passionately argues for an Asian theology of liberation, which is truly contextual and relevant. These phrases capture both the reality of theological context as well as the rootedness of his theology. As a symbol[546] of theological imagination, Pieris' phrase "the Jordan of Asian religion" states the profound fact of resourceful religiosity of Asia and issues an invitation to immersion in it. His second phrase "the Calvary of Asian poverty" acknowledges overwhelming poverty and demands the inevitability of sacrificial action. On the basis of these two paradigms, Pieris argues with unparalleled passion for the construction of this most urgent and relevant theological task of liberation.

One of the basic assumptions of Pieris is that the Asian church is a church *in* Asia and not the church *of* Asia. The church *in* Asia is, in fact, a local church of the west planted in Asia "to continue their alliance with neo-colonialism to survive."[547] This perception is the basis for his stringent critique of the present day church in Asia. In response to what he thinks is the church's failure, he engages in creative theologizing. The only way the church in Asia can acquire true status of the church of Asia is through the praxis of liberation in complete solidarity and humility with the religious poor of Asia.

As was pointed out in the first chapter, Pieris argues that the Asian situation must be recognized in terms of its rich and varied religious heritage and back-breaking poverty among the masses. On this basis, Pieris criticizes Kappan and Balasuriya for their lopsided emphasis on the problem of the poor and at the same time, theologians such as Kadowaki and Abhishiktananda are taken to task for being equally one sided in favor of the problem of religions in their theological reflections.[548] Such correction relates to the very heart of what Pieris considers to be the task of theology in the Asian context. The inseparable realities, in his own words, are the "overwhelming poverty" and its "multi-faceted religiousness" that "constitute in their interpretation what might be designated as the *Asian context,* the matrix of any theology truly Asian."[549] Situated within these realities, Pieris' theology relentlessly argues for the understanding of the cross of Jesus Christ as one of the two foundational paradigms for doing theology in the Asian context. Inextricably related to each other, these two paradigms, namely, the Calvary of Asian poverty and the Jordan of Asian religiousness, define the why, how and what of Jesus' ultimate purpose. Thus, Tombs states that Pieris' interpretation of the two events provides the liberating images of Christ.[550]

Clearly, in search of the meaning and purpose of Christian faith, Pieris engages in hermeneutics that is relevant and contextual to the Asian situation.[551] Based on his hermeneutical explanation of the baptism-event in Jordan, Pieris provides both Christological and missiological principles for contemporary implications. Different from both M. M. Thomas and Martin Luther, Pieris interprets the cross as planted on Calvary by "the money-polluted religiosity of his day," helped by "a foreign colonial power." Thus, for him, the cross exclusively refers to the empowerment of the poor for the one and only purpose of liberation.[552] On the cross Jesus' mission of making people conscious of their liberative role against mammon was consummated.[553]

Pieris' writing has been described as "heavy reading"[554] due to its scholarly nature and condensed style. Nevertheless, a theological theme that dominates his thoughts is clearly evident. His criticism of the Chalcedonian Christology and Latin American liberation theology along with his passionate contention for radical change in understanding the meaning of following Christ has rendered him a forceful voice to reckon with in any theological construction in Asian reality. His writings are worthy of admiration and salutary particularly for his vigorous denunciation of the present day church's complicity with mammon, his scathing critique of the process of inculturation without due regard to the issues of the poor, and his challenge to inter-religious dialogue to go beyond the mere textual comparison.[555]

Notwithstanding Pieris' stimulating and creative construction of theology in the South Asian context, he seems to have left out some issues that need further investigation and clarification. First, Pieris' positive evaluation of the Buddhist monastery for the sake of liberation has some powerful insights including the visible life of renunciation. He also argues that religion-based voluntary poverty in institutions like a monastery, Ashrams and *Sangha* is a potent way to fight mammon and thus a sure way to liberation for those who live in 'enforced poverty'. Though one can see theoretical justification for this ideal, however, it is not substantiated by the history of these movements. The combat spirituality against mammon that Pieris claims, unfortunately is not the dominant feature of them. Instead, in most cases the spirituality in monastic institutions is "oriented towards inner spiritual discipline, meditation and reflection that do not translate themselves into involvement with the challenges and concerns of the society."[556] It is rather difficult to imagine an institution being able to effect the radical movement needed to deal with Asian poverty, especially in the light of monaticism's decline in the modern age.

Although Buddhist *Sangha* is lauded for its potential liberative dimensions, yet it is not beyond the clutches of caste, which, by its very definition, renders all efforts for liberation null and void. Moreover, Pieris' vision of the ideal liberative community is inclusive of people of all religions.[557] In communities like monastics, Ashrams and *Sanghas*, highly insulated from other religions, this ideal would be extremely hard to imagine and thus will be proved not only less than motivating but in one sense self-contradictory.

Emphasis on the category of poverty as the focus of his theological endeavor has power and relevance. Yet his immediate context of Sri Lanka, especially its context of prolonged and violent ethnic conflict, has not been given space in his theology. Thus, another Sri Lankan theologian, R. Isvaradevan challenges Pieris and says, "the prophetic core of his faith must also passionately penetrate to the deeper core of his spirituality to integrate the ethnic issue as an inseparably challenging dimension of his social concern."[558] This is especially pertinent because Buddhist *Sanghas* play decisive roles in the political process of the country with its strong sense of Buddhist culture enshrined in the Sinhalese language to the neglect of the minority Tamil language and culture. Ramachandra also substantiates that while monks may be economically poor they command a very high social esteem and enjoy power and prestige in Asian traditional societies. He, thus, claims that Pieris fails to develop an adequate critique of the monastic privilege in his assessment of the Buddhist *Sangha*.[559]

Second, while recognizing Pieris' contribution in rediscovering a biblical epistemology "through the obedience to the truth in the concrete historical situation," another Sri Lankan theologian raises concern, as Pieris seems to betray a pervasive tendency to identify sin and evil with mammon—which restricts the "biblical diagnosis" of sin.[560] As we have already seen, Luther's understanding is that the cross relates to the reality of sin as alienation from God, which condemns all attempts to perceive reality of sin in any other category than as one turned in upon oneself. Even the best of human efforts, without the recognition of this fundamental view of humanity and the world, is bound to end up in pride and self-centeredness. In Pieris' theological equation, human beings in the category of the poor are understood only as victims of mammon, and hence, in need of redress and justice. Thus, instead of a savior a liberator is needed. This will further raise the question of Christology in Pieris' theology of the cross.

However, the point Pieris is raising can only be ignored at the risk of losing the relevance of the gospel in the Asian situation. In his critique of the church and of Asian theology, Pieris is able to make it very clear that the church in Asia cannot be the church of Asia without a self-conscious effort to find its authentic self in the poor. One of the valuable insights, which can be seen in Pieris' emphasis on doing theology in the Asian situation, is his unrelenting persistence in recognizing both the liberative aspects of Asian religions and Asian poor.

Third, Pieris' Christological assertions are largely determined by his interpretation of the baptism of Jesus in the Jordan and on the cross, which is fresh and challenging. In this, he is different from Latin American theologians such as Boff and Segundo as their works relate to the earthly life of Jesus. Pieris, further, recognizes Jesus' baptism as an act of "entering into the soteriological nucleus of his culture" to argue that only in this way Jesus evolved his self-understanding and his salvific mission as well.[561] Thus, reflecting on his radical Christological assertions, David Tombs rightly concludes: "Pieris' liberating theological praxis rests on his Christology of liberation and reflects his radical liberation of Christology."[562]

However, in any debate over his Christological claims we must ask a series of questions based on the scripture that Pieris has used so meticulously, although very selectively: Did Jesus consciously consider all the options (as Pieris assumes) before opting for John the Baptist's offer of baptism in the Jordan? Could the acts of mercy, justice and solidarity of Jesus be understood apart from his many exclusive assertions about himself as the Son of God and inaugurator of God's kingdom? How does scripture account for the reason why Jesus was crucified? Was it Jesus' actions alone or was it his claim of divinity that ultimately led to his crucifixion? Why did people believe in Jesus even after his apparently most wretched death? In what way does the cross remain a scandal and foolishness in the scheme of Pieris?

Many of his Christological problems remain unresolved between the tensions of Christology and insistence on non-exclusiveness. Jesus is clearly defined as having a divine pact with the poor in the fight against mammon. Pieris refers to this as the second Biblical or Christological axiom and also stresses that this is not to be found in any other religions. Here, contrary to his expressed view against exclusiveness, he can be judged to be exclusive as he claims that no religion is endowed with the insight of the pact between God and the poor. Fleming states that, "This suggests that Jesus is the unique and universal saving reality for the world, present through the poor by option *and* the poor by circumstance, which goes beyond the voluntary poverty found in Buddhism."[563]

No doubt, Pieris has sought to "expand the existing boundaries of orthodoxy"[564] by claiming liberation to be the *reason d'tre* of theology as well as dialogue, "rather than ontological statements about the divinity and uniqueness of Jesus."[565] By doing this, however, Pieris is not able to free himself from the theological problems arising out of this position. The sole and exclusive insistence on the concept of liberation seems to acquire ontological characteristics in defining and portraying God.[566] In this, it will appear equally exclusive as it denies any other criteria to view reality.

Fourth, Pieris' reference to the meta-cosmic and cosmic religions of Asia smacks of the same error that he so vigorously fights against, namely, hierarchy among religions. It would seem that in the absence of a written and "sophisticated" philosophy, religious traditions of, for example, tribal religions are considered less than meta-cosmic. Although Pieris recognizes the liberative religiosity of the cosmic religions, the fact remains that his theology has not been able to avoid a hierarchy among religions. Moreover, a hierarchical understanding will further undermine his main and worthy thesis of doing theology for and with the marginalized, i.e. the poor.

Notwithstanding the critical remarks about the theology of Pieris, it will be difficult not to agree with R. Isvaradevan, who states that Pieris is "widely regarded as perhaps the most stimulating, original and creative thinker in Asia today."[567] With his energy for persistent contention for liberation and insights for a relevant church, he remains a powerful force to reckon with in theological reflection in South Asia.

CHAPTER 5

The Theology of the Cross Amidst Many Religions and Many Poor

In the last chapter we encountered two prominent Asian expressions of the theology of the cross in which we noted their theologically-valid demand for a theology that takes Asian realities of poverty and religion as defining issues for the understanding of Christian faith. Aloysius Pieris, in particular, made it very clear that the Asian church can only be truly Asian when it is baptized in the waters of Asian religions and redeemed in the Calvary of Asian poverty. Thomas' emphasis on humanization as understood closely in relation to salvation established an integral relation between the two in the Asian situation.

In this chapter we will argue that Pieris' legitimate concern for openness towards other religions and his deep commitment for the poor can be made part of theology without relinquishing the particularism of the theology of the cross. Further, Thomas' concern for humanization can be given a sharper focus in the theology of the cross even while keeping the two dimensions of proclamation and praxis in dialectical relationship. For this to happen, we must relate the theology of the cross to the religious plurality of South Asia. Moreover, our thesis demands adequate consideration of the issue of religious pluralism for two reasons. First, as an incarnational faith Christianity must take the realities of its context with utmost seriousness. By its very nature faith in Jesus Christ will intentionally address the issues found in its context. Secondly, the declared position of the study is to affirm that the uniqueness and finality of the Christ event demands theological justification amidst the plurality of religions. Thus, we will be particularly concerned with the following questions: Why and how can the particularism of the theology of the cross still be an adequate framework for theology amidst many religions in South Asia? How and why must theological reflection in a situation of the plurality of religions and devastating poverty take the theology of the cross into serious consideration? What does it mean to confess Jesus to be Lord and Savior in such a situation? However, it must be said that we will not undertake any exhaustive discussion of the many issues related with religious pluralism. Our objective is rather modest and will be limited to presenting some of the avenues of understanding that the theology of the cross provides for a relevant theology for this context. Nonetheless, a survey of the pluralistic debate and a close evaluation of the pluralistic proposal will still be in order.

Though the three categories, namely, exclusivist, inclusivist and pluralist[568] are helpful ways to understand the different approaches to other religions, one must be careful to note that they remain "three points on a broader continuum of perspectives, with both continuities and discontinuities on various issues across the paradigms, depending upon the particular question under consideration."[569] The term exclusivist is used to refer to those with the traditional position of orthodoxy. An exclusivistic approach to other religions has three theological perspectives: The Bible is authoritative revelation and this is to be preferred in case of any conflict with other religious texts. Since Jesus Christ is the unique incarnation of God who is fully God and fully human, salvation is only possible through him. Salvation is not possible through the teachings, and rituals of other religions.[570] Interestingly, exclusivism as a term was used by critics to reject the position of the evangelicals[571] who joined the pluralism debate rather late.[572] The inclusivist position refers to Jesus Christ as unique, normative and superior to other religious figures and thus it is through him salvation is attained. For this position, God's grace and salvation are also available through other religions. Hence, other religions are considered positive and a part of God's creation. One fundamental characteristic of this position is that of deliberate openness and acceptance of other religions as part of God's creation.[573] The third category of pluralistic approach is most categorically represented by the publication of *The Myth of Christian Uniqueness* in 1987.[574] As one of the approaches to the other religions, the pluralistic position refers to the recognition of all major religions as equally salvific and no religion as normative and unique.

It is evident that a pluralist will raise many objections against the finality and uniqueness of Christ, inherent in Luther's theology of the cross, in the South Asian situation. Some of the prominent objections are[575]: First, since Asian religions are more ancient than Christianity and have more followers than Christianity, any claim for finality is only superficial. Even after colonial help in proselytization, Christians remains a tiny minority in South Asia. Second, amidst profound and long religious traditions of the context any claim for uniqueness and finality is sheer arrogance that is a product of western imperialism towards non-Christian faiths. Third, since all religions are culturally conditioned human efforts to know God who is unknowable, Christianity's claim to finality is at best spurious. Fourth, any exclusive claim is by definition divisive and breeds conflict and, hence, must be abandoned. Fifth, the implication of the doctrine of incarnation that Jesus is truly God is to be rejected as logical impossibility. Sixth, the Asian mind set of both/and over against western attitude of either/or renders any exclusive claim unacceptable.

At first glance many of the abovementioned criticisms seem quite reasonable. Even for many Christian people the most acceptable theological view in the modern debate about pluralism could be that there are many revelations and many ways of salvation, but one God who is the ultimate reality. This would mean what Samartha says about Christianity being norm for Christians and not for other religions.[576]

However, in actuality this view will prove Christian faith to be ethnic[577] and parochial. This will have serious implications for Christian faith. Needless to say the pluralistic position is not compatible with that of the assumption of this study. However important and valuable the insights, and legitimate and just the concern of the pluralistic position, its fundamental presuppositions are, however, controversial and even untenable. Thus, before we go any further, it is important to show the inner contradiction of this approach to other religions. First, the claim that all religious truths are relative to their context and hence devoid of any ultimate claim, in the final analysis, will prove to be an absolute statement itself valid for all time and thus, self-contradictory. Second, the presupposition that all religions are historically and culturally determined and hence express relative religious truths has greater and more radical implications for contextual theology such as this project itself. If all religions were culturally relative then all would receive a particular God construct in a specific cultural context. Such a parochial and ethnic understanding, even apart from the theological and historical self-perception of Christianity, would condemn the present exercise in contextual theology as irrelevant and unnecessary. Hence, in this logic Christian faith, even in its most humble and generous form, will have nothing to say in South Asian context. Accordingly, any question of contextualization of theology is necessarily out of question.

Third, how does this presupposition explain the origin of many religious faiths such as Hinduism, Buddhism, Jainism, Sikhism in one Indian cultural soil? How would this assumption account for the fact that all religions by virtue of being historical (in terms of having a date of origin) necessarily superseded, replaced or altered the previous religions? Because this took place in the same culturally specific area the pluralist presupposition is clearly untenable. Why didn't just one religion that came into existence remain the only valid perception of the truth or ultimate reality? The very existence of many religions in one context debunks such an argument. Fourth, it would be equally presumptuous to claim that all religions are equal, especially if one is making this claim on behalf of those whose religious experience is all but theoretical.[578] Fifth, such a well intentioned, yet simplistic understanding fails to deal with the profound differences and sometimes internal contradictions of the faith traditions. Sixth, in the final analysis it cuts the theological undergirding of any genuine conversion. We should remember that Christianity came into existence in a context of religious pluralism and it was "the converts from different religions who constituted its membership."[579] Seventh, this will not be true only for Christianity but also for all missionary religions such as Islam, Buddhism, etc. The number based argument can be raised against all religions. One can argue that Buddhism is not a very credible religion because the people where it originated did not accept it.

Eight, all religions claim to possess a core of unique content and can justly be called distinct from others. Ninth, the objections to the Christian claim of finality and uniqueness and its relation to violence and conflict can be shown to be rather more complex in light of the long history of communal conflict between Hindus and Muslims in India. It can even be argued that the ethnic assertion leads to conflict and hence must be abandoned as in the case of Tamil and Sinhalese in Sri Lanka. Such logic will be utterly intolerant of any diversity, which is truly imperialism.

Many of the pluralistic arguments and presuppositions are further contested and exposed by theologians like Jürgen Moltmann, Gavin D'Costa, Leslie Newbigin, Wolfhard Pannenberg, John B. Cobb, M.M. Thomas and others in the book *Christian Uniqueness Reconsidered: The Myth of a Pluralistic Theology of Religions*.[580] I would highlight just a few points to demonstrate the serious flaws in a pluralistic approach towards religions. Newbigin criticizes the epistemological presuppositions of Kaufman, Hick and Gilkey for their Kantian turn of making the subject all important to the neglect and finally elimination of the object of knowledge namely God. He is particularly critical of the tendency to bypass the question of truth and the criterion with which reality and truth are disclosed.[581] Jürgen Moltmann further scrutinizes this epistemological issue while considering the question of the nature and basis of dialogue presented by the pluralistic model. He rejects the relationship between religions based on the ideology of pluralism as the only relationship for dialogue for he detects the subjective tendency in the modern world, which privatizes and considers commitment a matter of taste. His critique of such a pluralistic model as nothing but "consumerism" is right because, although it allows "everything as subjective possibilities" however, it turns out to be "repressive in respect to skepticism about any objective reality being adequately mediated by religious symbols."[582]

John Hick is not only the foremost proponent of the pluralistic model but has been both a pioneer and very influential in this debate. However, Gavin D'Costa criticizes Hick's version of pluralism as an attempt to accommodate all religions of the world, which ends up accommodating none.[583] He accuses Hick of neglecting the fact that God is only known through particular revelation and cannot be divorced from the context. Even the basic coherence of the pluralist presupposition that all religions are a culturally determined response to the divine allows such particularity. In order to de-center the fact of incarnation in the Christian faith, Hick moves to theocentrism and mythological language. Along with his instrumentalist view of language and his inability to talk about reality in non-mythological language, Hick "severs any ontological connection between our human language and the divine reality."[584] As a consequence of such a mythologizing hermeneutic, for Hick all religious truth claims are undermined.[585] Leslie Newbigin argues against the pluralistic version of exclusivism on the basis of liberation. He says, "it is impossible to make any absolute claims for Jesus or for any other name in the history of religions. But it is possible and necessary to claim absolute validity for the praxis of justice and liberation."[586] He further says that this replacement of name by abstract noun is in order to control and, hence, it promotes self, because a principle is easy to manipulate for promoting one's own agenda. Citing the example of Hitler he argues that the rationale was the claim of justice for Germans under foreign rule. The result is not unknown. Thus, "when we absolutize words like *justice* and *liberation,* we remain locked into our own definitions of what these words mean." [587] Replacing one absolute claim with another, thus, is neither helpful nor needed to deal with other religions. Aloysius Pieris takes the liberationist approach as the valid approach, which faces difficulty in the light of bloody ethnic war fought on the basis of two different understandings of justice and liberation in Sri Lanka.

However, there is no doubt that Hick and his co-sponsors of the pluralistic approach to religions have noble intentions and just objectives. Hick's critique of Christian theology arises from the legitimate opposition to undifferentiated condemnation of non-Christian religions. His complaint that the absolutism of Christianity has contributed to the exploitation of the non-Christian world is valid given the many examples of the hands-in-gloves relationship of missionaries with exploiting colonial powers in the 18th and 19th centuries. In the same way, Paul Knitter realizes the need to promote justice and calls for a new attitude toward other faiths because, for him, to assert Christianity as the norm for all religions amounts to exploitation and injustice.[588] With a little knowledge of the past and sensitivity, any one will be sympathetic and even supportive of these objections as there is nothing objectionable. Especially while engaging in the theology of the cross, all possibility of arrogance and superiority is to be thoroughly negated. However, the claim of the theology of the cross for the particularity of the revelation of God will still be a serious issue, which will be incompatible with this form of the pluralistic framework. Not only are they incompatible with each other, they are, in fact, downright opposed to each other. While, on the one hand, the pluralistic model will not allow any particularity or uniqueness, let alone any finality there of, the theology of the cross, on the other hand, as we have seen in Luther's understanding, by virtue of its very definition cannot *not* affirm the finality of God's revelation in vulnerability. Hence, the obvious question at this juncture is whether the legitimate concern of the pluralistic model, namely, recognition of the intrinsic value of all religions and just and equal treatment of all religions, is possible within the paradigm of the theology of the cross? In other words, how can a theology that claims uniqueness and finality for God's revelation possibly be truly open to other religions?

Preparatio Evangelica

We will consider this by taking into consideration how Asian theologians have dealt with the particularity of Jesus Christ amidst other religions. Understandably this will be a very short overview, but it should be adequate to demonstrate indigenous efforts to respond to the issue of particularity. Nehemiah Goreh (1825-1895), an Indian convert who was well versed in Hindu *Sastras* (scriptures), was convinced that in some unknown way God had been preparing their hearts and minds to receive the Christian revelation. He writes, " 'Providence has certainly prepared us, the Hindus, to receive Christianity, in a way, in which, it seems to me, no other nation—excepting Jews, of course—has been prepared.'"[589] He further claims that there are certain ideas in orthodox Hinduism, which point beyond themselves to their fulfillment in Christ. Thus, he concludes, such ideas in Hinduism might be considered *preparatio evangelica*.[590] Others have also taken the same line of thoughts with regard to Hinduism.

Tambaram Debate[591]

One of the significant events with regard to the theological attempt to understand other religions can be seen in the Tambaram Conference. In re-examining the issues of Tambaram our vantage point is Luther's theology of the cross. Hendrick Kraemer's book *The Christian Message in a Non-Christian World,* written in preparation for the Conference elicited strong and critical responses from many quarters. One of the major controversies arose due to Kraemer's assertion of discontinuity between Christian faith and Hinduism. While discussing the Tambaram debate Wesley Ariarazah summarizes Kraemer's conclusion in the following words:

> Hinduism and Christianity are based on two entirely different apprehensions of reality, one prophetic and the other naturalistic-monistic, making it impossible for them to be compared or to see them in any kind of continuity....Since the gospel is the crisis of all religions it cannot be seen as the

fulfillment of Hinduism or Hindu values. The relationship of the gospel to Hinduism is one essentially of 'discontinuity'.[592]

P. Chenchiah (1886-1959), who belonged to the famous "Rethinking Group"[593] criticized Kraemer's presupposition and conclusion of discontinuity. Kraemer's approach of discontinuity spelt a profound problem for Chenchiah both at the personal and theological levels as a Hindu convert who wished to see his new obedience to Christ in continuity with his spiritual tradition. With "his own vivid awareness of a personal relationship with Christ and his emphasis on the "new creation" as the proper framework of this relationship,"[594] Chenchiah believes that Hinduism can change with the power of the Christian gospel. He states that "Christianity will produce the same effect on Hinduism as the moon on the sea. It would create tidal waves of spirituality to reform within Hinduism."[595] But by no means was Chenchiah uncritical of Hinduism; in fact, he could not follow the highly regarded 'Advaita' because it did not permit the possibility of the incarnation of Jesus Christ.

It is important to note that Chenchiah affirms the uniqueness of the Christ event while being truly open to Hinduism primarily due to the incarnation. Such a christological emphasis echoes the theology of the cross. However, unlike Luther, it is in this context of incarnation that Chenchiah concludes that the Old Testament is not necessary for salvation. Although he approved of prophetical teachings, yet his opinion towards the Old Testament is negative. The rationale for this rejection is that in his view it cannot help in the understanding of the incarnation which can be grasped only through Greek or Hindu thought forms, since it is wholly alien to Jewish thought, as it is to Islam. He has a biblical basis in Paul's arguments against circumcision for the new converts. He believes that Paul considers the Old Testament unnecessary in his rejection of circumcision. This leads him to ask why Hindu *Sastras* (scriptures) cannot be regarded as God's chosen *preparatio evangelica* for the people of India. He argues that just like Matthew, prophetical references can be found in the Hindu *sastras* to indicate the coming of the Messiah. However, on the whole, Indian theologians have refused to follow Chenchiah in this regard.[596] Nonetheless, Chenchiah's insistence on the continuity, with equal insistence on the particularity of the incarnation, provides new vistas for creative theological reflection, which certainly has impacted consequent endeavors.

In the final analysis, Luther's theology of the cross would insist on discontinuity rather than continuity in the framework of the controversy. However, Luther's discontinuity would be on the basis of the individual as opposed to Kraemer's view of religion. The rationale is human depravity and human inability to do anything about one's salvation. In this regard, Luther considers all humanity the same and hence, he leaves no room for pride and arrogance.[597] On the other hand, the continuity is not hard to be seen in God's final revelation on the cross of Jesus Christ for the sake of the world. Thus, it is neither the discontinuity of Barth or the continuity of the pluralist position but in tension of the cross as judgment and justification that one experiences both condemnation and promise of salvation. The discontinuity and continuity can also be established on the basis of scriptural witness. When Jesus Christ claims exclusive Sonship to the Father and consequently witnesses to be the Savior of the world, the discontinuity with other religions is not to be missed. However, many instances in the scripture suggest continuity. For example, the Magi have a vision of the star (Matthew 2:1-12); the centurion's faith puts the followers of Jesus to shame (Matthew 8:5-13); Cornelius was a devout man even before his baptism (Acts 10:2). Moreover, the many conversion stories of men and women testify to the fact that they were favored while they were still uninitiated (not baptized). Even for Saul, the persecutor's life was not beyond the grace and face of Jesus Christ. Thus, both continuity and discontinuity should be maintained in the creative tension of the cross because all the examples mentioned above can only be meaningful in the reference to Jesus of Nazareth.

The other controversy of Tambaram was the understanding of church versus the Kingdom.[598] Stanley Jones vociferously opposed the church-centered missionary approach of Kraemer in favor of a kingdom-oriented understanding of the task of mission. V. Chakkarai, a prominent member of the Madras group, spoke of the church as only a witness to the kingdom and hence, it must die in order that the kingdom may emerge. Thus, he was with Jones in this regard whereas another Indian theologian, P. D. Devanandan, sided with the 'church-group.'[599] Though this approach helped the cause of partnership between churches of the west and of the mission field for the future of mission, it smothered the little openness that the previous missionary council had achieved towards other religions.[600] Luther's theology of the cross does not recognize the visible church to be the true church and hence it cannot promote the mission of the church. In his stringent critique of the church, Luther did away with the narrow and unbiblical category of church-oriented mission and ministry. However, in some ways the debate and controversy of Tambaram continues in the theology of missions even today.

Opposed to the narrow mission of the church and based on the values of the Kingdom of God, Aloysius Pieris represents a pluralistic position that is not only open to other religions but, in fact, recognizes that all other religions are equally valid means of salvation. Thus, he does not think of the relationship of Christian faith with Buddhism as one of continuity because, however open this is towards the other, for him it is still affording Christian faith with uniqueness of fulfilling that which Buddhism lacks. His theology of religions, based on, and oriented solely towards, liberation, argues for cooperation between the religions so that mammon can be fought and the poor can be freed from the enslaving situation of poverty. While arguing for transcending Christological categories, his position is similar to that of S. J. Samartha, a South Indian theologian, who speaks of theocentric pluralism based on his understanding of God as the Mysterious Other. Samartha asserts:

> The Other [God as the Mysterious Other] relativizes everything else. In fact, the willingness to accept such relativization is probably the only real guarantee that one has encountered the Other as ultimately real.[601]

Thus, true religion is always relative for Samartha. Accordingly, the incarnation is a symbol of the divine rather than a normative historical happening. He maintains that even though the death and resurrection of Jesus Christ are the revelation of God, they cannot be made a universally valid paradigm. He, nonetheless, affirms the humanity and divinity of Jesus Christ but he is unwilling to acknowledge Jesus to be God. It is because, for him, "an ontological equation of Jesus and God would scarcely allow any serious discussion with neighbors of other faiths or with secular humanism."[602] Both Pieris and Samartha are profoundly concerned about the integrity of all religions and at the same time they are equally concerned about the closedness of any claim of Jesus Christ as the finality. Their concern is valid and must be taken with utmost seriousness.

Based on the pluralistic paradigm, Pieris and Samartha and others argue for a theocentric approach to faith instead of a Christocentric approach. A fundamental basis for this assertion is Jesus himself, for according to them Jesus' message was theocentric. His mission of the Kingdom was, in fact, God-centered. "All his powers were to serve this God and this kingdom; all else took second place."[603] The fact that Jesus always refers to himself as the Son of Man in the synoptic gospels suggests his self-understanding of his life mission as God-centered and God-dependent. Pluralists like Wesley Ariarajah then point out a shift from the theocentric Jesus to the Post Easter confessions. Ariarajah argues that gradually Jesus is brought to the center and God is pushed to the periphery.[604] Like Samartha, any exclusive claim of Jesus for him is to be understood only in the context of the faith community, as they are statements of confession.[605] Though pluralist interpretation of the synoptic gospels is not without some historical veracity, yet, at the same time it is also not beyond the tendency toward historical reductionism. To think that the synoptic gospels are more pristine and hence a more authentic representation of Jesus compared to the "confessional statements" is to ignore the historical chronology of the texts. Moreover, a tendency to differentiate in the texts between confessional and non-confessional materials is to seriously undermine the fact that the text followed the faith community that came into existence in response to Easter morning. Still, the pluralist position raises the Christocentric question inbuilt in the theology of the cross with utmost seriousness.

Thus, the question remains whether a true openness is possible within the framework of the theology of the cross? In other words, is it not possible to maintain the uniqueness of Jesus Christ and commitment to his finality without making a judgment on other religions?

We have been arguing while doing the theology of the cross that the concern for openness toward other religions and for liberation is possible. Not only are these concerns possible but also, in fact, they are mandated in any discourse on the crucified God. An affirmation of uniqueness of a God who is helpless on the cross and a commitment to his finality in his vulnerability cannot entertain any pride, arrogance and disrespect towards other religions or people of other faiths. By the very fact that it is the theology of the cross this can only be done from the vantage point of marginality.

Nonetheless, the insistence on uniqueness from a historical point of view is unavoidable. This is the self-perception of Jesus in his public declaration as the Son of God, as manifested in many of his claims.[606]

In their opposition to such exclusive claims, many pluralists assume that in a world of many religions and cultures it is neither possible nor helpful to maintain the claims of Jesus Christ. As we said earlier, Jesus' world was no less pluralistic and therefore, to consign these claims to the cul-de-sac of the past is at the least not recognizing the reality of his world. Even Pieris recognizes the multiple options within Judaism itself that Jesus had.[607]

A New Grammar to Talk about God

The theology of the cross demands in no uncertain terms that God is to be known through and only through the cross of Jesus Christ. Such a categorical and decisive statement about God's revelation is a major challenge in the Asian context as there are many living faiths that even predate Christianity.

It is further accentuated and taken further when New Testament writers assert the uniqueness, normativeness and exclusiveness of Jesus Christ, the Crucified God amidst a pluralistic context. Hence, Paul says, "God was in Christ reconciling the world unto himself" (2 Cor. 5:17); for John, Jesus is the "Lamb of God that takes away the sin of the world" (Jn 1:29); and "God so loved the world" as to give his "only Son" (3:16). As a consequence, Jesus is to be proclaimed to all nations (Mk 16:15). Thus, the particularity of Jesus is the very core of Christian *kerygma*, which has been a central emphasis throughout the history of Christianity. In this light, suddenly dialogue seems to be impossible. Christian faith seems to be insensitive, inconsiderate and triumphalistic.

Thus, it seems to be closed and rigid. Yet, the claim remains that God cannot be perceived anywhere else than in the cross of Christ. A closer look at the cross as God's revelation, however, will facilitate for us both the content and theological contours of the cross that would enable us to understand this in a relevant way even in a pluralistic context. God's revelation on the cross means that in the shame, humiliation and tragedy of the cross God's power of salvation is revealed. For Christians the implication is that they cannot but confess a God who is perceived in what is the most heinous place and way to die, the cross. The implication of such compulsion of being Christian is no small thing as it forces believers to humility and to the power in suffering and rejection.

It is also true that amidst many claims of authentic ways to God, mostly based on power, the theology of the cross does not permit Christians any other way to talk about God except in terms of suffering, rejection and vulnerability. The theology of the cross will not allow power in terms of control, ego, authority and supremacy. On the contrary, the only possible way to understand God's power is in the power of the cross. Thus, instead of control, God's power is seen in helplessness; instead of authority it is perceived in total surrender; and instead of glory and respect it is to be understood in vulnerability and rejection. This only way is no other than the way of the cross. Thus, the grammar of the cross is a scandal to the Jews and folly to the gentile (1 Cor. 1:23). God-talk can be done properly only in terms of suffering and the cross. Therefore, a God-talk that may at first sound closed and rigid, is actually vulnerable and relational, and thus open. As we have seen earlier the theology of the cross recognizes the universal sinfulness of humanity. It begins with self-criticism and hence cannot be understood in terms of superiority.

Uniqueness Reconsidered

The issue of the uniqueness of Christ seems to be most problematic, as it is understood to relegate all other faiths to the category of ordinary and also it promotes an imperialism associated with colonial Christians of the past era. Christ's uniqueness is not a claim to moral superiority, nor to deeper spirituality. In fact, the theology of the cross is a total reversal of any of such claim, emphasizing on the contrary that we are "justified by faith apart from works of the law" (Rom 3:28). As such, Christianity is precisely unable to make any claim to moral or spiritual virtue, let alone superiority. The scandal of the cross is that it is the "end of the law" (Rom 10:14) and it is folly precisely because there is nothing human wisdom can do. However, this particular claim will offend many modern ears and sound arrogant to modern sensitivity nonetheless; because it excludes any possibility of relativism, it remains a scandal and foolishness even today. It is the Christ who, having superseded the law, abolished the "dividing wall of hostility" between Jews and Gentiles. If the Christian gospel is to give offense, let it be the offense of the cross and not the offense of the proud Christian superiority.[608]

The uniqueness of Christian faith must be seen in its ability to maintain the particularity of the scandal of the cross yet, at the same time, be radically open to the other. Christians have to give others their due, and "even count others better" (Phil. 2:3). On the cross, Christ hangs stripped and naked for the sake of the world, so also the followers of such a crucified God can do no other than be totally open to the other in complete vulnerability.

While engaging in dialogue one must not forget that the theology of the cross, especially in the case of Luther, is a stinging critique of the church, theologians and church practice. Thus, the theology of the cross demolishes any confidence and security we might have in us or in tradition. Luther's last word before his death would serve us well in this regard : *"wir sind Bettler; hoc est verum"* (We are beggars, that is true).[609] Douglas John Hall develops a theology of beggars from this.[610] To live the life of a beggar is to live a life of insecurity, risk and complete vulnerability. Even with the particularity and exclusiveness of Jesus our Lord and Savior, we remain beggars and this should speak volumes about our attitude towards people of other faiths. Paul Althaus calls the theology of the cross a theology of *Anfechtung*. It is in the midst of temptation, uncertainty and struggle that the faith is found. In some strange way, this is true in the context of the plurality of religions. However, one must remember that Luther carefully distinguishes between human security and the certainty of faith. The denial of all forms of security does not mean the rejection of the certainty inherent in faith.

The inbuilt vulnerability of the cross not only insists on doing away with the walls of human security but also denies any approach of negating its own resourcefulness. Our concern, "cannot be whether our context pushes us to open appreciation of other religious or secular stances (as it surely does), but whether internal dimensions of our own faith require such openness."[611] As a response to the God on the cross, we are not only open but we also become vulnerable. Thus, it is indeed an opportunity for Christians to learn many things about spirituality from Hindus, Muslims and Buddhists, etc. With the crucified God Christians have something astounding to bring to the table too, something that the world cannot know on its own, that would never hurt but always attempt to heal.

In the light of the fact of the theology of the cross the assumption that the uniqueness of Jesus Christ among many saviors/ways of salvation is inherently divisive and disrespectful of other religions is a statement devoid of historical verification. Any claim of superiority is nothing but sheer distortion as the life of Jesus himself is a testimony. How was Jesus, even with all his exclusive claims to divinity, able to live a life that has become the basis for so many, including pluralists like Pieris, for ideal life in the Asian situation? How can a faith tradition that existed on the brink of society even as an illegitimate sect for well over three hundred years be a basis of arrogance and domination? How can a faith, which is only a minority religion, brag about any superiority? We must make it absolutely clear that it is not to deny scores of examples in which Christianity was claimed and proclaimed on the basis of theology of the glory in cohort with powers that be, especially with colonial powers. In opposition to such unfounded military and crusading spirit of the Constantanian Church, the theology of the cross stands as a stark reminder of the total depravity of all humankind; both the so called guardians of the gospel and perceived targets.

The Thing What It Is

Theology of the cross affirms the reality in terms of human sinfulness to talk about redemption. As we have seen, Luther primarily spoke in terms of human sinfulness as the fundamental reality of human life;[612] however, its recognition of the presence of many religions may be equally valid. N.K. Weng speaks of two kinds of pluralism, namely, descriptive and prescriptive, to argue that Christians should affirm descriptive pluralism manifested in the plurality of social structures indicating God's rich creation.[613] For him, prescriptive pluralism as the ideology of epistemological relativism should be challenged as it undermines religious commitment. He opposes the pluralist argument that social tolerance is possible only when prescriptive pluralism is accepted.[614]

Likewise, the claim of the finality of Jesus Christ is understandably unacceptable to pluralists for the same reason of affording Christianity a position of advantage vis-á-vis other religions. Again the opposition to Christ's finality on this basis is not unreasonable. However, our investigation into the theology of the cross leaves us with no choice but to affirm that God has chosen the cross over anything else to reveal the God-self. We believe that the finality of the cross should be affirmed even in the context of many religions for the following reasons: First, only the claim to finality can maintain a required dimension of transcendence to avoid the problem of allowing humanity to work out its own salvation. In order to uphold what we understand as the sacramental aspect of the theology of the cross, the transcendental nature is to be insisted. Without this, there will not be any theological basis for us to remain Christians; for example, in India Gandhi would turn out to be a better example than Jesus for the ideal of our lives.[615] Without the transcendental dimension the religious faith would run the danger of being reduced to socio-political activism alone.

Second, only the claim of finality can hold accountable those who confess and acknowledge Jesus of Nazareth to be the Lord for both radical openness to the other and genuine commitment towards the neighbor. Such a sense of finality is to be understood when Bonhoeffer states "when Christ calls a man he bids him come and die."[616] The danger of relativism lies in the fact that no one can be held accountable to the very concerns that it so passionately espouses. Thus, a self-defeating position, unfortunately with all good intentions, is inevitable. Third, it is incumbent upon a contextual theology to acquire depth and breadth in the light of the situation. The finality of the theology of the cross, thus, provides an adequate paradigm not only to address the situation of the plurality of faiths and plethora of the poor but also amidst such context to find greater and sharper expression of what it means to believe in crucified God. Fourth, only a claim to the finality of Christ can help account for Christological conversion. We are aware of the many very legitimate problems of conversion in the South Asian context, yet any theological validity for Christianity's self-understanding as a missionary faith, and also for any genuine Christological conversion, requires the finality of Jesus of Nazareth. Even in the process of dialogue change is not to be denied. Sometimes, people think of dialogue in terms of a static process of informing and being informed about religions. On the contrary, dialogue often is a dynamic process and requires change on the part of those who participate. Without openness and willingness to change, dialogue remains nothing but a ritual stripped of any meaning.

To deny finality to the cross, according to Luther, would amount to allowing means other than the cross to contribute to one's salvation. The soteriological problem cannot be avoided, as it would also imply that Jesus on the cross is less than final in his ability to save. We have already seen how Luther invested everything in condemning any move that establishes other ways to salvation than faith in Jesus Christ as a theology of glory. Moreover, it would utterly undermine the inner coherence of the framework of grace in the theology of the cross.

A New Grammar for Dialogue

But, how one deals with exclusive claims of Jesus, even for the most desirable phenomenon of inter-religious dialogue, is no less a difficult problem. From the very beginning we have maintained that the theology of the cross affords us certain trajectories and understandings of reality to speak of Christian faith in a faithful way and also to witness among many religions in relevant and sensitive ways. Thus there emerges a new grammar to understand "dialogue" with other religions. It has not always been easy to profess different faiths and share one geographical locatedness, as can be amply verified by the many unfortunate incidents of communal animosity that still raises its ugly head in the form of communal clashes between Hindu-Muslim, Hindu-Christian, Muslim-Christian, Hindu-Sikh, etc. Thus, it is not a matter merely of theory to talk about life in pluralistic context. Neither is it a matter of glossing over the differences between religions, as some dialogue-oriented theologians have tried to do. One must remember the fact of the raw nature of their living faith, for which the adherents actually engage in violence to the extent of killing and being killed for the sake of their religions. It is clear that we are surrounded by a host of issues and challenges in a very existential way in the midst of faith commitment and commitment to faiths.

On the other hand, a dialogue that begins with a reductionist theological stance is less than a genuine interaction of faith and can degenerate into merely a fad. To borrow the language of George Lindbeck, any interfaith relation which discards the "grammar" or "communally authoritative rules of discourse, attitude and action"[617] of either of the partners in dialogue precludes the possibility that real communication between historic faith communities will occur. Thus, authenticity is a prerequisite of any genuine dialogue. Luther was categorical about God's revelation in Jesus Christ on the cross and nowhere else. The approach for dialogue is to be understood in Jesus' life of interaction and death of condemnation. For example, the Canaanite woman (Matthew 15:21-28) insists that even dogs are entitled to the crumbs that fall from the table of the children. In this, dialogue leads to expansion of a life-giving promise of Jesus. Even on the cross Jesus is in dialogue with two thieves (Luke 23: 39-43).

While dying an utterly helpless death, Jesus is not helpless in promising the second thief a radical new future. It is interesting that the accusatory statement of the first thief is not condemned by Jesus but by the second thief.

Two comments are in order for dialogue and theology of the cross. First, even the exclusive claim of Jesus is not without the possibility of inclusive blessings. However, it takes a determined woman (Matt. 15) who would not give up for the sake of life of her child. Second, even in condemnation and persecution, there remains not only the possibility of dialogue but the promise of assurance for a better and desirable future (Lk. 23). If Jesus of Nazareth could live a life of openness and justice amidst many religions and philosophies, it is not only desirable for his followers but also required of them to live a life of equal openness while living and witnessing among people of many faiths. In the light of the preceding understanding of what it means to engage in the theology of the cross, the statement of Leslie Newbigin about Christianity's relation with other faith traditions summarizes the point well:

> [The relation of Christianity to other religions] is exclusivist in the sense that it affirms the unique truth of revelation in Jesus Christ, but it is not exclusivist in the sense of denying the possibility of the salvation of non-Christian. It is inclusivist in the sense that it refuses to limit the saving grace of God to the members of the Christian church, but it rejects the inclusivism which regards the non-Christian religions as vehicles of salvation. It is pluralist in the sense of acknowledging the gracious work of God in the lives of all human beings but it rejects a pluralism which denies the uniqueness and decisiveness of what God has done in Jesus Christ.[618]

Theology of the Cross among the Poor

The finality of God's revelation on the cross only acquires an even more radical dimension in dealing with poverty, injustice and a life of suffering. Luther does not downplay the importance of our responsibility toward our neighbor, as some have tried to portray him. He says "Christ is yours, presented to you as a gift. After that it is necessary that you turn this into an example and deal with your neighbor in the very same way, be given also to him as a gift and an example... This double kindness is the twofold aspect of Christ; gift and example."[619] This is a radical statement about the Christian's life and his attitude toward his neighbor. In following Christ we must do what Christ has done for us: become vulnerable unto giving our life for others.

This claim is critical of both the so-called narrow evangelical concern of saving souls and also the liberal concern of liberation.[620] In other words, if one is to affirm the sacramental aspect of theology of the cross with utter disregard for the *exemplum* aspect, according to Luther one has not grasped the true meaning of the theology of the cross. Conversely, if one is to accept only the *exemplum* of the cross without its *sacramentum* validity, one is still far from grasping the fundamentals of the theology of the cross. Both dimensions must be held in tension of authenticity and unity of complementary. Thus, Christians' socio-political engagement is not a work but a privilege and opportunity to live life firmly grounded in the theology of the cross.

Luther's idea of giving oneself as a Christ to one's neighbor is revolutionary when rightly understood and faithfully followed. After receiving the riches of God's righteousness and salvation in Christ, Luther says, "I will therefore give myself as a Christ to my neighbor, just as Christ offered himself to me; I will do nothing in this life except what I see necessary, profitable, and salutary to my neighbor." [621] In it lies the true possibility of the radical relevance of Christian faith in the world. We have seen how Luther understands a life that is redeemed by God's grace as one that is radically open to the need of one's neighbors.[622] We may recall Luther's statement when he argues that one is to be committed to the neighbor in his/her need. It is not simply charity that Luther is talking about nor is it just verbal advocacy for the poor, but rather one's daily care and involvement in the lives of people even to the extent of suffering on their behalf. It is remarkable that Luther even exhorts those saved by the grace of Christ to die for the sake of their neighbors. Thus, neighbor-concern is no less valuable even when the theology of the cross speaks of uniqueness and finality of the cross.

Many theologians have rightly argued passionately about the mandatory nature of action or praxis in Asia. This has been a clear emphasis of Aloysius Pieris. Especially in the developing countries theologians have emphasized the kingdom of God and Christian responsibility towards its values in terms of a preferential option for the poor. This is of immense value and cannot be replaced in Christian theology. Following Christ in action and acting on behalf of the poor and the marginalized is absolutely essential for the witness of the good news of Jesus Christ. In other words, it is precisely because God has identified with us to the very death that we must follow him.[623]

However, the insight of the theology of the cross as theology of God's location has a great deal to contribute towards relevance with regard to the poor. In recognition of the desperate situation of the world of the poor, many theologians with legitimate hope have stressed the urgency for action based on what Jesus did. However, in this zealous effort, many hardly pay any attention to where Jesus is. In the majority of cases, while Jesus' actions of liberation are imitated and argued for, Jesus' location amidst the poor and the despised too often is willfully ignored. Jesus allowed the vagaries of life common to all, especially to the poor, to impact his life as well. In this Jesus transcended the condescending attitude of the powerful and the charity of the rich, which, in fact, accorded authenticity to his actions because they were part of how he lived his life.

Since the theology of the cross is about the location of God, it requires that a theologian of the cross also be found in a location of pain and suffering. Too many theologians of the cross/liberation seem to make a mockery of this when they theologize without any experience of being located in the soil and turmoil of everyday life of the poor. Too many times theologians fail to realize the utter irony of their vocation when they gather to "discuss" poverty over the gluttony of sumptuous meals in an air-conditioned location of absolute insulation from the maddening and deathly cries of the poor.[624] How does the example of Jesus' actions on behalf of the poor and the marginalized, the foundation for today's relevant life of the church and Christians, miserably fail to acknowledge his location *with* the poor? As a theology of location, the theology of the cross stands in sharp critique of all of our passion for action without our being located with the victims of oppression.[625]

How can an appeal for the poor, passionate and persuasive as it might seem, ever carry any credibility if it is drafted in the comfort of an air-conditioned room? How can our frantic appeal for ending hunger ever be truthful if we have pampered ourselves while drafting the appeal? How can our protest and plethora of theologically powerful papers against marginalization and dehumanization have any meaning if we have never shared life with the marginalized? The questions can continue, but the heart of the matter is that we have so comfortably accepted Christ's action for others but have miserably failed to understand his very existence with the people with regard to that of our existence.

True theologians of the cross will not compromise with the determinative significance of the deliberate location of their life without which all theological endeavors are only mere words devoid of meaning and credibility and full of self-contradictions. If the action of Jesus Christ is to be our example, his presence with the suffering people is to be our paradigm. In short, Jesus' presence with the lost and the least was a prerequisite for the praxis. Even a context of the third world is not always devoid of elite islands for those who professionally use the issues of the place yet remain insulated in the four walls of seminary.[626] In a world of increasing institutionalization of life, in which credentials and career seem to dictate where one would seek one's location in life, the theology of the cross becomes increasingly difficult for those who wish to be called "professional theologian." In one sense, the rational tradition that took root before Luther's time continued to expand in seminaries and universities in the pursuit for intellectual sophistication and in mega-institutions of inter-church and para-church organizations which, in their professional demand for sophistication, continue to dislocate theologians from the context of pain and suffering. Even theologians from third world contexts have fallen prey to the temptation of power and privilege doled out by these institutions and structures. However, this is not to deny the many saints who have consciously sought to overcome institutional temptation by locating their lives with common people.[627]

Luther's theology of the cross continues to speak to today's theologians as it was addressed to the professional theologians of his time. Moreover, we believe that in understanding the theology of the cross as theology of location, a new paradigm of life with the poor will emerge. In this light, Moltmann's critique of Luther's theology of the cross being restricted to only religious world[628] seems less accurate especially when its impact is considered. We must remember that during Luther's time the religious world dominated all spheres of societal living. Thus, what James Atkins says about the theology of the cross critiques the "professional" tendency among today's theologians as well as underlines the possibility for its true significance:

> Luther's theology was shattering to the church precisely because he carried through his theological perceptions into

the sphere of church practice and daily living. He set Christ in the center of theological schools, Christ in the center of man's everyday life. Had his Christology remained a debate among the schoolmen, Luther would have no more significance than any other of the many contemporary German professors. By pursuing it to its proper end he lifted Christianity off its hinges and rehung it.[629]

Conclusion

We have argued that a theology of the cross amidst many religions and many poor will acknowledge these realities, which will enlarge the theological expanse to relate to the people of other faiths with openness and deepen the theological depth of vulnerability in the face of mass poverty. For these timely concerns to be incorporated in the exercise of contextual theology, we noted, the uniqueness and finality of the theology of the cross need not be compromised. In fact, we attempted to show that the inbuilt uniqueness and finality of the Christ event is both helpful and relevant for the absolute demand of the cross.

Though the theologies of Chenchiah, Appasamy, Chakkeriah and others took Hinduism seriously enough to develop a Christian theology based on it, they missed the central aspect that Hindu scripture has never been a scripture for all Hindus in the sense that the Bible is for all Christians. It is rather a monopoly of the Brahmins, who are a tiny minority within Hinduism. In fact, the Hindu scripture has been used to perpetuate the deplorable and inhuman caste system. All of these theologians who argued for Hindu scripture having a central role in Indian Christianity come from either the Brahmin caste or one of the higher castes. This explains why they have a positive attitude towards Hindu scripture. Further, attempts like this are in the category of indigenization that tends to be past-oriented and remains a static concept with its stress on the relation of the gospel to the traditional cultures.

The theology of the cross is a theology of God's life on the earth that will remove speculation from our life, establish that suffering of all kinds is valuable since God is revealed in such situations and finally draw out a response of faith to God as well as love to the neighbor. The theology of the cross, in its unrelenting insistence that God can only be known through the cross of Christ, requires total trust in such a suffering God. One cannot remain an aloof spectator to this crucified God, for one's response to this God necessarily will lead one to become as vulnerable as the crucified God himself to neighbor, history and creation. This would be an adequate response to plurality and diversity on the one hand, and to disturbing poverty and the agonizing suffering of the people, on the other. Such theology based on the thin tradition, i.e., theology of the cross, would be truly a contextual theology that would be open and dynamic and future-oriented, concerned with the totality of human existence—including proclamation and practice of what God has called us to live for: a life of vulnerability on the way to the cross.

CHAPTER 6

Markers of a South Asian Theology of the Cross

Having argued against the relativistic pluralist position as inadequate for its inherent contradictions and its untenable position as better than any other, we would further explicate an Asian theology of the cross in terms of some of its markers. In articulating the characteristics of the theology of the cross we would demonstrate that with its claim of uniqueness and finality, the theology of the cross is capable of reorienting both the Christian's life and the church's ethos for a proper attitude to live life with and among people of other faiths and poverty. What McGrath says indicates such possibility:

> The theology of the cross, however, is more like a tent pitched by a nomadic tribe as they wander from one situation to another. It adapts itself to the situation in which it finds itself, but is not bound by it—and upon being transferred to another cultural context, it is able to cast off its acquired cultural mantle in order to take root there.[630]

Now we are in a position to argue that Luther's theology of the cross lays a foundation upon which the theology of the cross of Thomas and Pieris brings significant insights to bear to expand its horizon. In a significant way, their contextual insights and theological insistence reshape contours of theological parameters of the understanding of the cross. However, we will not repeat one major characteristic of an Asian theology of the cross, which was argued as theology of location in the previous chapter.

Theology of the Cross as Theology of Perpetual Self-Criticism

Much of theology today is replete with criticism of one sort or the other. The evangelical theologians are critical of liberation theologians and liberation theologians are equally critical of evangelical theologians. Few have tried to maintain a creative tension between these two emphases of Christian witness. Still fewer have ever paid any attention to what we have seen in Luther's language *CRUX sola nostra theologia*[631] as a theology that functions critically.[632] The critical dimension of the theology of the cross should become a fundamental aspect of the Asian theological reflection. There is an inbuilt function that calls into question any attempt at theology and discipleship which is less than the standard of the cross. Thus, Luther asserts: *Crux probat omnia.*[633]

First of all it reveals our inability to do absolutely anything about salvation by exposing human sinfulness. Human shortcomings are interpreted by Luther as radical helplessness to do anything for their salvation except stand before the cross in stupefied gratitude for the sheer gift of faith and grace for salvation. Alfred Poirier recognizes the cross to be the epicenter of intense and pervasive criticism of humanity.[634] Faced with the scriptural assertion that all have sinned and fallen short of the glory of God, all of us come to realize our true status before God.[635] In short, the cross is the critique of us as doomed sinners. It divests us of any worth and levels us with all others. Faced with the cross we remain exposed as sinners and condemned. Thus, amidst many people of many faiths the cross remains, in some way, an equalizer that affords us a vantage point from which to do theology with a sense of equality with all others.

Secondly, even while speaking of the theology of the cross one needs to be aware of the condemnatory nature of this theology. It is to be seen in terms of "its principle of inner identity and self-criticism"[636] which is able to transcend any self-understanding.

In the academic world this is of particular significance. We may speak of the theology of the cross without any experience of confessing the scandal, on the one hand, and participating in what this folly of the cross entails in reference to one's neighbor, on the other. Thus, no theologian is immune to the danger of theologizing from an academic ghetto of sheer speculation. In recognition of this, Tomlin concludes that *theologia crucis* "stands as a critique of theology which becomes exclusively academic."[637] It is not to be overcritical but to be deeply aware of one's perpetual precarious situation *Coram Deo* in the exercise of theology. The cross carries the meaning of condemnation and consolation.

Thirdly, the theology of the cross perpetually questions our theologies, intentions, priorities and discipleship. In this light the comment of Elie Wiesel, a Holocaust survivor, seems appropriate: "Every question possessed a power that did not lie in the answer."[638] The cross represents such questions against all human endeavors of preaching and praxis.[639] This will mean that Christian living and witness is an existence with constant critique of the cross which avoids arrogance and facilitates humility. Such an understanding of the theology of the cross will facilitate a posture of humility and a praxis of gratitude in the non-Christian and poverty-stricken world of South Asia.

Finality of the Cross: Revelation of Crucified God

For many, the cross, without initiating any controversy, is understood as the final event of Jesus' earthly life. Moreover, in the estimate of the historian, the crucifixion is considered to be the final Roman judgment for Jesus. However, our concern here is how this finality of the cross is to be understood theologically. All three theologians, namely Luther, Thomas and Pieris, understand the cross to be final because they perceive it in terms of revelation. The revelation of God in and through the cross of Jesus of Nazareth determines what it means for them to talk about God in their respective contexts.

As we have seen, Luther's theology of the cross presupposes the finality of the cross. It is where God is revealed for the salvation of humankind. Nowhere else but on the cross, can one recognize and see God truly. The crucified God who is undergoing untold misery and unfolding embarrassment on the cross is none other than the God who is dying for the sake of the world (for you). Outside the cross, there is only the devil and illusion.[640]

Thomas argues for the finality of the cross as the possibility of the new beginning. The crucified and risen Jesus is the new human. For Pieris this finality is considered only in terms of its radical power for discipleship. As the ultimate paradigm of self-sacrifice, the cross remains final for all who follow. All those who follow the crucified God must also imitate his ultimate sacrifice on the cross in their life for the sake of liberation.

These concerns can adequately be addressed by underlining four aspects for the finality of the cross in the Asian situation. First, the cross is final because it is the ultimate paradigm for the final revelation of God. Contrary to rationalistic speculation and philosophical articulation, and also to many religious concepts about God, the cross of Jesus of Nazareth reveals the ultimate revelation of the truth of God in terms of the crucified God. Second, the cross is final because it relates to the innermost questions of human existence: who is a human being? What is the meaning of human life? How is this life related to the creator? In short, the question is, was Jesus' death on the cross of ultimate significance? Jesus of Nazareth on the cross responds to these questions both as sacrament and example. Much to the dismay of liberals and evangelicals,[641] these two aspects cannot be bypassed without doing violence to the Christian identity and relevance. Thirdly, it is final in the sense that Käsemann expresses in his characteristic phrase that the cross is "the signature of the one who is risen,"[642] which became the basis of Christian conviction and proclamation. Fourthly, the cross is final because it is not about principle but about a person that encounters people with a question, "who do you say that I am?"(Matt. 16:15). There is finality in this question.

However, McGrath challenges any attempt at the finality of the cross. It is true that in following the theology of the cross one would do well to remember that it defies intelligibility, let alone any systematic treatment.[643] McGrath's contention is that:

> We must learn to abandon any pretence to finality in our understanding of its significance, and any suggestion that one generation may dictate to another precisely what the meaning of the cross for them must be. Each and every generation, in whatever situation it may find itself, must learn to return to the cross itself, there to encounter the 'crucified and hidden God' (Luther).[644]

Though McGrath argues against the finality of any *understanding* of the cross, nonetheless, this very statement underlines the validity of our claim about the finality of the cross. It is in affirming this finality that its resourcefulness is realized in different situations. Moreover, the question of finality will determine one's ultimate commitment to the demands of the cross amidst other needs screaming for attention in this increasingly complex world. The church in Asia will require such a commitment for the other precisely as she knows the Crucified God in final terms.

Uniqueness of the Cross: Vulnerability

The question of uniqueness is fraught with much suspicion and doubt. In a world of many religions and cultures, any claim for uniqueness generally would be considered arrogant and presumptuous. Again, the question about uniqueness can be answered differently. At the historical level, it can be argued that the cross is unique among world religions for none of the historical persons after whom a faith movement began can claim to be hanged on the cross. In addition, it can also be counted as unique that in a world where the cross was considered, in the words of Josephus, "the most wretched of deaths," that apostles like Paul preached Christ crucified. Precisely in this line, our concern is that uniqueness can be construed in terms of the paradox of God being revealed in the pain and agony of the cross. Nowhere in the history of religion is found a parallel to this claim of God's revelation in Jesus of Nazareth dying helplessly on the cross. Thus, this uniqueness is to be understood this way: that the God revealed in the cross is a God of vulnerability, who is subjected to the utmost ignominy, as seen in the fact that he was crucified naked in public and the helplessness in his cry of abandonment. True to the spirit of the theology of the cross, even this cannot be claimed with any degree of arrogance but only in utter humility to remind us that the one who professes the crucified God is already crucified on the same shameless cross.

Contrary to many religious discourses in which the divine being is always portrayed as the source of ultimate power and might, the cross reveals a God who is profoundly vulnerable. The centurion who confesses Jesus to be the Son of God is moved not because Jesus commanded a miracle, as Jesus' adversaries required for belief, but because he saw how Jesus died.[645] Hence, Weeden concludes, "The only person with real power at the cross paradoxically verifies Jesus' divine status not because Jesus awed him with his power but because Jesus died a suffering, "powerless" death."[646] Interestingly, Pieris recognizes this acknowledgement by the centurion as a proof of how Jesus can be regarded to be relevant in the Asian context: Jesus' dying on the cross is, for him, a model for living. However, behind the centurion's remark is Jesus' own claim to be the Son of God which is not so in how Pieris interprets this. Nonetheless, Pieris' emphasis is also on the vulnerability of God in Jesus on the cross.

Even when the cross is understood to be the ultimate symbol of love and rightly so, as we saw in Thomas, God's vulnerability is undoubtedly implied. "To say that God is love is to say that God is vulnerable."[647] The cross is absurd yet God assumes it not to link it with himself but to overcome it with his love. This is made possible only via the risk of God's vulnerable self on the cross. The love of God is to be recognized in God's sending of his Son to the world, a risk unimaginable for humans, that God will become one with them (John 3:16).

This vulnerability of God does not make it any easier for people to accept the cross without a living and public faith. Against a ritual-based faith, the vulnerability of the cross constantly draws people into public where one is stripped of all securities. Much of the so-called evangelical[648] theology has regretfully helped to confine faith in the narrow and suffocating cage of private life. Mostly, and many times unconsciously, this is done by undue emphasis on the spiritual dimension alone in utter and unfounded disregard for the life in the world for which Jesus was crucified. Such unhealthy spiritualization of faith can only lead to sheer meaninglessness of the one who is running away from the world *in* the world. Those who remain stubborn and unrepentant in their attitude to dominion and control can domesticate even a powerful and irresistible theology of the cross. But, as Graham Tomlin puts it, the theology of the cross defies such domestication:

> The *theologia crucis* is for these theologians an insistence on the *paradigmatic* nature of the cross: it is not merely a soteriological event which remains locked in the past, but is a paradigm of the way in which God always works. For this reason, atonement theologies which regard the cross as purely a past action, the benefits of which one simply enjoys in the present, are inadequate if they fail to make the connection between God's action in the ongoing life of the church or the Christian.[649]

Against the privatization and domestication, thus, faith in the crucified God is a public faith. How can this faith be not public whose focus is on Jesus of Nazareth who inaugurated the Kingdom of God in public; who preached, taught and healed in public; challenged and refused rigid law in favor of redeeming love in public; was stripped, flogged, spat on, forced to drag the cross in public street and finally was hanged on the cross publicly? Such faith can only be made private at the expense of the very historicity of the gospel: a mistake that would ring a death knell for the historical faith as it is recorded in scripture.

On the other hand, a public faith in the vulnerable God reorients both the perception and the response to reality. Thus, the faith can only be understood vis-á-vis the worldly reality of joy and pain; celebration and suffering; birth and death, etc. The theology of the cross as theology of the vulnerable God particularly helps understand two things, which are related to public faith and public commitment. Firstly, that God is present amongst those vulnerable. The theology of the cross establishes that God employs the weakness and vulnerability of people to reveal the God-self. Secondly, that God's given vulnerability can truly be experienced in receiving the gift of faith in grateful participation in the struggles of those amongst whom the crucified God lived his earthly life. A context like that of South Asia portends well for bringing out the important dimension of the vulnerability of Christian life and thus to help shape Christian witness truly faithful to the crucified God.

Way of the Cross: Scandal and Foolishness

In order to properly assess and assimilate the raw meaning of the cross being "scandal" and "foolishness," one must go beyond both the spiritualization of the cross and the jargon of these terms. Though, as in Biblical times, they remain loaded with their negative, even appalling connotations, yet the full impact of the cross as scandal and foolishness is to be appropriated against the socio-cultural background of the first century world. Martin Hengel, in his book *Crucifixion*, facilitates a glimpse of utter degradation of crucifixion during the *Pax Romana*.[650] As a symbol of Rome's "most insidious and intimidating instrument of power and political control,"[651] the scandal and foolishness of the cross is to be perceived as Josephus calls it, "the most miserable of deaths," "accursed thing" or "plague."[652] For Jews, it was all the more scandalous as a crucified person was considered cursed. Deut. 21:23 refers to "anyone hung on a tree is under God's curse," thus, the inherent absurdity and offense of the cross is only more apparent for the Jews. Thus, it is no surprise that Christiaan Beker calls it "the most unreligious and horrendous feature of the gospel."[653]

The cross was more than a symbol of weakness, it was a sign of total impotence.[654] The scandal of the cross was not simply that Jesus was crucified as a criminal but was that it had "involved the display of his naked body in public—the final utter degradation."[655] Further, the scandalous dimension is to be noticed in the awkwardness with which the early Christians struggled while preaching the crucified Messiah as 'good news,' especially in a situation where escape from crucifixion and not punishment on the cross normally was, 'good news'.

The relevance of such a stark and apparently offensive portrayal is neither to evoke easy sentimentality nor to exploit fear in people but to re-imagine the scandalous basis of the gospel. In revisiting the reality of the passion of Jesus of Nazareth we hope to recreate the foolishness with which we find our being in Jesus Christ (Acts 17:28). It is important because we are too used to this crucified Messiah to realize either its scandal or its folly to avoid arrogance.

Boff argues that the cross is a scandal and must be interpreted as such. This scandal of the cross, for him, reaches its highest point in divine abandonment.[656] However, on this very point of divine abandonment, he criticizes Sobrino, Gutierrez and Moltmann for their understanding of it as a struggle between God the Father and God the Son. It is both absurd and irrational, according to Boff, to claim that God "effectuated the sacrifice of his son on the cross."[657] Nnamani interprets Boff's critique when he says, "We cannot preserve the scandalous character of the Cross, by conceiving it as a God-ordained instrument of divine salvation, nor can we achieve our aim by making God himself a perpetrator of Jesus' crucifixion."[658]

Willi Marxen would not, for the right reasons, dehistoricize or impersonalize it, "The cross is not just a little vexatious, it is an utter scandal."[659] On the other hand, following such a scandal would mean nothing but sheer folly. However, it is with the experience of real scandal and unsettling folly of the cross that the church can truly find authentic witness in a world of plurality of faith and mass poverty. As incomprehensible and unreasonable as it may sound, the scandal and folly of the cross can be the only basis to follow and witness God crucified in South Asia.

Power of the Cross: For the Sake of the Other

In this post-modern age, in which all relations are frequently characterized as power-relations, and as people living after Nietzsche, for whom power was the most important human experience,[660] we cannot omit power[661] from our consideration. Moreover, the church must deal with the issue of power "not only in response to immediate social pressures, but also as part of her own responsibility for the interpretation of the gospel in our time."[662] Thus, it is inescapable in the South Asian situation.

All along we have seen the cross to be strange and even despicable in the world. The power of the cross, consequently, is to be understood in strange and unconventional terms. We agree with what Tomlin says about the power of the cross as an alternative model of power:

> Because the *theologia crucis* depicts the God who does not abandon power, but who uses it for the healing and salvation of his creation, exercising his power in the foolish, powerless vulnerability of the cross, it can therefore offer an alternative model of power for the Christian community.[663]

When Paul spoke of the power of God in weakness and suffering, he did so against the background of Graeco-Roman and Jewish understandings of power.[664] While power was considered to be the prerogative of the gods and other superhuman entities in the ancient world, Paul's world saw imperial power as the greatest human power. The *Pax Romana,* or Roman peace, as a symbol of the emperor, was maintained with sheer power of muscle and authority. The emperor was perceived as divine; especially after death he was elevated to divinity, which is attested by the "imperial cult."[665] However, the Roman peace over which the emperor presided was, for many, nothing but oppression and domination. It was "the power to crush opposition, to expand borders, to colonize, to enslave and to crucify."[666] Further, in the Roman cultural context, "power' and "glory" or "honor" were associated with high culture and status. Achievements in the military, political, and social life, family heritage, status, physical appearance, learning, physical prowess, etc., provided power and glory.[667] Moreover, stars and other cosmic entities played an important role in the understanding of power.

For the people of Israel, the true and only supreme God, Yahweh, was believed to be all-powerful. This was expressed both in battle and deliverance as well as in creation because creation was understood as a powerful victory over the forces of chaos.[668] Paul is aware of the evil and hostile powers of his time. Neyrey argues that Paul's "cosmos is crowded with ...personified malevolent figures."[669] There are many instances of Paul's consciousness of such malevolent powers around him; two examples would suffice. In Romans 8:38-39, he speaks of a host of influences and powers in relation to his inseparability from the love of God.[670] In this, he speaks of both political and anthropological powers.[671] Further, while analyzing Paul's writing, James Dunn states that sin and death as powers are so fully personalized that they can be considered proper nouns.[672] It is against this background that Paul understood the liberating power of God in Jesus Christ.[673]

Contrary to the prevalent culture of power, Paul announces the power of the crucified Messiah. However, Paul understood that the gospel is more than a mere word in the sense that it accomplishes what it sets out to do.[674] In the words of Luke Johnson it is "a performative utterance,"[675] thus, it efffects God's power. The salvific power of the gospel is rooted and derived from the crucified God. Its power cannot be understood in worldly terms, as Paul affirms the weakness of crucified God. For Paul, Christ is *"God's power in weakness."*[676] In speaking of the cross, Paul asserts a benign yet forceful power that overcomes the "powers and principalities of this world." Knowledge of God's power is indeed true power and Paul knew this only in the knowledge of Christ crucified.

Further, Paul speaks of the power of the cross as the power of freedom. True Christian freedom is derived from the cross. However, as we have seen, the theology of the cross presupposes human inability to do anything with regard to salvation. Thus, rendered impotent, human beings cannot extricate themselves from the bondage to sin. The only way freedom is possible is through acceptance of one's helplessness and believing that in the crucified Jesus God has made one a new creation free from all requirements. 'The freedom wherewith Christ has made us free' (Gal. 5:1) is derived from what God has done in Jesus Christ on the cross. As all are in need of God's grace without any reference to works, so also all are given freedom in the cross. "Justifying faith then frees the believer from anxiety over his own salvation, identity, or value and gives him the dignity of being the free lord of all things."[677] Based on divine freedom such freedom is "for service and its characteristic mark is the cross, its willingness to give itself for the other."[678] Luther speaks of Christian liberty in terms of service to the neighbors.[679]

Käsemann says that the "power of Christ's resurrection becomes a reality, here and now, in the form of Christian freedom, and only in that."[680] Thus, freedom entails responsibility towards the world. Käsemann further insists, "Because Jesus' gift is Christian freedom and we live by that gift and grace of his, Christian freedom demands that we prove it on earth before it is perfected in heaven."[681] Along with its theological interpretation, freedom must be acknowledged as a socio-political issue. Thus, freedom of the cross is truly power for the sake of the world. "The freedom of the Christian is freedom in the world but not from the world, freedom for service."[682] However, it cannot be equated with the political power. Rather, Barr argues:

> The power of cross or more precisely, the power of the God who presents himself focally in the crucified Christ, is not separated from the situation in which power is exercised. The power of the cross is not simply identical with political power; it is rather the power that shapes ultimately the situation in which political power is to be understood and evaluated.[683]

Moreover, Christ-given freedom can only be understood meaningfully in the early Christian context in which early believers had to contend with the politics of the dominant ethos of the Roman Empire as they struggled to remain faithful to their commitment as followers of the "good news." "In their interaction with non-Christian communities they had to encounter the hostility meted out to them by asserting their right and freedom to choose a way of life which had been effectively outlawed by officialdom."[684] This suggests the deep and dangerous implications of freedom for faithfulness in following the crucified God.[685]

This is important because on the cross Christ has freed all to be totally free of all compulsion. During Luther's time, as we have seen, ordinary folks were subjected to ecclesiastical and spiritual powers of the church hierarchy that apart from other things kept them in bondage. By the power of the cross, Luther opposed the degrading power of the time. Thus, the power of the cross enables others. Barr concludes:

> Unlike oppressive forms of power, it does not render the other powerless nor hamper the full development of the other. Rather it empowers the other in a renewal of existence so that the other may become most fully and authentically her/himself.[686]

Thus, the power of the cross is ultimately shared power.[687] Not only did Jesus realize his power in the company of people in ancient Palestine but also his power is realized on the cross. Jesus promises the humble and repentant robber the kingdom (Lk. 23: 42-43) and a Roman soldier praises God and acknowledges Jesus to be innocent even on his death (Lk. 23: 47).

It is important at this point to respond to the feminist critique of Paul as the perpetuator of hierarchical power and the cross itself as the symbol of violence and subjugation for women. Joanne Carlson Brown and Rebecca Parker raise fundamental problems with the death of Jesus:

> Why we [women] suffer is not fundamentally different question than why Jesus suffered. It may be that this fundamental tenet of Christianity—Christ's suffering and dying for us—accepts actions and attitudes that accept, glorify, and even encourages suffering. Perhaps until we challenge and reject this idea we will never be liberated.[688]

Obviously, the charge against Christian faith is that the death of Jesus has provided a basis among Christians for other victimizations. Given the history of many places and many peoples around the world, such an allegation only brings to surface the painful experiences of injustice and subjugation of women. Further, one may not deny without bias that patriarchy has undermined woman emancipation. However, the question that such a feminist critique raises is whether the death of Jesus is the reason for all the models of patriarchal domination in the history? Is their claim "that classical atonement theories have been used to maintain and exonerate the purpose of a tyrannical God"[689] true or not? The matter of God's maleness and the claim that God behind the cross is sadistic and abusive are implied in these questions.

As is clear from the discussion on the power of the cross, contrary to a worldly concept of power, which is oppressive and dominating, the power of the cross is a power that opposes such powers. Having been subjected to nakedness, publicly and brutally dominated death on the cross, Jesus cannot be a symbol of further domination of any sort except by sheer misinterpretation. The problem is that Christ's followers often have been responsible for such misinterpretation. Many women have attempted to deal with these questions. One way to deal with the maleness of Jesus and thus patriarchy is to focus on Jesus' life instead of the cross.[690] Thus, Jesus' life-affirming human activities and his denunciation of the patriarchal and oppressive dominance of his culture take precedence over his death on the cross. There are others who replace dualistic anthropology with multipolar one.[691] In this Jesus' maleness is one of the many characteristics that make him human. Thus, maleness, his skill as carpenter, Jewishness, etc., all make up his humanness.

The theology of the cross and its insistence on the Incarnation would necessarily require the affirmation of the full humanity of Jesus.

Moreover, feminist theologian Elizabeth Moltmann-Wendel warns against the tendency of decrucifixion for a theologian of the cross. She argues that decrucifying fails to take seriously the suffering and violence of Jesus' death, which, in turn, downplays the reality of sin and suffering in human life.[692] Sally Purvis recognizes the positive impact of the cross and states, "The cross is not a dangerous symbol for Christian feminism but a resource we have both the right and the obligation to restore and enact."[693] She argues the cross to be a resource of power for love and life because "it breaks free from the control and violence it has confronted and moved through."[694] Though she recognizes the brutal and raw physical pain associated with the crucifixion, she claims that the suffering of Jesus is caused by love betrayed. In her emphasis of the positive aspects of the cross she reclaims its power as love. Thus, power understood as love, for her, changes the terms of the conversation; now instead of control, the cross is life-giving power; instead of violence, overcoming love.[695]

In spite of frequent misinterpretation, abuse, misuse and misapplication, the cross stands at the heart of the Christian gospel and as James Kay puts it "without a saving cross, would the Christian message still be Christian?"[696] Against much distortion, we argue that the power of the cross is not of domination and control but power of the "creative/redemptive giving of life, the power of conversion from the ways of death to the way of life, not only for the inner person but also for the totality of human and creaturely existence, including also social and natural relationships."[697] While Barr would readily admit the cross to be the power of solidarity, as we have seen in Moltmann, Pieris, Thomas and others, yet he rightly sees this as more than an act of solidarity and identity with the suffering humanity: "It is an act of radical protest against and the liberation of the creature, eschatologically, from a self and world-nihilating existence."[698]

Theology of the Cross vs. Incarnational Life

As we have seen, some feminist theologians have serious doubts about the relevance of the cross and, consequently, they argue for the incarnational life of Jesus Christ. This leads us to discuss the theology of the cross and incarnation in this section. The validity of the two statements that "the atonement is critical; it is the central doctrine of Christianity"[699] and Christianity is supremely "the religion of incarnation"[700] require examination for a theology of the cross in the South

Asian situation. There are two theological reasons for this. First, the systematic need to understand the relation between atonement and incarnation. Though we have argued that the theology of the cross is more than a theory of atonement, yet, soteriological implications are most definitely integral to it. Second, what is the nature of this relation that impacts Christian life amidst poverty and many religions?

Since the entire life of Jesus of Nazareth, his birth, his ministry, his teachings, crucifixion, and resurrection constitute God's incarnational life, atonement on the cross can only be understood in the light of Jesus' life of historical particularity. In this particularity alone is Christian identity and relevance to be perceived; likewise, in this alone is the inevitable relation between the cross and incarnation to be affirmed. Thus, Moltmann asserts, "There can be no theology of incarnation which does not become the theology of the cross."[701] Douglas John Hall also thinks that the cross is the logical necessary point towards which the incarnation moves. He says, "The theology of incarnation is and remains a theology of the cross, for it proclaims a God whose will is to be with us, where we are (Immanuel)."[702] Gustaf Aulen also sees the inseparability of the two: "The incarnation is the presupposition of the atonement and the atonement, the completion of the incarnation."[703] Ganse Little[704] rightly sees this relationship in "God was in Christ"[705] and "Christ died for us."[706] He further says that once continuity between these is realized "the indestructible logic that binds the incarnation to the atonement will be seen."[707] Thus, there is an inescapable relationship between the atonement and the incarnation.

In our interpretation of Luther's theology of the cross, we have also seen that Luther understood the cross both in terms of atonement and incarnation. To reiterate this conclusion, we recall how Luther uses the example of Philip as a theologian of glory because Philip attempted to locate the Father apart from Jesus of Nazareth.[708] Luther's strong condemnatory response to Philip's tendency to seek the Father elsewhere is a sign of his understanding of incarnation. Jesus is the true revelation of God and hence, his proclamation and claims; his preaching, and action must be understood in continuity with the event of the cross. Further, as pointed out earlier, Luther unlike Moltmann who speculates on the "sonlessness of the Father," speaks of Jesus' brotherliness with the people here and now, to prove as crucial a point as God's true and adequate revelation in Jesus. Thus, Luther is able to keep a critical and desirable tension between the cross and incarnation that facilitates a more contextual understanding of the theology of the cross. In this regard McGrath's conclusion is very instructive:

> A theology of the cross maintains that the cross remains the unequivocally *historical* event linking Christian faith to worldly reality. And that link must never be allowed to be broken if Christianity is to maintain its identity within and relevance for the world.[709]

Some theologians have confined the theology of the cross to the mere passion story of Jesus of Nazareth. For them the event of the crucifixion defines their theology of the cross. However, the complete neglect of Jesus' incarnational life in the understanding of the theology of the cross will seriously undermine both its usefulness as well as its content. It is important to understand the theology of the cross in terms of the incarnational life of Jesus to bring out the full significance of such theology for South Asia. The clarion call of Pieris for committed involvement and Thomas' insistence on *Karma Marga*[710] draw on both the way Jesus lived and died.

Thus, Sobrino concludes, Jesus' "historical career led to a historical cross." The life of Jesus cannot be spiritualized. The relation between the cross and the incarnational life is well expressed by the International Theological Commission of Roman Catholic Church:

> Theology can grasp the meaning and import of the resurrection of Jesus only in the light of the event of his death. Likewise, theology cannot understand the meaning of Jesus' death except in the light of his life, deeds, and message. The totality and coherence of the saving event which is Jesus Christ imply his life, death, and resurrection.[711]

It is in this understanding of his life that one is able to understand the full implications and effect of salvation.

However, the danger is to deduce from the principle of incarnation what McGrath calls the 'perversion of the doctrine of the incarnation' and he points out two fundamental ones.[712] Firstly, the perversion of misinterpretation of the statement that Christ is both God and man to deduce by pure logic the conclusion that man is now God. Unable to distinguish between God and man, McGrath speaks of many people such as Nietzsche who have replaced God with man. Secondly, the perversion is seen in the fact that "the principle of the incarnation establishes the essential harmony between God and humanity, so that human history may be viewed as a gradual process of evolution towards deification."[713] Undue emphasis on the humanity of Jesus to the neglect of the true meaning of his death and resurrection will always involve the danger of theology degenerating into ideology for humanistic objectives. Jesus of Nazareth cannot be reduced to a principle. He is a person with particularity in time and space who "does not encounter us at the level of principle, but in our historical existence."[714] Thus, the idea or the doctrine of incarnation cannot replace the person of Jesus Christ.

The discussion above may seem to be too Christocentric and closed. However, it would be difficult to deny the fact that the paradigm of the cross is a paradigm that can only be understood in reference to Jesus Christ the crucified God. From the New Testament it is not difficult to see the primacy of the cross and resurrection over the doctrine of incarnation. This primacy is a theological priority as the doctrine of incarnation in the final analysis is the interpretation of Christ event.[715] Thus, Martin Kähler observes, "The gospels are passion narratives with an extended introduction."[716] The event and its meaning cannot be separated from one another. In keeping the cross and incarnation as inevitable aspects of the theology of the cross in South Asia, theology acquires depth and expanse of Christian existence. The confession that Jesus died for us confirms our faith identity, so also, confessing that Jesus lives for us continues the relevance of faith.

To conclude, we can say that an Asian theology of the cross as a theology of self-criticism, vulnerability, revelation of the crucified God, and a way of scandal, foolishness and power for the sake of the other, can truly represent a Christian life and witness marked with true openness towards the people of other faiths and committed involvement in the lives of the poor.

Constructive Proposal:
Theology of the Cross as Theology of the Way

Many urgent as well as pressing concerns, challenges and conclusions for theological reflections in South Asian situation, that have been pointed out in the previous discussion could be helpfully understood in the theology of the cross as a theology of the way. We believe that understood as theology of the way the indispensable soteriological and epistemological as well as inevitable *sacramentum* and *exemplum* aspects of the theology of the cross will meaningfully be presented to those faithful followers of the cross for proclamation of the good news of Jesus Christ and also for practicing the way of the cross in relation to one's neighbor. Though the proposal is tentative yet its promises to validate our consideration.

It is obvious that the proposal relates to a metaphorical shift. The biblical account of God's activities is replete with various metaphors that help shape the meaning perception of the reality of God.[717] Although even a moderate study of metaphors in the Bible is beyond the scope of this preliminary proposal, a brief suggestion with purposeful potential with regard to the understanding of the theology of the cross as the "theology" of the way in South Asian context is, nonetheless, in order. The metaphor of the Way as tensive, epistemological and a meaning-maker signifies its value for doing contextual theology of the cross.

There are a number of important points one can underline with regard to this proposal. First, the Christian life was for the first time recognized as the way by those who were not part of Christian faith. The reference to this in Acts 9:2 suggests both their life and their identity as Christians.[718] Second, Jesus himself claims to be the way to the Father (John 14:6). Third, Jesus' whole life was destined to be a man on the way. For example, his parents were on the way when he was born; he had to be on the way to Egypt to escape Herod; his proclamation of the proximity of the kingdom of God takes place on the way; his miracles and important encounters with people take place as he meets with people on the way; his triumphant march to Jerusalem and difficult way to Golgotha are all indicative of the significance of his being on the way. Fourth, the way that Jesus is, is the way to the cross. His proclamation of the kingdom and practicing of its values lead him to the cross. His message and the meaning of his life can only be understood in terms of the way to the cross and the way of the cross.

Fifth, the metaphor of the way will underline the pilgrim character of Christian life. The prevalent self-understanding of the church as stationary institution is unhelpful in South Asia and everywhere else. Ancient symbol of Christianity as the way can still be understood afresh as a people's movement. Sixth, as a theology of the way, the theology of the cross will be more accessible to non-Christians in an Asian context as there are the somewhat equivalent concept of *Marga* (loosely translated it means way) in Hinduism and Buddhism. For many, due to historical reasons, the symbol of the cross is perceived as threatening and triumphalistic which, by articulating it in terms of a theology of the way, can be made accessible and non-threatening.

Seventh, the theological importance of the way to Emmaus is significant for such understanding. Jesus' choice to be with the disciples on the way after his resurrection without revealing his identity speaks of much more than simply the disciples' surprise at Jesus' ignorance. It is rather in the fact of posing questions and in accompanying the disciples as ignorant traveler that Jesus manifests the value of being on the way. His post-resurrection return to the way to accompany the two disciples is not without value for all those who follow after him. It is in the context of the way that the dialogue takes place, invitation is extended and, not the least, Jesus' identity is revealed in the breaking of the bread. Jesus' life comes full circle in returning to his disciples after his passion, crucifixion and resurrection. Jesus' led him to the death on the cross, whereas the victory over death, i.e., the resurrection, led him back to the community.

Both sacramental and exemplary aspects of the cross, as we have seen earlier, can be fruitfully joined in the metaphor of the way. Jesus is the way that suggests the truth of sacrament and also his life provides the true example to emulate. This is what many theologians intend to convey. For example, when Loewenich argues that the cross of Christ and the cross of Christians belong together and the cross's meaning can only be found in experience, he is, in fact, talking about two sides of one coin. This image can be understood in the metaphor of the way. For Christian life Jesus the way is at the same time the way of Jesus. In other words, confession of Jesus as the way constrains one to follow him by his example of both words and deeds. The way Jesus related to people occupies central importance for how one is to understand the relationship with the other. Moreover, his radical actions should equally be our inspiration for steps towards the establishment of justice and the affirmation of love in one's historical situation. Though Jesus the way is final, the way we follow him in our own unique situation translates finally the orientation of such confession.

As we have seen, there is an order of proper understanding in Luther's theology of the cross with regard to Jesus. For profound theological reasons, Jesus Christ the crucified must be regarded as sacrament before he is followed as example. The order of sacrament and example is important in order to realize the true depth and authentic expanse of what it means to believe and follow the crucified

Lord amidst many faiths and many poor. Similarly, the theology of the way refers to Jesus first as the way to salvation that leads a response of faith. In a response of faith Jesus also inspires those followers to take up their cross and follow him. The concept of the "way" projects the Christian life of faith response to Jesus as Lord and savior and faithful imitation of him on the way to the cross in terms of dynamism and vitality that would more truly relate to the metaphors of leaven, light and salt that Jesus intended for his followers. As pointed out earlier, such a life of faith will remain utterly open to the point of being vulnerable while relating to people of other faiths and also invests itself in grateful service for the sake of the other, especially those poor and marginalized.

Thus, the theology of the cross can be understood as the theology of the way in South Asia. However, it will always refer back to the historicity of the cross-event and hence to the Christ event. It is not to replace the cross but to re-appropriate it that we speak of the way. Christian witness rooted in the cross will not compromise with the foundation of faith, neither will it surrender the foolish and scandalous commitment to the crucified God to serve the neighbor. With its characteristics of a confessional, contextual, unified view of Jesus as sacrament and example, it promises to provide much needed direction to theological construction in South Asia today.

CHAPTER 7

Conclusions

Our emphasis has been on Luther's theology of the cross as a viable option for doing contextual theology in South Asia. While recognizing the challenges of the plurality of faiths and the poverty of the masses in the South Asian context, we have maintained, against the pluralist proposal, and argued that it is precisely in the affirmation of the uniqueness and finality of the cross that one is able to be truly open to the other (people and faith traditions) and genuinely committed to the poor. Thus, the theology of the cross represents the certainty of salvation as God's gracious gift that opposes both the prevalent relativism and the inner contradiction of the pluralist position. It also opposes the pluralists' radical break with the particularism of the biblical witness to the Christ event. Even though such a forthright contradiction to the seemingly justified pluralistic proposal would seem to be rather exclusive and closed, the deep and profound implications of the scandalous nature of God's self-revelation mandates inevitable openness and inbuilt vulnerability. The sacramental understanding of Jesus Christ is indispensable for a life of faith in Christ as Savior; however, it is also unavoidable to pattern such a life of faith after the example of Jesus Christ. Thus, the South Asian challenge of the poverty and suffering of the masses remains the context in which Luther is to speak of Christ as God's only gift for salvation, yet, at the same time, he would also with equal emphasis speak of giving oneself "as a Christ to my neighbor."[719] Thus, the challenge of identity amidst many faiths and the relevance of Christian faith for the poor in South Asia are to be responded to in a radical recognition of Jesus as both sacrament to be confessed and example to emulate.

As a missionary religion from its very inception, Christian faith has been encountering religions and cultures as it moves from one socio-cultural situation to the next. This has precipitated struggles for it in terms of both identity and relevance. True to its incarnational characteristic, Christian faith is impacted and enriched by new experiences of spirituality and cultural ethos. Faced with the South Asian context, this process must continue. As we have maintained, the theology of the cross is of foundational import for the Christian faith because it facilitates theological framework for the pastoral and prophetic contents to find new manifestations in different contexts. This is precisely why Luther's theology of the cross, though developed in the polemical context of 16th-century Europe, remains viable for doing contextual theology in South Asia. In fact, the intrinsic soteriological intention and inherent epistemological implication of the theology of the cross secures and substantiates its continuing relevance.

Against the theology of speculation, the official theology of the church of the time, Luther's theology of the cross proved to be a counter theology that spoke of God in terms of the crucified one. Not fully aware of its comprehensive depth and remarkable sweep, Luther in his theology of the cross nonetheless defended the views that God can only be known in suffering and the cross, which were to be expounded in later years. Luther's theology of the cross led him to deep and far-reaching conclusions in the understanding of who God is. So profound and decisive were the insights of Luther's theology of the cross for the understanding of God that they were to impact theologians and theologies for centuries, particularly for relating theology to burning questions of suffering, poverty, injustice, etc.

Luther's insistence that God be perceived in Jesus on the cross brought about an understanding of God that was radically final and finally radical. Radically final because it does not allow any speculation beyond the incarnation of Jesus of Nazareth and finally radical because it broke away the straight jacket of the concept of impassibility of God to allow him to be conceived as 'crucified.' Walter Kasper concludes this about the theology of the cross of Luther:

> Luther's *theologia crucis* breaks through the whole system of metaphysical theology. He tries consistently to see, not the cross in light of a philosophical concept of God, but God in the light of the cross. ...For Luther, the hidden God is the God hidden in the suffering and the cross. We should not try to penetrate the mysteries of God's majesty, but should be content with the God on the cross. We cannot find God except in Christ; anyone who tries to find him outside of Christ will find the devil.[720]

In some significant sense, thus, it led to the paradigm shift in the conception of God in modern times. Thus, contemporary theologians speak of "revolution,"[721] a "metaphoric shift,"[722] to indicate the import and impact of the theology of the cross.

In emphasizing the need of this shift, pluralist theologians like Pieris have compromised the soteriological foundation of the cross. Though their concern for openness to religio-cultural lessons from different faith traditions and acceptance of the otherness is legitimate, their conclusion that the uniqueness and finality of Jesus Christ is problematic is ill founded. For it is not difficult to see that these so-called problems of the Christian faith, in the light of the theology of the cross, are, in fact, the very reality that must help overcome the tendency of a superiority of faith and a lack of sensitivity towards other religions. It is because the uniqueness is of the one who claimed to be the savior of the world by going to the scandalous cross to die a helpless death. And its finality is only of the crucified God who is to be understood in terms of finally transforming one's life into a life of utter humility, self-criticism, and vulnerability.

For pluralist theologians, the problematic claim of uniqueness and finality for the Christ event relates to the sacramental nature of Jesus Christ. Nonetheless, as we have seen, by making any compromise with the sacramental nature of the cross, even under tremendous seemingly legitimate pressure on account of many faiths and their various ways of salvation, we would prove Jesus to be a parochial Savior or, even worse, less than a God. However, it is far from just simply affirming the traditional understanding of Jesus as the Savior of the world that we have maintained the primacy of Jesus' soteriological validity amidst many faiths; rather, serious theological reasons, understood according to the framework of Luther's theology of the cross, have predicated this. In fact, we would recall that Luther's theology of the cross was developed in sharp contrast to the prevalent official theological tradition of the contemporary church.

At the same time, our contention has been that the true and faithful appropriation of Jesus Christ as an example is most adequately possible within the sacramental framework that demands ultimate and unwavering loyalty from those who follow. We have seen that in the framework of the theology of the cross the order of sacrament and example is to be maintained for theological reasons. In fact, what Luther says should give heart to our deep concern about the actions of peace and love:

> Your salvation does not depend on the fact that you believe Christ to be the Saviour of the godly, but that he is a Saviour to you and has become your own. Such a faith will work in you love for Christ and joy in him, and good works will naturally follow. If they do not, faith is surely not present; for where faith is, there the Holy Ghost is and must work love and good works.[723]

Further, if we were to exclude the sacramental fact of the Christ event, we would seriously undermine the theological moorings of the phenomenon of "genuine conversion," persecution for the sake of faith, and even public proclamation of the gospel in South Asia. Thus, those who accept Christ as Savior would be theologically crippled for lack of sound theological foundation. Those persecuted for the sake of their faith would be proved to have made an ultimate faith commitment for empty promises. And the public proclamation of the gospel confined only to the four walls of the sanctuary would finally restrict even public commitment of the faithful. Needless to say, these theological and pastoral possibilities contradict what Luther's theology of the cross espouses. Instead of being helpful for our attempt at contextual theology, ultimately, it would be less than holistic. Further, if we were to undermine the sacramental aspect of the cross to afford, instead, salvific value to human actions, it would only jeopardize the harmonious relationships with the other faiths. Moreover, if human works were to be given salvific merit, it would only lead to an attitude of discrimination and judgment towards the other. Finally, its very logic would even blame the poor for their poverty as their actions could become the basis to judge. Thus, the affirmation of the uniqueness and finality is not only indispensable for theological integrity but also helpful for harmonious living together amidst plurality of faith and poverty.

As significant as the fact of grace and justification by faith understood in terms of Jesus Christ the sacrament has been in this dissertation, nonetheless, we would be served well to heed the warning of Käsemann against idle talk: "The fear of works, which sometimes seems to be all that remains in Protestantism from the Reformation, must not lead us to fall back on nothing but theology and idle talk."[724] Thus, the aspects of *sacramentum* and *exemplum* are indispensable for relevant and contextual theological reflection for the church in South Asia.

When one realizes that one is justified by grace through faith and stands face to face with the broken and battered Christ on the cross, he or she realizes that it is not cheap grace; it is not lip service that many confuse this with, but, rather, it is to be gripped with the sheer irrationality and undeservedness of such grace; it is to be taken up in God's vulnerability that we can do no other but be Christ[725] to all those under the yoke of poverty and oppression. Pieris speaks powerfully for this aspect of the theology of the cross. In fact, in his relentless effort for the church *in* Asia to become church *of* Asia, rooted and reoriented in the Asian ethos, we have glimpsed the expanding contours of the theology of the cross. The encounter of the cross with other faith traditions accentuates the sheer irrationality, folly, scandal and vulnerability for those who follow and carry the cross, while the poverty of the masses determines a life of faithful response to God as graceful affirmation in daily and decisive response to the poor. For Asian perception of the theology of the cross, Thomas and Pieris have emphasized that any theology of the cross can only be done with one's involvement in the process of humanization (Thomas) and critical participation in human liberation (Pieris). Though Thomas recognizes the plurality of religions, he remains within the paradigm of understanding other religions as being fulfilled in Christ. On the other hand, Pieris has argued for the recognition of the soteriological value of all the meta-religions of Asia. Moreover, his theology of the cross will require Christian followers to immerse themselves in the spirituality of the Asian religions to find authentic existence in relation with liberation. Pieris is right in his assertion; however, a Christian does not necessarily have to forgo the claim of uniqueness and finality to do this. On the other hand, faced with mass poverty of such an unprecedented scale, the theology of the cross in South Asia will redefine the church and the Christian life as being marked with their locatedness with the poor for the experience of God's hopeful future for all.

Though the inner resourcefulness of the theology of the cross has been affirmed, it is not, however, to deny the fact that the theology of the cross would fathom new depths of compassion in its interaction with Buddhism; generosity and tolerance with Hinduism; non-violence with Jainism; and a sense of order in its interaction with Islam. In its somewhat lopsided emphasis on the individual, though not without legitimate theological reasons, nonetheless one sided, the theology of the cross will find timely corrective in meeting with the primal religions, for example in North India. The indigenous/tribal-integrated worldview in which community is inclusive as it encompasses people, nature, ancestors and spirit, and the fact that human being, nature, spirit continuum makes a person a really complete person,[726] has something valuable to offer to the theology of the cross to be holistic in South Asia.

The precedence of *sacramentum* over *exemplum* might be a reason for joy to those who emphasize solely the spiritual and individual aspect of Christian life, whereas the predominance of exemplary aspect would satisfy those whose theology begins with human actions. Nonetheless, the theology of the cross remains a perennial critique of both conservative and liberal tendencies in theology. Both of them employ rationality to set their agenda and pursue them with sincerity. The conservative tendency seeks to establish the exclusive claim of the truth of God and the gospel of Jesus Christ on the basis of their rational theories and assertions, whereas the liberal tendency bypasses the person of Jesus to establish Jesus the principle by using the same method of rationality. Luther does not allow any rationality to have the last word when it comes to understanding God's revelation on the cross.

The aspects of *sacramentum* and *exemplum* of the theology of the cross remain beyond any compromise because a greater emphasis on Christ the *sacramentum* runs the risk of cheap grace against which Bonhoeffer warns, and at the same time, underestimating it in favor of Christ the *exemplum* endangers theology being reduced to mere social action. Thus, the theological and existential challenge is how we understand both and keep the dialectic such that they remain decisive part of Christian existence. Luther's theology of the cross, in our contention, does precisely this. We have seen that Luther's theology of the cross, with its emphasis on revelation, faith, incarnation, self-criticism, scandal and folly could helpfully present us with an alternative to find Christian existence marked with humility, genuine concern for the other, locatedness with those on the margin and vulnerability for the sake of the other. For an unknown professor of a nondescript school, Luther demonstrates the spirit of the theology of the cross in his righteous anger towards the church's serious compromise with God's grace that led to his theological conviction of as one who was willing to take risk for the sake of the truth. Thus, he criticizes self-deceived people, ill-informed priests and an overweening pope and also challenges those rich and powerful for benefiting from the sale of indulgences. His example of risking his life speaks out of theology of the cross. Such exemplary risk, we must emphasize, is for the sake of God's truth of grace in Jesus Christ. Thus, Luther's life and Christian life can only be thought of as faithful response to God and grateful affirmation among people of the fact that he or she is truly a new creation in Christ.

The dilemma of the twin aspects of the cross, namely, sacrament and example, can be resolved by using the metaphor of the way. The metaphor of the way seems helpful and promising for understanding the indispensable double dimensions of the theology of the cross. While Jesus as the way to salvation may not be compromised amidst plurality of faiths, Jesus' way as man for others even unto death, however, may also not be ignored without violating the authenticity of Christian existence.[727] Moreover, the 'thin tradition' or minority tradition of the theology of the cross appropriately relates not only to the minority metaphors of leaven, salt and light found in Jesus' teaching, it also approximates the minority Christian population in South Asia. In this light, one only hopes that the small church in the South Asian context would overcome its minority mentality of always being in need of security and privilege, on the one hand, and equally uncharacteristic attitude of concluding its influence to be ineffective and inadequate, on the other, with regard to the challenges that it encounters. Instead, as much as they seem insignificant both compared to the ocean of people in the region and also in the number politics of democracy, their lightness and tastefulness if lived under the cross would inevitably witness to the truth of both Christian identity in self-criticism and utter humility and relevance in radical commitment.

Constantly convicted and critiqued by the cross on a daily basis, a Christian attitude towards the other religions and people of other faiths cannot be one of judgment or superiority. In Luther's concept of simultaneously saint and sinner, Christians will always find themselves in the same boat with others constantly in need of God's grace in Jesus Christ. Hence, a more appropriate and helpful Christian approach towards other can begin to take shape in realizing the present folly and scandal of the cross while living life together in the community. As was pointed out, public faith and a conscious location with the vulnerable and the marginalized people for a shared life will help Christians experience what Thomas argues in terms of the acknowledged Christ of

Indian renaissance. Moreover, in being small christs to those in need, Asian Christians would realize the true meaning and significance of what Pieris intends in his passion for liberation. An Asian theology of the cross will take shape in daily encounter with and confession of Christ the way and draw believers to the way the Savior lived and died. Thus, the proclamation of the one who died for the world and the practice of the values of the one who inaugurated the Kingdom, promise true Christian identity and relevance in South Asia. Indeed, the theology of the cross is the theology of the way.

Acknowledgments

This work, that occupied several years of my energy, attention and labored efforts, has been no less than a community effort. I wish to acknowledge that community with my sincere and heartfelt gratitude. It has been an adventure in faith as I was never in doubt about God's abrupt intervention as I pursued the meaning and implications of Luther's theology of the cross. And I thank the triune God for his abiding faithfulness in this journey in which I was blessed with much motivation and sustained with divine wisdom, hopeful courage, and fruitful perseverance throughout.

Initially I had thought that I was at Luther Seminary, Saint Paul, Minnesota, by default as I followed my wife, Nijhar, but now with the benefit of the hindsight, I can say that it was God's divine provision for me as Luther seminary proved a very helpful place to undertake Luther research. I thank the seminary for financial help for my study. I owe much more than the words could ever convey to my wife, Nijhar, for her support and strength. While my efforts in scholarship produced one dissertation, Nijhar managed well multiple tasks; work in and out of home, care for three young children Maani Grace, Urbas Sawang and Puna Bel and also at the same time continued her own Ph.D. work at the University of Minnesota. In spite of all these, she remained an unwavering pillar of encouragement and tender refuge of companionship for me, for which I have only inadequate words to express my sense of deep gratefulness.

This book would not have taken its present shape and form without the help, guidance, and encouragement of many professors and friends at Luther Seminary. Particularly, I thank Professor Dr. Jim Nestingen for his prayerful support and readiness to offer assistance above and beyond the call of his duty. His suggestion to study Luther's *Church Postils* was valuable for this study. I also record my appreciation for Dr. Lois Malcolm for her interest and help, especially at the beginning of this project. Professor Dr. Marc Kolden, was a willing and perceptive reader, for which I am very grateful. His meticulous comments were helpful. Through Professor Dr. Charles Amjad-Ali's insightful conversation, thoughtful critique, personal interest in my project he became ever-encouraging friend and always-supportive older brother, for which I will always be deeply grateful. His precious time and energy amidst his own struggle with life-threatening illness became a lesson of witnessing in vulnerability of the cross, a profound insight that I have used in this book.

Many others outside the Luther Seminary community have upheld me and my family with prayers and support, for whom, I wish to record my deep sense of gratitude, especially, to dear "uncle" Rev. Dr. Duain Vierow and "aunt" Donna Vierow, beloved friends Patty Amundsen, Chance, Sommer, Nancy and David Hanson, Harriet Peterson, Rev. Del Jacobson, Daryl and Vicky Johnson, Pastor Melinda Melhus, Rev. Duane Olson, the late Rev. Paul Hanson, Martha Kunau, Jim and Lynne Moratzka, Sara Trumm for their many ways of support and encouragement. For the assistance that I received, I record my appreciation for the Luther Seminary library staff, especially, Bruce Eldevik, Sally Sawyer, and Judy Stone. I am very grateful to Rhoda Schuler for her technical assistance. Many thanks are also due to many friends who lifted my spirit and effort by their encouraging words, especially to Samantha and Orin Cummings, Lacee and Matt Anderson, Peter Bartimawus and Gaylan Mathiesen. For his arduous task of proof reading I record my deep appreciation and gratitude to Professor Emeritus Olaf Storaasli. My extended family in India deserves special recognition for their prayer and support.

Bibliography

Abhisiktananda, Swami *Saccidananda: A Christian Approach to Advaitic Experience*, rev. ed. Delhi, India: ISPCK, 1984.

Abraham, K. C., ed. *Third World Theologies: Commonalities and Divergences.* Maryknoll, NY: Orbis Books, 1990.

_____. "Pluralism as Oikomene of Solidarity." In *New Horizons in Ecumenism: Essays in Honour of Bishop Samuel Amritham*, ed. K. C. Abraham, 121-130. Bangalore, India: The Board of Theological Education of the Senate of Serampore, 1994.

Achtemeier, Paul J., ed. *Harper's Bible Dictionary.* San Francisco, CA: Harper & Row, 1985.

Althaus, Paul. *The Ethics of Martin Luther.* Translated by Robert C. Schultz. Philadelphia: Fortress, 1972.

_____. *The Theology of Martin Luther.* Translated by Robert C. Schultz. Philadelphia: Fortress, 1972.

Alves, Ruben. *Theology of Human Hope.* Washington, DC: Corpus Books, 1969.

Amjad-Ali, Charles, "A Theory of Justice for an Ecumenical Praxis: A Critique of Eurocentric Pseudo-Universals." Ph.D. diss., Princeton Theological Seminary, 1985.

_____. ed. *Liberation in Ethics: Essays in Religious Social Ethics in Honor of Gibson Winter.* Chicago: Center for the Scientific Study of Religion, 1985.

_____. "The Religious Dimension of Social Change" In *Christian Ethics in Ecumenical Context*, ed. Shin Chiba, George Hunsberger, and Lester Edwin J. Ruiz, 268-279. Grand Rapids, MI: William B. Eerdmans Publishing Company, 1995.

Amoladass, Michael. "Questions from the Local Churches from Asia." In *Trends in Mission*, ed. William Jenkinson and Helene O'Sullivan, 46-52. Maryknoll, NY: Orbis Books, 1991.

Anderson, Gerald H. and Thomas F. Stransky. eds. *Asian Voices in Christian Theology.* Maryknoll, NY: Orbis Books, 1976.

_____. eds. *Christ's Lordship & Religious Pluralism.* Maryknoll, NY: Orbis Books, 1981.

Anselm. *Anselm of Canterbury.* Edited and translated by Jasper Hopkins and Herbert Richardson. Toronto: The Edwin Mellen Press, 1976.

Ariarajah, Wesley. *Hindus and Christians: A Century of Protestant Ecumenical Thought.* Grand Rapids, MI: William B. Eerdmans Publishing Company, 1991.

_____. *The Bible and People of Other Faiths.* Geneva: WCC, 1985.

Atkinson, James. "Ecclesia Reformata Semper Reformanda." In *Luther for an Ecumenical Age*, ed. Carl S. Meyer, 271-290. St. Louis, MO: Concordia Publishing House, 1967.

Aulén, Gustaf. *Christus Victor: A Historical Study of Three Main Types of the Idea of Atonement*. Translated by A.G. Herbert. London: SPCK, 1950.

Baago, Kaj. *Pioneers of Indigenous Christianity*. Bangalore: Christian Institute for the Study of Religion and Society and CLS, 1969.

Baillie, Doanld M. *The Theology of the Sacrament*. London: Faber & Faber, 1964.

Bainton, Roland H. *Here I Stand*. New York: The New American Library, 1955.

_____. *The Age of Reformation*. Princeton, NJ: D. Van Nostrand Company, 1956.

Balasundaram, Franklyn J. *Contemporary Asian Christian Theology*. Delhi, India: ISPCK, 1991.

Balasuriya, Tissa. *Jesus and Human Liberation*. Colombo, Sri Lanka: Centre for Society and Religion, 1976.

Barnes, T.D. *Tertullian: A Historical and Literary Study* 2nd ed., rev. Oxford: Clarendon Press, 1985.

Barr, William. "Political Power and the Power of the Cross." *Lexington Theological Quarterly* 11 (1976) 3-8.

Bartsch, Hans W., ed. *Kerygma and Myth*. London: SPCK, 1953.

Bassler, Jouette M. "Cross." In *Harper's Bible Dictionary*, ed., Paul J. Achtemeier, 211-213. San Francisco: Harper & Row, 1985.

Bauckham, Richard. "Only the Suffering God Can Help: Divine Possibility in Modern Theology." *Themelios* 9 (1984) 6-12.

_____. "In Defence of The Crucified God." In *The Power and Weakness of God*, ed. Nigel M. de S. Cameron, 93-118. Edinburgh: Rutherford House Books, 1990.

Baum, Gregory, and Robert Ellesberg, eds. *The Logic of Solidarity*. Maryknoll, NY: Orbis Books, 1989.

Beker, J. Christaan. *Paul the Apostle: The Triumph of God in Life and Thought*. Philadelphia: Fortress, 1980.

Bell, T. *Divus Bernardus: Bernard von Clairvaux in Martin Luthers Schriften*. Mainz, Germany: P. von Zabern, 1993.

Bernard of Clairvaux. *Bernard of Clairvaux: On the Song of Songs*. Translated by K. Walsh. Cistern Fathers Series No. 7. Kalamazoo, MI: Cisterian Publications, 1976.

Boff, Leonardo. *Jesus Christ Liberator: A Critical Christology for Our Time*. Translated by Patrick Hughes. Maryknoll, NY: Orbis Books, 1979.

_____. *Passion of Christ, Passion of the World: Their Facts, Their Interpretation, and Their Meaning, Yesterday and Today*. Translated by Robert R. Barr. Maryknoll, NY: Orbis Books, 1987.

_____. *Way of the Cross-Way of Justice*. Translated by John Drury. Maryknoll, NY: Orbis Books, 1982.

Bonhoeffer, Dietrich. *The Cost of Discipleship*. 2d ed., rev. New York: Macmillian Publishing, 1976.

_____. *Life Together*. Translated by John W. Doberstein. New York: Harper and Brothers, 1954.

Boyd, Robin. *An Introduction to Indian Christian Theology*. Delhi: ISPCK, 1998.

Braaten, Carl E. "A Trinitarian Theology of the Cross." *Journal of Religion* 56 (1976) 113-121.

_____. *No Other Gospel! Christianity Among the World Religions*. Minneapolis: Fortress Press, 1992.

_____. *The Apostolic Imperative*. Minneapolis: Augsburg Publishing House, 1985.

Brecht, Martin. *Martin Luther: His Road to Reformation. 1483-1521*. Translated by James L. Schaaf. Philadelphia: Fortress, 1985.

Brock, Rita Nakashima. *Journeys by Heart: A Christology of Erotic Power*. New York: Crossroad, 1992.

Bronkamm, Heinrich. *Luther and the Old Testament*. Translated by Eric W. and Ruth Gritsch. Philadelphia: Fortress, 1969.

_____. *Luther's World of Thought*. Translated by Martin H. Bertram. St. Louis: Concordia Publishing House, 1958.

Brown, Joanne Carlson and Rebcca Parker. "God So Loved the World." In *Christianity, Patriarchy and Abuse: A Feminist Critique*, ed. Joanne Carlson Brown and Carole R. Bohn, 1-30. New York: Pilgrim Press, 1989.

Brueggemann, Walter and George W. Stroup, eds. *Many Voices One God: Being Faithful in a Pluralistic World*. Louisville, KY: Westminster John Knox Press, 1998.

Bultmann, Rudolf. "New Testament and Mythology." In *Kerygma and Myth*, ed. Hans Werner Bartsch, 1- 44. London: SPCK, 1953.

Calvin, John. *The Institute of the Christian Religion*. Vols. 1-2. Translated by Ford Lewis Battles and ed. John McNeill. Philadelphia: Westminster Press, 1960.

Cameron, Nigel M. de S., ed. *The Power and Weakness of God*. Edinburgh: Rutherford House Books, 1990.

Carino, Feliciano V. and Marina T. eds. *Faith and Life in Contemporary Asian Realities*. Hong Kong: CCA, 2000.

Carr, Dhyanchand. *Emerging Voices in Global Christian Theology*. Grand Rapids, MI: Zondervan Publishing House, 1990.

_____. ed. *God, Christ and God's People in Asia*. Hong Kong: CCA Theological Concerns, 1995.

Cessario, R. *The Godly Image: Christ and Salvation in Catholic Thought from Anselm to Aquinas*. Petersham, MA: St. Bede's, 1990.

Chacko, Mohan. *Interpreting Society: A Study of the Political Theology of M. M. Thomas and Its Implications for Mission*. Dehradun, India: Presbyterian Theological Seminary, 2000.

Chiba, Shin, George Hunsberger and Lester Edwin J. Ruiz. eds. *Christian Ethics in Ecumenical Context*. Grand Rapids, MI: William B. Eerdmans Publishing Company, 1995.

CIA. "World Fact Book: Country Profiles," http://cia.gov/cia/publications/factbook (accessed February 15, 2005).

Cooey, Paula M, et al., eds. *After Patriarchy: Feminist Transformation of the World Religions*. Maryknoll, NY: Orbis Books, 1991.

Cousar, Charles B. *A Theology of the Cross: The Death of Jesus in Pauline Letters.* Minneapolis: Fortress, 1990.

Cowdell, Scott. *Is Jesus Unique?* New York: Paulist Press, 1996.

Danahue, J. R. "Passion Narrative." In *Interpreter's Dictionary: Supplemetary Volume*, ed. Keith Crim, 643-644. Nashville, TN: Abingdon, 1976.

Dawson, Ann. *Freedom As Liberating Power.* Freiburg, Germany: Universitatsverlag, 2000.

D' Costa, Gavin, ed. *Christian Uniqueness Reconsidered: The Myth of a Pluralistic Theology of Religions.* Maryknoll, NY: Orbis Books, 1990.

_____. "The New Missionary: John Hick and Religious Plurality." *International Bulletin of Missionary Research* 15 (1991) 66-69.

Dietrich, Gabriele and Bas Wielenga. *Towards Understanding Indian Society.* Madurai, India: Tamilnadu Theological Seminary, 1997.

Dillenberger, John. *God Hidden and Revealed.* Philadelphia: Muhlenberg Press, 1953.

DiNoia, Joseph. *The Diversity of Religions: A Christian Perspective.* Washington DC: Catholic University Press, 1992.

Doble, Peter. *The Paradox of Salvation: Luke's Theology of the Cross.* New York: Cambridge University Press, 1996.

Dolan, John P. *History of the Reformation.* New York: Desclee Company, 1965.

Dreyer, Elizabeth. *Cross in Christian Tradition.* New York: Paulist Press, 2000.

Dryness, William A. *Learning About Theology from the Third World.* Grand Rapids, MI: Zondervan Publishing House, 1990.

Dunn, James D. G. *The Theology of Paul the Apostle.* Grand Rapids, MI: William B. Eerdmans Publishing Company, 1998.

Dupuis, Jacques. *Toward a Christian Theology of Religious Pluralism.* Maryknoll, NY: Orbis Books, 1997.

Ebeling, Gerhard. *Luther: An Introduction to His Thought.* Translated by R. A. Wilson. Philadelphia: Fortress, 1970.

_____. *Word and Faith.* Translated by James W. Leitch. Philadelphia: Fortress Press, 1963.

Eckardt, Jr., Burnell F. "Luther and Moltmann: The Theology of the Cross." *Concordia Theological Quarterly* 49 (1985) 19-28.

Elm, K., ed. *Bernhard von Clairvaux: Rezeption und Wirkung in Mitelalter und in der neuzeit.* Wiesbaden, Germany: Harrassowitz, 1994.

Elwood, Douglas J. *Asian Christian Theology: Emerging Themes.* Philadelphia: The Westminster Press, 1980.

_____. *What Christians Are Thinking.* Quezon City, Philippines: New Day Publishers, 1976.

England, John C. *Living Theology in Asia.* Maryknoll, NY: Orbis Books, 1982.

Fabella, Virginia. *Asia's Struggle for Full Humanity.* Maryknoll, NY: Orbis Books, 1980.

_____ and Sergio Torres, eds. *Irruption of the Third World.* Maryknoll, NY: Orbis Books, 1983.

_____, eds. *Doing Theology in the Divided World*. Maryknoll, NY: Orbis Books, 1985.

Ferguson, Sinclair B. and David Wright. eds. *New Dictionary of Theology*. Downer Grove, IL: Inter varsity, 1988.

Firth, C. B. *An Introduction to Indian Church History*. Madras, India: CLS, 1961.

Fitzgerald, Allan D., ed. *Augustine through the Ages: An Encyclopedia*. Grand Rapids, MI: William B. Eerdmans Publishing Company, 1999.

Flemming, Kenneth. *Asian Christian Theologians in Dialogue with Buddhism*. New York: Peter Lang, 2002.

Førde, Gerhard. *On Being a Theologian of the Cross*. Grand Rapids, MI: William B. Eerdmans Publishing Company, 1997.

Forester, D. B. "The Depressed Classes and Conversion to Christianity, 1860-1960." In *Religion in South Asia*, ed. G. A. Oddie, 35-66. Columbia, MO: South Asia Books, 1977.

Forman, Charles. *Christianity in the Non-Western World*. New Jersey: Prentice Hall, 1967.

Fretheim, T. *The Suffering of God*. Philadelphia: Fortress, 1984.

Gerrish, Brian. "To the Unknown God: Luther and Calvin on the Hiddenness of God." *Journal of Religion* 53 (1973) 263-292.

Gibbs, Philip. *The Word in the Third World: Divine Revelation in the Theology of Jean-Marc Ela, Aloysius Pieris, and Gustavo Gutierrez*. Roma: Pontifcia Universita Gregoriana, 1996.

Gillis, Chester. *Pluralism: A New Paradigm for Theology*. Louvain, France: Peeters Press, 1993.

Glebe-Moller, Jens. *Jesus and Theology: Critique of a Tradition*. Translated by Thor Hall. Minneapolis: Fortress, 1989.

Gonzalez, Justo L. *A History of Christian Thought*. 3 vols. Nashville, TN: Abingdon Press, 1980.

Gorman, Michael. *Cruciformity: Paul's Narrative Spirituality of the Cross*. Grand Rapids, MI: William B. Eerdmans Publishing Company, 2001.

Grant, Frederick C. *The Gospels: The Origin and the Growth*. New York: Harper and Bros, 1957.

Grislis, E. "Martin Luther's View of the Hidden God. The Problem of the *Deus Absconditus* in Luther's Treatise *De servo arbitrio*." *McCormick Quarterly* 21 (1967) 81-94.

Grimm, Harold J. *The Reformation Era 1500 - 1650*. New York: Macmillan Company, 1954.

Gundry, Stanley N. and Alan F. Johnson. eds. *Tensions in Contemporary Theology*. Chicago: Moody, 1976.

Gustafson, J. M. *Theology and Christian Ethics*. Philadelphia: United Church Press, 1974.

_____. *Christ and Moral Life*. New York: Harper and Row, 1968.

Gutierrez, Gustavo. *A Theology of Liberation: History, Politics and Salvation*. Maryknoll, NY: Orbis Books, 1973.

Hägglund, Bengt. *The Background of Luther's Doctrine of Justification in Late Medieval Theology*. Philadelphia: Fortress, 1971.

Hall, Douglas John. *God and Human Suffering: An Experience in the Theology of the Cross*. Minneapolis: Augsburg Publishing House, 1986.

_____. *Lighten Our Darkness: Toward an Indigenous Theology of the Cross*. Philadelphia: Westminster Press, 1976.

_____. "Luther's Theology of the Cross." *Consensus* 25 (1989) 7-19.

Hallencreutz, Carl F. *New Approaches to Men of Other Faiths*. Geneva: WCC, 1970.

Hallman, Joseph. *The Descent of God: Divine Suffering in History and Theology*. Minneapolis: Fortress, 1991.

Hamel, Adolph. *Der junge Luther und Agustin*. Gütersloh, Germany: C. Bertelsmann, 1934.

Hamilton, Andrew. "What has Asia to do with Australia: Reflections on the theology of Aloysius Pieris." *Pacifica* 3 (1990) 304-322.

Heim, S. Mark. *Salvations: Truth and Difference in Religion*. Maryknoll, NY: Orbis Books, 1995.

_____. *Is Christ the Only Way*. Valley Forge, PA: Judson Press, 1985.

Hengel, Martin. *Crucifixion*. Translated by John Bowden. London: SCM Press, 1977.

Hick, John and Paul Knitter. eds. *The Myth of Christian Uniqueness: Toward a Pluralistic Theology of Religion*. Maryknoll, N.Y.: Orbis Books, 1987.

_____. *A Christian Theology of Religions*. Louisville, KY: Westminster John Knox Press, 1995.

Hillerbrand, Hans. ed. *The Reformation: A Narrative History Related by Contemporary Observers and Participants*. New York: Harper and Row, 1964.

Hoffman, Bengt R. *Luther and the Mystics*. Minneapolis: Augsburg Publishing House, 1976.

Hogg, A. G. *The Christian Message to the Hindu*. London: SCM Press, 1947.

Hooker, Morna D. *Not Ashamed of the Gospel*. Grand Rapids, MI: William B. Eerdmans Publishing Company, 1994.

Horsley, Richard A., ed. *Paul and Empire: Religion and Power in Roman Imperial* Society. Harrisburg, PA: Trinity, 1997.

Hwa, Yung. *Mangoes or Bananas: The Quest for an Authentic Asian Christian Theology*. Oxford: Regnum Books, 1997.

International Theological Commission, *Select Questions on Christology*. Washington, DC: United States Catholic Conference, 1980.

Iserloh, Erwin. "Luther's Christ-Mysticism." In *Catholic Scholars Dialogue with Luther,* ed. Jared Wicks, 37-58. Chicago: Loyola University Press, 1970.

Isvaradevan, R. "Some Major Aspects of Aloysius Pieris' Liberation Theology: Critical Reflections." *The Asia Journal of Theology* 11 (1997) 48-68.

Jacob Satish, "Buddhism appeal to low-caste Hindus." *BBC* November 5, 2001. http://news.bbc.co.uk/1/low/world.south_asia/1639245.stm (accessed December 31, 2004).

Janz, D. R. *Luther on Thomas Aquinas: The Angelic Doctor in the Thought of the Reformer*. Wiesbaden, Germnay: Franz Steiner, 1989.

Jathanna, O. V. *The Decisiveness of the Christ-Event and the Universality of Christianity in a World of Religious Plurality*. Berne, Germany: Peter Lang, 1981.

_____. "Religious Pluralism: A Theological Critique." *Bangalore Theological Forum* 31 (1999) 1-19.

Jenkinson, William and Helene O., eds. *Trends in Mission*. Maryknoll, NY: Orbis Books, 1991.

Jensen, Gordon. "The Significance of Luther's Theology of the Cross for Contemporary Political and Contextual Theologies." Ph.D. diss., Toronto School of Theology, 1992.

Johnson, Elizabeth. *SHE WHO IS: The Mystery of God in Feminist Theological Discourse*. New York: Crossroad, 1993.

Johnson, Luke Timothy. *Reading Romans: A Literary and Theological Community*. New York: Crossword Publication, 1997.

Jungel, Eberhard. *God and the Mystery of the World: On the Foundation of the Theology of the Crucified One in the Dispute between Theism and Atheism*. Translated by Darrel L. Guder. Grand Rapids, MI: William E. Eerdmans Publishing Company, 1977.

Kadai, Heino O., ed. *Accents in Luther's Theology*. St. Louis, MO: Concordia Publishing House, 1967.

_____. "Luther's Theology of the Cross." In *Accents in Luther's Theology*, ed. Heino O. Kadai, 238-235. St. Louis, MO: Concordia Publishing House, 1967.

Kappen, Sebastian. *Jesus and Freedom*. Maryknoll, NY: Orbis Books, 1977.

Käsemann, Ernst. *Jesus Means Freedom*. Philadelphia: Fortress, 1969.

_____. *Perspectives on Paul*. London: SCM., 1971.

_____. "The Pauline Theology of the Cross." *Interpretation* 24 (1970) 151-177.

_____. "The Saving Significance of the Death of Jesus in Paul." In *Perspectives on Paul*. Translated by Margaret Kohl. 32-59. Philadelphia: Fortress, 1971, reprint Mifflitown, PA: Sigler, 1996.

Kasper, Walter. *Jesus the Christ*. Translated by V. Green. New York: Paulist Press, 1976.

Kattenbusch, F. "Deus absconditus bei Luther." In *Festgabe für D. Dr. Julius Kaftan zu seinem 70. Geburtstag*, Germany: Tübingen,1920.

Kay, James. "Word of the Cross at the Turn of the Ages." *Interpretation* 53 (1999) 44-56.

Kee, Alistair. "The Imperial Cult: The Unmasking of an Ideology." *Scottish Journal of Religious Studies* 6 (1985) 112-128.

Kehm, George H. and Wolfhart Pannenberg. *Basic Questions in Theology*, Vol. 2. Philadelphia: Fortress, 1970.

Kelber, Werner H., ed. *The Passion in Mark*. Philadelphia: Fortress, 1976.

Kern, H. *Manuel of Indian Buddhism*. Delhi, India: Motilal Benarasi Das, 1974.

Kitamori, Kazoh. *Theology of the Pain of God*. Translated by Shinkyo Suppanskha. Richmond, VA: John Knox Press, 1965.

Knitter, Paul F. *No Other Name? A Critical Survey of Christian Attitude Towards the World Religions*. Maryknoll, NY: Orbis Books, 1985.

Koyama, Kosuke. *Mount Fuji and Mount Sinai*. Maryknoll, NY: Orbis Books, 1984.

_____. *Water Buffalo Theology*. Maryknoll, NY: Orbis Books, 1974.

Kraemer, Hendrick. *The Christian Message in a Non-Christian World*. London: Harper Co.,1938.

Krey, Philip. "Martin Luther." 516-518 in *Augustine Through Ages: An Encyclopedia*. Edited by Allan D. Fitzerald. Grand Rapids, MI: William B. Eerdmans Publishing Company, 1999.

Küng, Hans. *Freedom Today*. Translated by Cecily Hastings. New York: Sheed and Ward, 1966.

———. "What is True Religion? Toward an Ecumenical Criteriology." In *Christian Revelation and World Religion*, ed. L. Swidler, 231-250. Maryknoll, NY: Orbis Books, 1987.

———. *On Being Christian*. Translated by Edward Quinn. Garden City, NY: Double day, 1976.

———. and Helmut Schmidt. eds. *A Global Ethic: The Declaration of the Parliament of the World's Religion*. New York: Continuum, 1993.

Kurien, C. T. *Poverty and Development*. Madras, India: CLS, 1974.

Kuruvilla, Kadakkal Pothen. "The Incarnation and the Cross: The Inseparable Paradigm for an Indian Christian Theology of Inculturation and Liberation." Ph.D. diss., Lutheran School of Theology at Chicago, 1999.

Lage, Dietmar. *Martin Luther's Christology and Ethics*. Lewiston, NY: The Edwin Mellen Press, 1990.

Lee, Bernard J. *Jesus and the Metaphors of God*. New York: Paulist Press, 1993.

Lienhard, Marc. *Luther: Witness to Jesus Christ, Stages and Themes of the Reformer's Christology*. Translated by Edwin H. Robinson. Minneapolis: Augsburg Publishing House, 1982.

Lindbeck, George. *The Nature of Doctrine: Religion and Theology in a Post liberal Age*. Philadelphia: Westminster Press, 1984.

Little, Hervey Ganse. "Christ for Us and in Us." *Interpretation* (1956) 144-156.

Loewenich, Walter von. *Luther's Theology of the Cross*. Translated by Herbert J. A. Bouman. Minneapolis: Augsburg Publishing House, 1976.

———. Review of *Luther's Theology of the Cross,* by Lowell C. Green. *Lutheran Quarterly* 29 (May 1977) 196-198.

Lohse, Bernard. *Martin Luther: An Introduction to His Life and Work*. Translated by Robert C. Schultz. Philadelphia: Fortress, 1986.

———. "Luther und Bernard von Clairvaux." In *Bernhard von Clairvaux: Rezeption und Wirkung in Mitelalter und in der Neuzeit*, ed. K. Elm. 23-51. Wiesbaden, Germany: Harrassowitz, 1994.

Lull, Timothy. "Luther Writings." In *Cambridge Companion to Martin Luther,* ed. Doanld K. McKim, 39-61. Cambridge: Cambridge University Press, 2003.

Lukito, Daniel Lucas. *Making Christology Relevant to the Third World*. Berne, Germany: Peter Lang, 1998.

Luther, Martin. *Luther's Works*. Edited by Jaroslav Pelikan and Helmut T. Lehmann. 56 vols. Philadelphia: Fortress; St. Louis, MO: Concordia Publishing House, 1955-86.

———. *Church Postils*. Translated and edited by John Nicholas Lenker. 4 vols. Reprint, Grand Rapids, MI: Baker Books,1995.

———. *D. Martin Luthers Werke*. Krirische Gesamtausgabe. Weimar: Herman Böhlaus Nachfolger, 1883-.

Luz, Ulrich. "*Theologia Crucis* als Mitte der Theologie im Neuen Testament." *Evangelische Theologie* 34 (1974) 116-141.

Maiyam, T. A. P. *Profiles of Poverty and Networks of Power.* Madurai, India: DACA Publication, 2001.

MacMullen, Ramsay. *Roman Social Relations: 50 B.C. to A.D. 284.* New Haven, CT: Yale University, 1974.

Malina, Bruce J. *The New Testament World: Insights from the Cultural Anthropology.* rev. ed. Louisville, KY: Westminster Press, 1993.

Marxen, Willi. *Jesus and the Church: Beginnings of Christianity.* Translated by Philip E. Devenish. Philadelphia: Trinity Press International, 1992.

Maschle, Timothy, Franz Posset and Joan Skocir. eds. *Ad Fontes: Toward the Recovery of the Real Luther.* Milwaukee, WI: Marquette University Press, 2001.

Matthew, C. P. and M. M. Thomas. *Indian Churches of Saint Thomas.* Delhi, India: ISPCK, 1967.

McGrath, Alister. *Luther's Theology of the Cross.* Oxford: Basil Blackwell, 1985.

_____. *The Intellectual Origins of the European Reformation.* Oxford: Basil Blackwell, 1978.

_____. *The Mystery of the Cross.* Grand Rapids, MI: Zondervan Publishing House, 1988.

McKim, Doanld K., ed. Cambridge Companion to Martin Luther. Cambridge: Cambridge University Press, 2003.

McSorley, Harry J. *Luther: Right or Wrong: An Ecumenical Theological Study of Luther's Major Work, "The Bondage of the Will."* New York: Newman Press: 1969.

McWilliams, Warren. *The Passion of God: Divine Suffering in Contemporary Theology.* Macon, GA: Mercer University Press, 1985.

_____. "The Pain of God in the Theology of Kazoh Kitamori." *Perspectives in Religious Studies* 7 (1981) 184-200.

Meyer, Carl S., ed. *Luther for an Ecumenical Age.* St. Louis, MO: Concordia Publishing House, 1967.

Michalson, Carl. *Japanese Contributions to Christian Theology.* Philadelphia: Westminster, 1960.

Minz, Nirmal. "Religion and Culture as Power in the Context of Tribal Aspiration in India." *Religion and Society* 23 (1986) 45-54.

Moltmann, Jürgen. *The Crucified God.* Translated by R.A. Wilson and Herbert J. Bowden. New York: Harper and Row, 1974.

_____. "Is "Pluralistic Theology" Useful for Dialogue of World Religions?" In *Christian Uniqueness Reconsidered: The Myth of a Pluralistic Theology of Religions*, ed. Gavin D'Costa, 149-156. Maryknoll, NY: Orbis Books, 1990.

_____. *Jesus Christ for Today's World.* Minneapolis: Fortress, 1994.

_____ and Elizabeth Moltmann-Wendel. *God: His & Hers.* New York: Crossroad, 1991.

Morris, Leon. *The Cross in the New Testament.* Grand Rapids, MI: William B. Eerdmans Publishing Company, 1965.

Morris, L. L. "Atonement." In *New Dictionary of Theology*, ed. Sinclair B. Ferguson and David F. Wright, 54-57. Downer Grove, IL: Inter varsity, 1988.

Mozley, John. *The Impassibility of God: A Survey of Christian Thought.* Cambridge: Cambridge University Press, 1926.

Nestingen, James A. *Martin Luther: A Life*. Minneapolis: Augsburg Fortress, 2003.

_____. "Luther's *Heidelberg Disputation*: An Analysis of the Argument." *Word and World Supplement Series* (1992) 147-154.

Netland, Harold. *Encountering Religious Pluralism*. Downers Grove, IL: Intervarsity, 2001.

Neyrey, Jerome H. *Paul, In Other Words: A Cultural Reading of His Letters*. Louisville, KY: Westminster, 1990.

Newbigin, Leslie. *The Gospel in a Pluralistic Society*. Grand Rapids, MI: William B. Eerdmans Publishing Company, 1989.

_____. "Religion for the Marketplace." In *Christian Uniqueness Reconsidered: The Myth of a Pluralistic Theology of Religions,* ed. Gavin D'Costa, 135-148. Maryknoll, NY: Orbis Books, 1990.

Ngien, Dennis. *The Suffering of God according Martin Luther's Theologia Crucis*. New York: Peter Lang, 1995.

Nicholls, Bruce J., ed. *The Unique Christ in Our Pluralistic World*. Grand Rapids, MI: Baker Book House, 1994.

Niebhuhr, H. R. *Christ and Culture*. New York: Harper Collins, 2001.

Niles, Damayanthi Mercy Arulratnum. "Religion and Christian Faith in South Asia: A Critical Inquiry into the Writings of Hendrick Kraemer, Lynn De Silva and M. M. Thomas with regard to the use of understanding of religion in the Theological Task." Ph.D. diss., The University of Chicago, 1998.

Niles, Preman "Report of the Consultation of Theologians, Hong Kong, October 10-15, 1976." In *Asian Theological Reflections on Suffering and Hope,* ed. Kim Hao Yap, 8-14. Singapore: CCA, 1977.

Nirmal, Arvind P. *Heuristic Explorations*. Madras, India: CLS, 1990.

_____., ed. *A Reader in Dalit Theology*. Madras, India: Dept. of Dalit Theology, Gurukul, 1991.

_____. "Towards a Christian Dalit Theology," In *A Reader in Dalit Theology*, ed. Arvind P. Nirmal. 53-70. Madras, India: Dept. of Dalit Theology, Gurukul, 1991.

Nnamani, Amuluche Gregory. *The Paradox of a Suffering God*. New York: Peter Lang, 1995.

Norris, Richard A., ed. and trans. *The Christological Controversy: Sources of Early Christian Thought*. Philadelphia: Fortress, 1980.

Oberman, Heiko A. *Luther: A Man between God and the Devil*. New Haven, CT: Yale University Press, 1989.

_____. *Dawn of the Reformation*. Edinburgh: T. T. Clarke Ltd., 1986.

Oddie, G. A., ed. *Religion in South Asia*. Columbia, MO: South Asia Books, 1977.

Okholm, Dennis L. and Timothy R. Phillips, ed. *Four Views on Salvation in a Pluralistic World*. Grand Rapids, MI: Zondervan, 1996.

O' Leary, Joseph Stephen. *Religious Pluralism and Christian Truth*. Edinburgh: Edinburgh University Press, 1996.

Oliver, Daniel. *The Cause of the Gospel in the Church*. Translated by John Tonkin. St. Louis, MO: Concordia Publishing House, 1982.

Pannenberg, Wolfhart. "A Theology of the Cross." *Word and World* 8 (1988) 162-172.

_____. "The Appropriation of the Philosophical Concept of God as a Dogmatic Problem of Early Christian Theology." In *Basic Questions in Theology*, Vol. 2., Translated by George H. Kehm. Philadelphia: Westminster Press, 1971.

_____. "The Religions from the Perspective of Christian Theology and the Self-Interpretation of Christianity in Relation to the Non-Christian Religions." *Modern Theology* 9 (1993) 285-297.

Pelikan, Jaroslav. *The Growth of Medieval Theology*. Chicago: The University of Chicago, 1978.

_____. *Reformation of the Church and Dogma (600-1300)*. Chicago: The University of Chicago Press, 1983.

Persaud, Winston D. *The Theology of the Cross and Marx's Anthropology*. New York: Peter Lang, 1991.

Philip, T. M. *Encounter Between Theology and Ideology: An Exploration into the Communicative Theology of M. M. Thomas*. Madras, India: CLS, 1986.

Pieris, Aloysius. *A Theology of Liberation in Asian Churches?*. Quezon City, Philippines: Socio-Pastoral Institute, n.d.

_____. *An Asian Theology of Liberation*. Maryknoll, NY: Orbis Books, 1988.

_____. "Asia's non-semitic religions and the mission of the local Churches." In *Asian Expression of Christian Commitment* ed. T. Dayanandan Francis and Franklin Balasundaram. 45-64. Madras, India: CLS, 1996.

_____. "Christianity and Buddhism in Core-to-Core Dialogue." *Cross Currents* 37 (1987) 47-75.

_____. "God-Talk and God Experience in a Christian Perspective." *Dialogue* 2 (1975) 116-128.

_____. *God's Reign for God's Poor*. Kelayina, Sri Lanka: Tulana Research Center, 1998.

_____. *Fire and Water: Basic Issue in Asian Buddhism and Christianity*. Maryknoll, NY: Orbis Books, 1996.

_____. "Liturgy and Dialogue with Buddhism: An Experiment." *Dialogue* 15 (1968)1-25.

_____. *Love Meets Wisdom: A Christian Experience of Buddhism*. Maryknoll, NY: Orbis Books, 1988.

_____. "Mission of the Local Church in Relation to Other Major Religious Traditions." *CCA-CTC Bulletin* 4 (1983) 36-49.

_____. "Political Theologies in Asia." In *The Blackwell Companion to Political Theology*, ed. Peter Scott and William T. Cavanaugh. Malen, MA: Blackwell Publishing Ltd., 2004.

_____. "The Place of Non-Christian Religions and Cultures in the Evolution of a Third-World Theology." *CTC Bulletin* 3 (1982) 43-61.

_____. *Theology of Liberation in Asian Churches?* Quezon City, Philippines: Socio-Pastoral Institute, n.d.

_____. "Towards an Asian Theology of Liberation: Some Religio-Cultural Guidelines." *Dialogue* 6 (1979) 29-52.

Pinomma, Lennart. *Faith Victorious: An Introduction to Luther's Theology*. Philadelphia: Fortress 1963.

Poirier, Alfred. "The Cross and Criticism." *Journal of Biblical Counseling* 17 (1999) 16-20.

Pollard, T. E. "The Impassibility of God." *Scottish Journal of Theology* 8 (1955) 353-364.

Prabhakar, M. E. ed., *Towards a Dalit Theology*. Delhi, India: ISPCK, 1988.

Prabhu, George Soares. "Class in the Bible: The Biblical Poor a Social Class?" In *Voices from Margin*, ed. R. Sugirtharajah, 147-171. Maryknoll, NY: Orbis Books, 1991.

Purvis, Sally P. *The Power of the Cross*. Nashville, TN: Abingdon Press, 1993.

Prenter, Regin. *Luther's Theology of the Cross*. Philadelphia: Fortress, 1971.

Price, S. R. F. "Rituals and Power." In *Paul and Empire: Religion and Power in Roman Imperial Society*, ed. Richard A. Horsley, 47-71. Harrisburg, PA: Trinity, 1997.

Race, Alan. *Christian and Religious Pluralism*. London: SCM Press, 1983.

Rajashekar, Paul, ed. *Religious Pluralism and Lutheran Theology*. Geneva: Lutheran World Federation, 1988.

Ramachandra, Vinoth. *The Recovery of Mission*. Delhi, India: ISPCK, 1996.

Richard, Lucien. *What Are They Saying about the Theology of Suffering?* New York: Paulist Press, 1992.

Ruge-Jones, Philip Lawrence. "Cross in Tension: Theology of the cross as Theologico-social Critique." Th.D. diss., Lutheran School of Theology at Chicago, 1999.

Rupp, Ernest Gordon. "Luther's *Ninety-five Theses* and the Theology of the Cross." In *Luther for an Ecumenical Age*, ed. Carl C. Meyer, 67-81. St. Louis, MO: Concordia Publishing House, 1967.

_____. *Luther's Progress to the Diet of Worms*. London: SCM Press Ltd., 1951.

_____. *The Righteousness of God*. London: Hodder and Stoughton Ltd., 1953.

Ryan, Samuel. "M. M. Thomas - Response-ability." In *Christian Witness in Society*, ed. K. C. Abraham. 1-14. Bangalore: BTE-SSC, 1998.

_____. "Reconceiving Theology in the Asian Context." In *Doing Theology in a Divided World*, ed. Virginia Fabella and Sergio Torres, 124-142. Maryknoll, NY: Orbis Books, 1985.

_____. "Theological Priorities in India Today." In *Irruption of the Third World*, ed. Virginia Fabella and Sergio Torres, 30-41. Maryknoll, NY: Orbis Books, 1983.

Samartha, Stanley J. *Between Two Cultures: Ecumenical Ministry in a Pluralistic World* Geneva: WCC Publications, 1996.

_____. *Courage for Dialogue: Ecumenical Issues in Inter-Religious Relationships* Maryknoll, NY: Orbis Books, 1982.

_____. *One Christ Many Religions: Towards a Revised Christology*. Maryknoll, NY: Orbis Books, 1991.

_____. "The Cross and the Rainbow: Christ in a Multi-religious Culture." In *Asian Faces of Jesus*, ed. R. S. Sugirtharajah, 104-123. Maryknoll, NY: Orbis Books, 1995.

Sanneh, Lamin. *Encountering the West*. Maryknoll, NY: Orbis Books, 1993.

Scaer, David P. "Theology of Hope." In *Tensions in Contemporary Theology*, ed. Stanley N. Gundry and Alan F. Johnson. 197-234. Chicago: Moody, 1976.

Scott, Peter and William T. Caranaugh, eds. *The Blackwell Companion of Political Theology*. Malen, MA: Blackwell, 2004.

Shah, Ghanshyam. *Caste and Poverty*. Surat, India: privately printed by author, 1987.

Sheth, D. L. "Nation-Building in Multi-Ethnic Societies: The Experience of South Asia," *Alternatives* 14 (1989) 15-29.

Sobrino, Jon. *Christology at the Crossroads: A Latin American Approach*. Maryknoll, NY: Orbis Books, 1978.

Soelle, Dorothee. *Suffering*. Translated by Everett Kalin. Philadelphia: Fortress, 1973.

Song, Choan-Seng. *Jesus, the Crucified People*. New York: Crossroad, 1990.

_____. *Jesus in the Power of the Spirit*. Minneapolis: Fortress, 1994.

_____. *Theology from the Womb of Asia*. Maryknoll, NY: Orbis Books, 1979.

_____. *Third-Eye Theology*. Maryknoll, NY: Orbis Books, 1979.

Song-mee, Chung. "Continuity and Change? A Quest for a Relevant Christology in the Mayasian Multi-religious Society." Ph.D. diss., Luther Seminary, 2001.

Strange, J. F. "Method of Crucifixion." In *Interpreter's Dictionary of the Bible, Supplementary Volume*, ed. Keith Crimm et al., 199-200. Nashville, TN: Abingdon Press, 1976.

Stuhlmacher, Peter. *Reconciliation, Law and Righteousness: Essays in Biblical Theology*. Philadelphia: Fortress, 1986.

Sugirtharajah, R. S. *Seeking the Asian Face of Jesus*. Oxford: Regnum, 1997.

_____. ed. *Asian Faces of Jesus*. London: SCM Press, 1993.

_____. ed. *Frontiers in Asian Christian Theology: Emerging Trends*. Maryknoll, NY: Orbis Books, 1980.

_____. ed. *Voices from Margin*. Maryknoll, NY: Orbis Books, 1991.

Sumithra, Sugand. *Revolution as Revelation: A Study of M. M. Thomas' Theology*. New Delhi, India: Theological Research and Communications Institute, 1984.

Tauler, Johannes. *Johannes Tauler: Sermons*. Translated by Maria Schrady. Marwah, NJ: Paulist Press, 1985.

Tavard, George H. "Medieval Piety in Luther's Commentary on the *Magnificat*." In *Ad Fontes: Toward the Recovery of the Real Luther*, ed. Timothy Maschke, Franz Posset and Joan Skocir, 281-301. Milwaukee, WI: Marquette University Press, 2001.

Tertullian, *Adversus Marcionem*. Edited and translated by E. Evans. Oxford: Oxford University Press, 1972.

_____. *Tertullian's Treatise against Praxeas*. Edited and translated by E. Evans. London: SPCK, 1948.

_____. *Tertullian's Treatise on Incarnation*. Edited and translated by E. Evans. London: SPCK, 1956.

Thangaraj, M. Thomas. *Crucified Guru: An Experiment in Cross-Cultural Christology.* Nashville, TN: Abingdon Press, 1994.

Thapa, Shanker. *Buddhist Monasticism: Theory and Practice.* Kathmandu, Nepal: Walden Book House, 1995.

Thomas Aquinas. *Summa Theologiae.* Translated by Fathers of the English Dominican Province, revised by Daniel J. Sullivan. Chicago: Encyclopedia Britannica, 1952.

Thomas, M. M. *Christian Response to Asian Revolution.* SCM: 1966.

_____. *Ideological Quest within Christian Commitment.* Madras, India: CLS, 1983.

_____. *Man and the Universe of Faiths.* Madras, India: CLS, 1975.

_____. *New Creation in Christ: Twelve Selected Sermons.* Delhi, India: ISPCK, 1976.

_____. *Religion and Revolt of the Oppressed.* Delhi, India: ISPCK, 1981.

_____. *Realization of the Cross: Fifty Thoughts and Prayers Centered on the Cross.* Madras, India: CLS, 1972.

_____. *Revolution in India and Christian Humanism.* New Delhi, India: Forum for Christian Concern for People's Struggle, 1978.

_____. *Risking Christ for Christ Sake: Towards an Ecumenical Theology of Pluralism.* Geneva: WCC, 1987.

_____. *Salvation and Humanization.* Madras, India: CLS, 1971.

_____. *Some Theological Dialogue.* Madras, India: CLS, 1977.

_____. *The Christian Response to the Asian Revolution.* London: SCM Press Ltd., 1966.

_____. *The Acknowledged Christ of the Indian Renaissance.* London: SCM Press Ltd., 1969.

_____. *The Secular Ideologies and Meaning of Christ.* Madras, India: CLS, 1976.

_____. *Towards a Theology of Contemporary Ecumenism.* Madras, India: CLS, 1978.

Thomas, T. Jacob. *Ethics of World Community: Contribution of Dr. M. M. Thomas Based on Indian reality.* Calcutta, India: Punthi Pustak, 1993.

Thomson, Deanna Alicia. "Theological Proximity to the Cross: A Conversation between Martin Luther and Feminist Theologians." Ph.D. diss., Graduate School of Vanderbilt University, 1998.

Tinder, Galen. "Luther's Theology of Christian Suffering and Its Implications for Pastoral Care." *Dialog* 25 (1986) 108-113.

Tillich, Paul. *Systematic Theology.* Vol.1. Chicago: University of Chicago Press, 1951.

Tobin, Thomas H. *The Spirituality of Paul,* Message of Biblical Spirituality 4, Collegeville, MN: Liturgical, 1991.

Todd, John M. *Reformation.* New York: Doubleday and Company, 1971.

Tombs, David. "Liberating Christology: Images of Christ in the Works of Aloysius Pieris." In *Images of Christ,* ed. Stanley Porter, Michael A. Hayes and David Tombs, 173-188. Sheffield, England: Sheffield Academic Press, 1997.

Tomlin, Graham. *The Power of the Cross.* Cumbria, UK: Paternoster Press, 1999.

_____. "The Theology of the Cross: Subversive Theology for a Postmodern World." *Themelios* 23 (1997) 59-73.

Transparency International. "Transparency International Corruption Perception Index 2004." http://www.transparency.org (Accessed December 7, 2004).

Vercruysse, Joe E. "Luther's Theology of the Cross at the Time of the *Heidelberg Disputation*." *Gregorianum* 57 (1976) 523-548.

Weber, Hans-Ruedi. *The Cross: Tradition and Interpretation*. Translated by Elke Jessette. Grand Rapids, MI: Eerdmans Publishing House, 1975.

Weeden, Theodore J. "The Cross as Power in Weakness." In *The Passion in Mark,* ed. Werner H. Kelber, 115-129. Philadelphia: Fortress Press, 1976.

Wells, Harold. "The Holy Spirit and the Theology of the Cross: Significance for Dialogue." *Theological Studies* 53 (1992) 476-492.

Weng, Ng Kam. "Pluralism and Particularity of Salvation in Christ." *Transformation* 15 (1998) 10-15.

Wengst, Klaus. *Pax Romana and the Peace of Jesus Christ.* Translated by John Bowden. Philadelphia: Fortress, 1987.

Wiesel, Elie. *Night.* New York: Farrar, Straus & Giroux, 1960.

William, Sam K. *Jesus' Death as Saving Event: The Background and Origin of a Concept.* Missoula, MT: Scholar's Press, 1975.

Williams, Delores. "Black Women's Surrogacy and the Christian Notion of Redemption." In *After Patriarchy: Feminist Transformation of the World Religions,* ed. Paula M Cooey, et al. 1-14. Maryknoll, NY: Orbis Books, 1991.

Wingren, Gustaf. *Luther on Vocation.* Translated by Carl C. Rasmussen. Philadelphia: Muhlenberg Press, 1957.

Wolters, Hielke T. *Theology of Prophetic Participation: M. M. Thomas' Concept of Salvation and Collective Struggle for Fuller Humanity in India.* Delhi, India: ISPCK, 1996.

Wondra, Gerald. "The Pathos of God." *The Reformed Review* 18 (1964) 28-35.

Woollcombe, K. J. "The Pain of God." *Scottish Journal of Theology* 20 (1967) 129-148.

World Bank. "South Asia: Data Reports Studies Statistics Projects." http://lnweb18.worldbank.org/sar/sa.nsf (accessed March 17, 2004).

Yap, Hao Kim, *Asian Theological Reflections on Suffering and Hope.* Singapore: CCA, 1977.

Young, William G. Review of *An Asian Theology of Liberation,* by Aloysius Pieris. *Scottish Bulletin of Evangelical Theology* 9 (1991) 72-73.

Zahl, Paul F. M. *A Short Systematic Theology.* Grand Rapids, MI: William B. Eerdmans Publishing Company, 2000.

Endnotes

[1] That these countries are increasingly realized to be one segment for the development of the region is substantiated by the creation of the South Asia Association of Regional Cooperation (SAARC) in 1980s.

[2] The population of the South Asian countries are as follows: India 1,065,070,607; Pakistan 159,196,336; Bangladesh 141,340,476; Sri Lanka 19,905,165; Nepal 27,070,666; Bhutan 2,185,569 and Maldives 339,330. See CIA, "World Fact Book: Country Profiles," http://www.cia.gov/cia/publications/factbook (accessed February 15, 2005).

[3] World Bank, "South Asia: Data Reports Studies Statistics Projects," http://lnweb18.worldbank.org/sar/sa.nsf (accessed March 17, 2004). Samuel Ryan emphasizes this aspect of Asia when he asserts, "Before and above all else, Asia is persons." Not only for number, he explains, but more importantly for their significance in the fact that persons belong and they matter in life of the community. See Samuel Ryan, "Reconceiving Theology in the Asian Context," in *Doing Theology in a Divided World*, ed. Virginia Fabella and Sergio Torres (Maryknoll, NY: Orbis Books, 1985) 125.

[4] World Bank, "South Asia : Data Reports Studies Statistics Projects," http://lnweb18.worldbank.org/sar/sa.nsf (accessed March 17, 2004).

[5] India is the largest democracy in the world. Along with Pakistan it shares nuclear capabilities that have enhanced their geo-political significance in recent years.

[6] C. T. Kurien, *Poverty and Development* (Madras, India: CLS, 1974) 74.

[7] The British ruled the united India that included Pakistan and Bangladesh then, from 1857 to 1947. However, the British East India Company ruled certain parts of India from as early as late 17th century.

[8] Preman Niles, "Report of the Consultation of Theologians, Hong Kong, October 10-15, 1976," in *Asian Theological Reflections on Suffering and Hope*, ed. Kim Hao Yap (Singapore: CCA, 1977) 9. Many other theologians recognize that colonial experience of Asian countries has left behind the dominative structure and a culture of dependency. See, for example, Franklin Balasundaram *Contemporary Asian Christian Theology* (Delhi, India: ISPCK, 1991) 1-3.

[9] For the adverse impact and theological critique of globalization, see Feliciano V. Carino and Marina T., eds. *Faith and Life in Contemporary Asian Realities* (Hong Kong: CCA, 2000).

[10] Indian data is more or less representative. A study by Gabriele Dietrich and Bas Wielenga shows that India economy has grown considerably in the last 40 years; production of food grains has trebled since 1950; industrial production has increased; economic growth has kept ahead of

population growth that has impacted per capita income positively. See *Towards Understanding India Society* (Madurai, India: Tamilnadu Theological Seminary, 1997).

[11] Quoted by Kadakkal Pothen Kuruvilla, "The Incarnation and the Cross: the Inseparable Paradigm for an Indian Christian Theology of Inculturation and Liberation" (Ph.D. diss., Lutheran School of Theology at Chicago, 1999) 16.

[12] Samuel Ryan, "Theological Priorities in India Today," in *Irruption of the Third World*, ed. Virginia Fabella and Sergio Torres (Maryknoll, NY: Orbis Books, 1983) 31.

[13] See Tissa Balasuriya, *Jesus and Human Liberation* (Colombo, Sri Lanka: Centre for Society and Religion, 1976); Aloysius Pieris, *An Asian Theology of Liberation* (Maryknoll, NY: Orbis Books, 1988); Sebastian Kappen, *Jesus and Freedom* (Maryknoll, NY: Orbis Books, 1977).

[14] George Soares Prabhu, "Class in the Bible: The Biblical Poor a Social Class?" in *Voices from Margin*, ed. R. Sugirtharajah (Maryknoll, NY: Orbis Books, 1991) 168. For relation between poverty and caste, see Ghanshyam Shah, *Caste and Poverty* (Surat, India: privately printed by Author, 1987); T. A. P. Maiyam, *Profiles of Poverty and Networks of Power* (Madurai, India: DACA Publication, 2001); Kuruvilla, "The Incarnation and the Cross." 36. In response to dehumanizing segregation in Indian society, Dalits have been expressing strong resentment against the caste system. True to the Dalit nature of the Church in India, a profound voice of Dalit theology is being argued which takes into serious consideration the implications of the caste system. See A. P. Nirmal, *Heuristic Explorations* (Madras, India: CLS, 1990); M. E. Prabhakar, ed., *Towards a Dalit Theology* (Delhi, India: ISPCK, 1988); A. P. Nirmal, ed., *Reader in Dalit Theology* (Madras, India: Dept. of Dalit Theology, Gurukul, 1991).

[15] Aloysius Pieris, "Mission of the Local Church in Relation to Other Major Religious Tradition," *CCA-CTC Bulletin* 4, (1983) 41.

[16] Tissa Balasuriya, *Jesus and Human Liberation* (Columbo, Sri Lanka: Center for Society and Religion, 1976) 103.

[17] Ryan, "Theological Priorities in India Today," 37.

[18] See Pieris, *An Asian Theology of Liberation*. Michael Amoladass speaks of Asian search for integral humanism. See "Questions from the Local Churches from Asia," in *Trends in Mission*, ed. William Jenkinson and Helene O'Sullivan (Maryknoll, NY: Orbis Books,1991) 48. M. M. Thomas understands the same goal of liberation as humanization; see *Salvation and Humanization* (Madras, India: CLS, 1971).

[19] See CIA, "World Fact Book: Country Profiles," http://www.cia.gov/cia/publications/factbook (accessed March 18, 2004)

[20] Includes Hindu, Christian and others.

[21] Sunni 77% and Shia 20%.

[22] Only Hindu state in the world.

[23] Lamaitic Buddhism.

[24] Almost all are Muslims and they are Sunni.

[25] Samuel Ryan speaks of Asian sense of the sacred, transcendent, depth, meaning, mystery, communion and hope that have found expression in rich religious literature, stories, songs,

myths, theologies, criticism and humor. He also speaks of renunciation, worship and ritual with flower, water, fire, word and fragrance, art as the deep expression of Asian spirituality. See Samuel Ryan, "Reconceiving Theology in the Asian Context," in *Doing Theology in the Divided World*, ed. Virginia Fabella and Sergio Torres (Maryknoll, NY: Orbis Books, 1985)125-126.

[26] The tradition of St. Thomas in Kerala, South India goes back to the earliest centuries of Christian existence. However, there are many theories about the time and nature of Christian existence; many scholars believe that there was a vibrant Christian community from the middle of fourth century onwards. See C. P. Matthew and M. M. Thomas, *Indian Churches of Saint Thomas* (Delhi, India: ISPCK, 1967) 14-19; C. B. Firth, *An Introduction to Indian Church History* (Madras, India: CLS, 1961) 20.

[27] C. T. Kurien speaks of this influence in Indian context, which is also true in South Asia: "religion is the foremost influence in life from birth to death, deciding what one may eat, what vocation to go into, whom one may marry (or not marry), whether one is to be buried or cremated when dead. Of course, it is not the same for everyone, but it is religion all the same." C. T. Kurien, "The Role of Religion," unpublished paper, quoted by K. C. Abraham, "Pluralism as Oikomene of Solidarity," in *New Horizons in Ecumenism: Essays in Honour of Bishop Samuel Amritham*, ed. K. C. Abraham (Bangalore, India: The Board of Theological Education of the Senate of Serampore, 1994) 126.

[28] Charles Amjad-Ali, "The Religious Dimension of Social Change" in *Christian Ethics in Ecumenical Context*, ed. Shin Chiba, George Hunsberger, Lester Edwin J. Ruiz (Grand Rapids, MI: William B. Eerdmans Publishing Company, 1995) 270.

[29] For the first use of these terms, see Alan Race, *Christian and Religious Pluralism* (London: SCM Press, 1983). Since then, they have been used extensively.

[30] O. V. Jathanna, *The Decisiveness of the Christ-Event and the Universality of Christianity in a World of Religious Plurality* (Berne, Germany: Peter Lang, 1981) 4-5.

[31] O. V. Jathanna, *Decisiveness of Christ-Event*, 5 ff.

[32] Hans Küng, *On Being A Christian,* trans. Edward Quinn (Garden City, NY: Double day, 1976) 174.

[33] Bangladesh was a part of Pakistan and existed as East Pakistan from 1947 to 1971, but the difference in ethnicity and language proved to be too powerful for the people of the East Pakistan to remain a part of Pakistan. However, there were other factors both political and geographical that contributed to cessation of East Pakistan from Pakistan.

[34] D. L. Sheth, "Nation-Building in Multi-Ethnic Societies: The Experience of South Asia," *Alternatives* 14 (1989) 19.

[35] Many scholarly writings tend to bypass these two realities; especially the issue of corruption has not been given adequate attention by theologians. In our opinion this is an issue that the Church cannot afford to ignore in its task of witness.

[36] Graham Steines was burnt alive along with two of his children in a remote village in Eastern State by a mob of people.

[37] See D. B. Forester, "The Depressed Classes and Conversion to Christianity, 1860-1960" in *Religion in South Asia* ed. G. A. Oddie (Columbia, MO: South Asia Books, 1977) 49-50.

[38] It is very interesting to note that the leaders of Dalit society organized this conversion rally in Delhi while the Bhartiya Janata Party (Indian People's Party) ruled in the center. This party along with Shiv Sena is generally known to be the political face of Hindu fundamentalist parties in India such as Rastiya Swamsevak Sangh (National Volunteers Organization), Bajrang Dal etc. that are vehemently opposed to conversion out of Hindu fold and claim India exclusively for Hindus. In somewhat democratic spirit the participants were given the freedom to choose the religion of their choice. As a result most opted for Buddhism where as some converted to Christianity. See Satish Jacob, "Buddhism appeal for low-caste Hindus," *BBC* Monday, 5 November 2001, http://news.bbc.co.uk/1/low/world/south_asia/1639245.stm (accessed on December 31, 2004).

[39] Transparency International, "Transparency International Corruption Perception Index 2004," http://www.transparency.org (Accessed December 7, 2004).

[40] One of the more public displays of corruption within the Church is to be witnessed during the time of election of the bishop. In many instances the election process is not complete without court litigations and stay orders from the court. The use of money and power to influence constituents is clear indication of the corruption within the Church. Such investments have long implications as the winner (the Bishop) takes sole control of the many appointments in many Church-run schools, management of many mega shopping complexes, etc.

[41] The problem of poverty is assumed to include the problem of corruption, and in the issue of plurality of faith the issue of conversion is implied throughout this thesis.

[42] Hence, many theologians use theological framework of other faith traditions to make sense of Christian faith. For example, many have argued for the concept of Advaita to understand Christian faith in Indian context; see Swami Abhisiktananda, *Saccidananda: A Christian Approach to Advaitic Experience,* rev. ed. (Delhi, India: ISPCK, 1984). On the other hand, some others have completely ignored the gospel's implication for a context of poverty. Examples of it are to be found in many forms such as other worldly theology, prosperity theology of many T. V. preachers, docetic tendency in theology, etc.

[43] Douglas John Hall, *Lighten Our Darkness: Towards a Theology of the Cross* (Philadelphia: Westminster Press, 1976) 115ff.

[44] Gustaf Aulén, *Christus Victor: An Historical Study of Three Main Types of the Idea of Atonement,* trans. A. G. Herbert (London: SPCK, 1950) The objective view shows that the demands of justice have to be satisfied before forgiveness can take place. The debt of sin is so heinous that only God can pay it and yet it has to be paid from the human side as they are the debtors. Thus, Jesus, the God-man satisfies God's justice by his death on the cross. This theory does not compromise with the divine justice. Humans have no part as it is an action primarily between God and Christ. God imputes the merits of Christ to humans, thus justification is a second and separate act. Anselm argued for this theory that takes human sin and human inability for any solution very seriously.

The subjective view propounded by Abelard affirms Jesus' death to be fundamentally a demonstration of God's love, which, in turn, evokes repentance. Such astounding love of God displayed on the cross is bound to elicit a response of love, leading to forgiveness and a fresh obedience to God's will. What needs to be changed is not God but humans. Because of its emphasis on God's love it held great appeal for liberals of the 19th and 20th century.

The third type advocated by Aulén himself has roots in Irenaeus and Luther. It is generally called the classic or *Christus victor* view of atonement. It sees the cross as the decisive moment in a cosmic drama between good and evil, in which victory over hostile powers results in a new and reconciled relation between God and the world. Jesus' death is victorious in that it liberates sinful humanity from devil.

[45] Bengt Hägglund, *The Background of Luther's Doctrine of Justification in Late Medieval Theology* (Philadelphia: Fortress, 1971) 1.

[46] Luther's discovery of the righteousness of God will be discussed in later section to prove its role in the development of the theology of the cross.

[47] Charles B. Cousar, *A Theology of the Cross: The Death of Jesus in Pauline Letters* (Minneapolis: Fortress, 1990) 27. Others have also concluded the centrality of the cross in Pauline corpus, for example, Ernst Käsemann, "The Pauline Theology of the Cross," *Interpretation* 24 (1970) 167, 172; Peter Stuhlmacher, *Law and Righteousness: Essays in Biblical Theology* (Philadelphia: Fortress, 1986) 156.

[48] Cousar, *A Theology of the Cross*, 28-29.

[49] Ibid., 179.

[50] Ibid., 181.

[51] Wolfhart Pannenberg, "A Theology of the Cross," *Word and World* 8 (1988) 163-164. 52; Cousar, *A Theology of the Cross*, 42; Käsemann, "The Pauline Theology of the Cross," 154.

[53] Ulrich Luz, "*Theologia Crucis* als Mitte der Theologie im Neuen Testament," *Evangelische Theologie* 34 (1974) 124. ("In Paul's theology of the cross he has to do with the godness of God.")

[54] We will undertake a discussion in later sections to show why and how Luther responded to the practice of indulgence and growing deeper theological malaise in the teaching of the Church.

[55] Ernst Käsemann, *Perspectives on Paul* (London: SCM, 1971) 41.

[56] Ibid., 55-56.

[57] Walter von Loewenich, *Luther's Theology of the Cross*, trans. Herbert J. A. Bouman (Minneapolis: Augsburg Publishing House, 1967) 22.

[58] *First Lectures on the Psalms* (1513), *LW* 10:119-120; *Lectures on Isaiah* (1527), *LW* 17:131ff; *Lectures on Galatians* (1535), *LW* 26:113,228; *Heidelberg Disputation* (1518), *LW* 31:52.

[59] We will see that Luther was the first in the history of theology to challenge the notion that God is a dispassionate God. As passionate God, God is involved in the suffering of his people. There is a radical suggestion that the redemption of God's people is possible only through suffering; a suffering that carries a divine significance.

[60] Tertullian, *Adversus Marcionem*, ed. and trans. E. Evans (Oxford: Oxford University Press, 1972) 131.

[61] Ibid.,131.
[62] Tertullian, *Tertullian's Treatise against Praxeas*, ed. and trans. E. Evans (London: SPCK, 1948) 74.
[63] Tertullian, *Tertullian's Treatise on Incarnation*, ed. and trans. E. Evans (London: SPCK, 1956) 19-20.
[64] Graham Tomlin, *The Power of the Cross* (Cumbria, U.K.: Paternoster Press, 1999) 120.
[65] Tertullian, *Tertullian's Treatise against Praxeas*, 177.
[66] Ibid.
[67] Ibid., 178.
[68] T. D. Barnes, *Tertullian: A Historical and Literary Study*, 2d ed., rev. (Oxford: Clarendon Press, 1985) 213.
[69] Ibid., 219.
[70] Adolph Hamel, *Der junge Luther und Agustin* (Gütersloh, Germany: C. Bertelsmann, 1934) 197.
[71] *Heidelberg Disputation* (1518), *LW* 31:75.
[72] Marc Lienhard, *Luther: Witness to Jesus Christ, Stages and Themes of the Reformer's Christology*, trans. Edwin H. Robinson (Minneapolis: Augsburg Publishing House, 1982) 26.
[73] Jaroslav Pelikan, *Reformation of the Church and Dogma 600-1300* (Chicago: The University of Chicago Press, 1983) 164. Also see Luther's comments in *Lectures on Galatians* (1535), *LW* 27: 34, 238ff; 30:117.
[74] Philip D. Krey, "Martin Luther," in *Augustine through the Ages: An Encyclopedia*, ed. Allan D. Fitzerald (Grand Rapids, MI: William B. Eerdmans Publishing Company, 1999) 517.
[75] Ibid.
[76] Tomlin, *The Power of the Cross*, 122.
[77] Anselm, *Anselm of Canterbury*, ed. and trans. Jasper Hopkins and Herbert Richardson (Toronto: The Edwin Mellen Press, 1976) 100.
[78] Ibid., 58-59.
[79] Quoted by Tomlin, *The Power of the Cross*, 123.
[80] Tomlin, *The Power of the Cross*, 124.
[81] Thomas Aquinas, *Summa Theologiae*, trans. Fathers of the English Dominican Province, rev. Daniel J. Sullivan (Chicago: Encyclopedia Britannica, 1952) 3a.49.3.
[82] See R. Cessario, *The Godly Image: Christ and Salvation in Catholic Thought from Anselm to Aquinas* (Petersham, MA: St. Bede's, 1990) 19, 132-134.
[83] *Summa Theologiae*,3a. 46.12.
[84] Tomlin, *The Power of the Cross*, 124-125.
[85] D.R. Janz, *Luther on Thomas Aquinas: The Angelic Doctor in the Thought of the Reformer* (Stuttgart, Germany: Franz Steiner Verlag Wiesbaden, 1989).
[86] Tomlin, *The Power of the Cross*, 125.
[87] Ibid., 126.
[88] Richard Bauckham, "Only the Suffering God Can Help: Divine Passibility in Modern Theology," *Themelios* 9 (1984) 7. Many scholars have discussed the debate on passibility-impassibility of

God. See John Mozley, *The Impassibility of God: A Survey of Christian Thought* (Cambridge: Cambridge University Press, 1926); Warren McWilliams, *The Passion of God: Divine Suffering in Contemporary Theology* (Macon, GA: Mercer University Press, 1985); Joseph Hallman, *The Decent of God: Divine Suffering in History and Theology* (Minneapolis: Fortress, 1991); T.E. Pollard, "The Impassibility of God," *Scottish Journal of Theology* 8 (1955) 353-364; Dennis Ngien, *The Suffering of God according to Martin Luther's* Theologia Crucis (New York: Peter Lang, 1995); Gerald Wondra, "The Pathos of God," *The Reformed Review* 18 (1964) 28-35; Wolfhart Pannenberg, "The Appropriation of the Philosophical Concept of God as a Dogmatic Problem of Early Christian Theology," in *Basic Questions in Theology*, vol. 2., trans. George H. Kehm (Philadelphia: The Westminster Press, 1971); Lucien Richard, *What Are They Saying about the Theology of Suffering?* (New York: Paulist Press, 1992).

[89] Ngien, *The Suffering of God according to Martin Luther's* Theologia Crucis, 3.

[90] McWilliams, *The Passion of God: Divine Suffering in Contemporary Theology*, 10-11.

[91] Jürgen Moltmann, *The Crucified God*, trans. R.A. Wilson and Herbert J Bowden (New York: Harper and Row, 1974) 228.

[92] Mozley, *The Impassibility of God*, 119.

[93] John Calvin, *Institutes of the Christian Religion*, vol. 1, trans. Ford Lewis Battles & ed. John McNeill, (Philadelphia: Westminster Press, 1960) bk.II. xii.2, 484.

[94] Mozley, *Impassibility of God*, 121.

[95] Ngien, *The Suffering of God*, 17. See also K. J. Woollcombe, "The Pain of God," *Scottish Journal of Theology* 20 (1967)137-138.

[96] Galen Tinder, "Luther's Theology of Christian Suffering and Its Implications for Pastoral Care," *Dialog* 25 (1986) 111.

[97] Ibid.

[98] Ngien, *The Suffering of God*, 17.

[99] Mozley, *The Impassibility of God*, 121.

[100] Kazoh Kitamori, *Theology of the Pain of God*, trans. Shinkyo Suppanskha (Richmond, VA: John Knox Press, 1965).

[101] For Luther's influence in 20th century, see Douglas John Hall, "Luther's Theology of the Cross," *Consensus* 25 (1989) 10-11.

[102] Kitamori is important for three reasons. First, he is an Asian and this dissertation purports to be a critical theological engagement for South Asia. Second, he is the first theologian to talk about the pain of God in modern time. Third, inspired by Luther's theology of the cross, Kitamori is in critical conversation with Luther in Asian situation.

[103] Kitamori, *Theology of the Pain of God*, 44-49.

[104] Kitamori, *Theology of the Pain of God*, 111-112. See also Warren McWilliams, "The Pain of God in the Theology of Kazoh Kitamori," *Perspectives in Religious Studies* 7 (1981) 190.

[105] Kitamori, *Theology of the Pain of God*, 95.

[106] Choan-Seng Song, *Third-Eye Theology* (Maryknoll, NY: Orbis Books,1979) 61.

[107] Ibid.

[108] Moltmann, *The Crucified God*, 47.

[109] Carl Michalson, *Japanese Contributions to Christian Theology* (Philadelphia:Westminster Press, 1960) 73. Although this comment was made in 1960s, it holds true even today.

[110] M. M. Thomas, *Realization of the Cross: Fifty Thoughts and Prayers Centered on the Cross* (Madras, India: CLS, 1972) 3.

[111] M. M. Thomas, *The Acknowledged Christ of the Indian Renaissance* (Madras, India: CLS, 1970) 117.

[112] Way of Action.

[113] Aloysius Pieris, *An Asian Theology of Liberation* (Maryknoll, NY: Orbis Books, 1988). A comprehensive account of his theology of the cross will be presented in a later chapter.

[114] Leonardo Boff, *Jesus Christ Liberator: A Critical Christology for Our Time,* trans. Patrick Hughes (Maryknoll, NY: Orbis Books, 1979) 55.

[115] Jon Sobrino, *Christology at the Crossroads: A Latin American Approach.* Maryknoll, NY: Orbis Books, 1978).

[116] Ibid., 216.

[117] Ibid., 192.

[118] Ibid., 193.

[119] Moltmann, *The Crucified God*.

[120] Ibid., 72.

[121] Richard Bauckham, "In Defence of The Crucified God," in *The Power and Weakness of God*, ed. Nigel M. de S. Cameron (Edinburgh: Rutherford House Books, 1990) 94.

[122] Moltmann, *The Crucified God*, 7.

[123] We will discuss Moltmann's theology of the cross in detail in later chapter.

[124] Moltmann, *The Crucified God*, 47.

[125] Tomlin, *The Power of the Cross*, 172.

[126] Tomlin, *The Power of the Cross,* 112, 116. Tomlin quotes Theo Bell who says, "es wurde doch zu wenig nach den Quellen dieser Theologie in der mittelalterlichen Theologie und Frömmigkeit geforscht," T. Bell, *Divus Bernardus: Bernard von Clairvaux in Martin Luthers Schriften* (Mainz, Germany: P. von Zabern, 1993) 375 argues the scarcity of research in the area of sources of the theology of the cross in medieval theology and spirituality. Tomlin argues that Luther appropriated the theology of the cross, kept alive in the popular devotion of medieval time. See *Power of the Cross*, 112, 113, 129-153.

[127] Alister McGrath, *The Intellectual Origins of the European Reformation* (Oxford: Basil Blackwell, 1978) 40.

[128] Moreover, Luther used rhetoric for the sake of preaching and proclaiming God's word whereas other humanists considered rhetoric as an end in itself. Not only was Luther influenced by humanism, in early years of reformation he was also supported by the humanists.

[129] *First Lectures on Psalms II* (1513-1515), *LW* 11:451.

[130] Jaroslav Pelikan, *The Growth of Medieval Theology* (Chicago: The University of Chicago, 1978)155.

[131] Bernard Lohse, "Luther und Bernard von Clairvaux," in *Bernhard von Clairvaux: Rezeption und Wirkung in Mitelalter und in der Neuzeit*, ed. K. Elm (Wiesbaden, Germany: Harrassowitz, 1994) 271-301.

[132] *Bernard of Clairvaux: On the Song of Songs*, trans. K. Walsh. Cisterian Fathers Series No. 7 (Kalamazoo, MI: Cisterian Publications, 1976) 223.

[133] Ibid., 146, 224.

[134] Ibid., 155-156.

[135] Ibid., 48-50.

[136] Graham Tomlin, *The Power of the Cross*, 133. Moreover, the monastery at Erfurt, which Luther joined as young monk, shared widespread interest in meditating upon the sufferings of Christ.

[137] Gordon Jensen, "The Significance of Luther's Theology of the Cross for Contemporary Political and Contextual Theologies," (Ph.D. diss., Toronto School of Theology, 1992) 48, footnote 2.

[138] Dietmar Lage, *Martin Luther's Christology and Ethics* (Lewiston, NY: The Edwin Mellen Press, 1990) 55.

[139] Ibid., 53.

[140] Marc Lienhard, *Luther: Witness to Jesus Christ, Stages and Themes of the Reformer's Christology*, trans. Edwin H. Robinson (Minneapolis: Augsburg Publishing House, 1982) 48.

[141] Bengt R. Hoffman, *Luther and the Mystics* (Minneapolis: Augsburg Publishing House, 1976) 145.

[142] Johannes Tauler, *Johannes Tauler: Sermons*, trans. Maria Schrady (Marwah, NJ: Paulist Press, 1985) 166.

[143] Ernest Gordon Rupp, *The Righteousness of God* (London: Hodder and Stoughton Ltd., 1953) 119.

[144] Lage, *Martin Luther's Christology and Ethics*, 49.

[145] Heiko A. Oberman, *Luther: A Man between God and the Devil* (New Haven, CT: Yale University Press, 1989) 182.

[146] Lage, *Martin Luther's Christology and Ethics*, 76.

[147] Marc Lienhard, *Luther: Witness to Jesus Christ*, 36; John P. Dolan concludes that many have tried to undermine the importance of Luther as a reformer. He says, "To consider him merely as the enunciator of ideas traceable to a number of early theologians or to maintain as Haller does, that his contribution to the Reformation was small (that it was, as it were, the spark that ignited the powder and that it was an occasion, not a cause of the Reformation) is a view that no serious student of the period now accepts." See John P. Dolan, *History of the Reformation* (New York: Desclee Company, 1965) 251.

[148] Jensen, *Significance of Luther's Theology of the Cross*, 62 (note 2).

[149] Lienhard, *Luther: Witness to Jesus Christ*, 36. Though, it must be remembered that Tauler and others did not consider Christ only in terms of an example as mentioned above. But they do not have the emphasis in the sacramental quality as Luther does.

[150] Erwin Iserloh, "Luther's Christ-Mysticism," in *Catholic Scholars in Dialogue with Luther*, ed. Jared Wicks (Chicago: Loyola University Press, 1970) 40-41.

[151] *Operationes in Psalmos* (1519-1521) WA 5/176, 32-33.

[152] There is a long history of communal violence in this part of the world. Especially in India the communal riots between Hindus and Muslims for a very long time stands as a sad witness to deep antagonism between these two communities but it also proves the adherents of these religious faiths are willing to defend their faith even if it means dying for it.

[153] Roland H. Bainton, *The Age of Reformation* (Princeton, NJ: D. Van Nostrand Company, 1956) 12.

[154] Many forms of this include a share in dowry in South Indian Church. While the ecclesial positions were sold during Luther's time, the South Asian protestant Churches' election to the Bishops is seldom complete without scores of court litigations. Thus, the scrambling for power and positions by self-righteous power mongers in the Church is so similar to the power hungry Church leaders of Luther's time.

[155] Justo L. Gonzalez, *A History of Christian Thought*, vol. 3. (Nashville,TN: Abingdon Press, 1980) 26.

[156] This is seen in his interaction with Staupitz.

[157] Martin Brecht, *Martin Luther: His Road to Reformation. 1483-1521*, trans. James L. Schaaf (Philadelphia: Fortress, 1985) 77.

[158] For the lack of English equivalent this deeply comprehensive German word is explained in terms of "despair"; "anguish"; "temptation"; "attack"; "uncertainity" etc.

[159] Bernard Lohse, *Martin Luther: An Introduction to His Life and Work*, trans. Robert C. Schultz (Philadelphia: Fortress, 1986) 43.

[160] *Early Sermons* (1510?-1517), *LW* 51: 26-31.

[161] See Harold J. Grimm, *The Reformation Era 1500 - 1650* (New York: Macmillan Company, 1954) 50 -51.

[162] Grimm, *The Reformation Era*, 91.

[163] John M. Todd, *Reformation* (New York: Doubleday and Company, 1971) 152.

[164] Gonzalez, *A History of Christian Thought*, 27.

[165] Bainton, *The Age of the Reformation*, 25.

[166] Grimm, *The Reformation Era*, 83.

[167] In Luther scholarship the term 'discovery' is used to refer to this development in Martin Luther's theological development. While reading the scripture Luther applied Christological interpretation and discovered that in Roman 1: 17 the phrase the 'righteousness of God' actually referred to Christ and not to the demand of justice of God. Thus, for Luther justification by faith in Jesus Christ became the foundational doctrine to understand everything. There is a direct connection between this new understanding and the theology of the cross, which we will discuss in later.

[168] Grimm, *The Reformation*, 50.

[169] James Atkinson, "Ecclesia Reformata Semper Reformanda," in *Luther for an Ecumenical Age*, ed. Carl S. Meyer (St. Louis, MO: Concordia Publishing House, 1967) 181.

170 Timothy Lull, "Luther Writings" in *Cambridge Companion to Martin Luther*, ed. Doanld K. McKim (Cambridge: Cambridge University Press, 2003) 39. See also Deanna Alicia Thomson, "Theological Proximity to the Cross: A Conversation between Martin Luther and Feminist Theologians," (Ph.D. diss., Graduate School of Vanderbilt University, 1998) 5.

171 *Ninety-five Theses* (1517), *LW* 31: 25 -33.

172 *Explanations of the Ninety-five Theses* (1518), *LW* 31: 77-252.

173 Heiko Obermann points out that, by Luther's own admission, the part of *Ninety-five Theses* did not originate with him alone or first. At least Karlstadt and Armsdorf were part of Wittenberg School-team. However, Luther, Obermann acknowledges, exceeded many in radically understanding many of the themes. See Obermann, *Dawn of the Reformation,* 80-81.

174 Luther's sermon of July 27, 1516; October 31, 1516; and February 24, 1517. See *LW* 51: 14-31.

175 *Ninety-five Theses* (1517), *LW* 31:25.

176 Ibid., 28.

177 Ernest Gordon Rupp, "Luther's *Ninety-five Theses* and the Theology of the Cross," in *Luther for an Ecumenical Age.* ed. Carl C. Meyer (Saint Louis, MO: Concordia Publishing House, 1967) 68ff. McGrath also argues that there is a connection between Luther's breakthrough and his theology of the cross, see McGrath, *Luther's Theology of the Cross,* 99 ff.

178 *Ninety-five Theses* (1517), *LW* 31:25.

179 Harold Grimm in the introduction to the 95 Theses in *LW* 31:22.

180 Rom. 3:23; 5:8; I Tim. 1:15.

181 *Explanations of the Ninety-five Theses* (1518), *LW* 31:89.

182 Ibid.,104.

183 *Ninety-five Theses* (1517), *LW* 31:31.

184 Ibid., 33.

185 Ibid., 30.

186 Ibid., 28.

187 Ibid.

188 Ibid., 30.

189 Ironically, the war against the Turks had been financed by the money raised through the sale of indulgences in the 11th century. Those who were unable to go to the Holy Land contributed by giving money to the cause of crusade. See Roland H. Bainton, *Here I Stand* (New York: The New American Library, 1955) 54.

190 *Ninety-five Theses* (1517), *LW* 31: 29-32 (Theses 37; 60; 62; 79; 93; 94).

191 *Explanations of the Ninety-five Theses* (1518), *LW* 31:224.

192 Ibid.

193 Ibid., 227.

194 Ibid., 79.

195 Ibid., 250.

196 *Heidelberg Disputation* (1518), *LW* 31: 36-71.

[197] Joe E. Vercruysse, "Luther's Theology of the Cross at the Time of the *Heidelberg Disputation*," *Gregorianum* 57 (1976) 524. He states "Luther uses the expressions *theologia crucis and theologus crucis* ... in only five texts. Four of them were written in the spring of 1518, namely the *Asterisci Lutheri adversus Obeliscos Eckii*, the *Lectures on Hebrews*, the *Resolutiones disputationum de indulgentiarum virtute* and finally the Heidelberg disputation. The fifth one is to be found in the *Operationes in Psalmos*, Luther's second course on the Psalms.

[198] This conclusion is drawn by Gerhard Førde. See *On Being a Theologian of the Cross* (Grand Rapids, MI: William B. Eerdmans Publishing Company, 1997) 19ff.

[199] These writings included *Asterisci Lutheri adversus Obeliscos Ecki,* which Luther wrote in response to Eck's criticism of Luther's *Ninety-five Theses*, see WA/1: 281 ff; *Lecture on Hebrews* (1518) *LW* 29: 109-241, and the *Resolutiones disputationum de indulgentiarum virtute* WA/1: 522 ff.

[200] Graham Tomlin, *The Power of the Cross*, 115.

[201] Loewenich, *Luther's Theology of the Cross*, 20.

[202] *Heidelberg Disputation* (1518), *LW* 31:39.

[203] James A. Nestingen, *Martin Luther: A Life* (Minneapolis: Augsburg Fortress, 2003) 36.

[204] *Lectures on Genesis* (1535-1536), *LW* 2: 40, 140, 300-301; *Sermons on the Gospel of John* (1537-1540), *LW* 22: 138, 179, 346 (cf. Ps. 14: 2-3; 116: 11; Rom. 3: 10; 11: 32).

[205] Tomlin, *The Power of the Cross*, 298.

[206] Ibid.

[207] *Heidelberg Disputation* (1518), *LW* 31: 42.

[208] Ibid., 37.

[209] James A. Nestingen, "Luther's *Heidelberg Disputation*: An Analysis of the Argument," *Word and World Supplement Series* (1992) 147.

[210] *Heidelberg Disputation* (1518), *LW* 31: 40.

[211] Ibid., 40.

[212] Ibid., 52-53.

[213] Althaus, *The Theology of Martin Luther*, 26.

[214] John 3:16.

[215] Nestingen, "Luther's *Heidelberg Disputation*: An Analysis of the Argument,"153.

[216] Many theologians will vigorously argue for expurgation of all exclusiveness of Christian faith especially amidst the plurality of faiths in our world. In a later chapter we will undertake a discussion on the theology of religions of John Hick and Paul Knitter in which we will argue that a Christian does not need the help of an unfounded crutch of the theology of religions (as argued by Hick and Knitter) to live a meaningful life even in a world of many cultures and religions.

[217] I owe credit to Prof. Charles Amjad-Ali for this section. He has emphasized and elaborated on the vulnerability of God in a number of his lectures and seminars.

[218] Luke 2:5ff.

[219] Matthew 2:13-16.

220 Luke 9:58.

221 Matthew 26:36ff; Mark 14:32ff: Luke 22:39ff; John 18:1ff.

222 John 20:27. Instead of a nail, Jesus invites Thomas to put his finger into his wound for reassurance of who Jesus was. This invitation of putting finger is full of significance as it reenacts Jesus' passion but also sustains his eternal purpose that he is for the world even in resurrected state.

223 On the way to Emmaus c.f. Luke 24:13 ff. This image of the risen Lord will be important for our discussion on the theology of the cross as a theology of the way in the final chapter.

224 The notable examples are Moltmann's *The Crucified God*; Douglas John Hall's *Lighten Our Darkness*; however, Hall pays attention to theses 16-20 but he also disregards the insight of a theology of the cross under justification; Heino Kadai also considers theses 19 and 20 to discuss Luther's theology of the cross, see Heino O. Kadai, "Luther's Theology of the Cross" in *Accent to Luther's Theology* (St. Louis, MO: Concordia Publishing House, 1967) 238-245.

225 *Heidelberg Disputation* (1518), *LW* 31:40.

226 Ibid.

227 Førde, *On Being a Theologian of the* Cross, 69.

228 *Heidelberg Disputation* (1518), *LW* 31: 41.

229 Philip Lawrence Ruge-Jones, "Cross in Tension: Theology of the cross as Theologico-social Critique," (Th.D. diss., Lutheran School of Theology at Chicago, 1999) 116.

230 Harold Grimm, "Introduction to the *Heidelberg Disputation*," *LW* 31:37.

231 Jos E. Vercruysse, "Luther's Theology of the Cross at the Time of *Heidelberg Disputation*," 538.

232 Nestingen, "Luther's *Heidelberg Disputation*: An Analysis of the Argument," 151-152.

233 As is evident in *Heidelberg Disputation* (Theses 4 and 11), God condemns before he saves. The works of man (Theses 2 and 5) even the law of God (Theses 1 and 23) make them neither sinless nor ready for the grace of God unless they are humbled and despaired about their helplessness and acknowledge sinfulness for God to begin his work in them (Theses 18 and 24). God uses law to achieve necessary desperation in the sinner (Theses 1, 2, 3, 5,7, 8, 9, 10, 23). Contrary to common perception, the law of God rather hinders a human than advances him in righteousness (Theses 1). Luther argues that the experience of suffering and despair; unattractive and apparently evil things are not to be avoided (4, 20). Humility, for Luther, plays an important role in salvation (Theses 4, 8, 16).

234 Nestingen, "Luther's *Heidelberg Disputation*: An Analysis of the Argument," 153.

235 Tomlin, *The Power of the Cross*, 115.

236 Kadai, "Luther's Theology of the Cross," 238.

237 Ruge-Jones, "Cross in Tensions," 127-128.

238 The reference to 1 Corinthians 1 [:25] makes it clear that it is pronounced in the context of proclamation amidst many not only not believing but apparently ridiculing Jews and Greeks.

239 *Heidelberg Disputation* (1518), *LW* 31:52-53.

240 Theses 19-21.

[241] Lowenich, *Luther's Theology of the Cross*, 27.
[242] Kadai, "Luther's Theology of the Cross," 246.
[243] Tomlin, *The Power of the Cross*, 115.
[244] *Heidelberg Disputation* (1518), *LW* 31:53.
[245] Ruge-Jones, "Cross in Tension," 128.
[246] Vercruysse, "Luther's Theology of the Cross," 541.
[247] Ibid.
[248] *Heidelberg Disputation* (1518), *LW* 31: 53.
[249] Ngien, *The Suffering of God according to Martin Luther's Theologia Crucis*, 53.
[250] Hall, *Lighten Our Darkness*, 123.
[251] Loewenich, *Luther's Theology of the Cross*, 20.
[252] Indian saying to refer to the one who acts illogically to his own disadvantage and injury.
[253] *Heidelberg Disputation* (1518), *LW* 31 53; c.f. John 14:8.
[254] Ibid.
[255] Ibid.
[256] Ibid., 52.
[257] Ibid.
[258] McGrath, *Luther's Theology of the Cross*,150.
[259] *Heidelberg Disputation* (1518), *LW* 31:56.
[260] Loewenich, *Luther's Theology of the Cross*, 38.
[261] It is a devotional tract composed in 1521. This is addressed to Prince John Frederick of Saxony, the elector's nephew. He was to become the ruler of Electoral of Saxony (1532-1547). In fact Luther was interrupted by the Diet of Worms in the writing of the commentary on the *Magnificat*. In the Diet of Worms, Luther was commanded to recant his stand with regard to evangelical theology.
[262] Although Luther's writing of it was disrupted by Diet of Worms.
[263] Heino O. Kadai, "Luther's Theology of the Cross," 250-251.
[264] *The Magnificat* (1521), *LW* 21: 298.
[265] Ibid.
[266] Ibid., 302.
[267] Ibid., 321.
[268] Ibid.
[269] Ibid., 325.
[270] Ibid., 309.
[271] In many cases Luther followed Augustine, but, in this case Luther called upon the temporal powers to reform the Church whereas Augustine the Church to carry authority and responsibility.
[272] *The Magnificat* (1521), *LW* 21: 305.
[273] Ibid., 317.

274 George H. Tavard, "Medieval Piety in Luther's Commentary on the *Magnificat*," in *Ad Fontes: Toward the Recovery of the Real Luther*, ed. Timothy Maschke, Franz Posset and Joan Skocir (Milwaukee, WI: Marquette University Press, 2001) 287.

275 *The Magnificat* (1521), *LW* 21:332.

276 McGrath, *Luther's Theology of the Cross*, 99.

277 *Operationes in Psalmos* (1519-1521) WA 5/176.32-33. (The cross alone is our theology).

278 Ibid., WA/5:179.31. (The cross tests everything).

279 Since we are dealing with the theology of the cross of Luther, it would be important for us to show how his gradual understanding of the righteousness of God not only proves to be critical for theology of the cross but eventually becomes the basis of unyielding conviction for the primacy of God's final and decisive judging action in the death of Jesus Christ. To put it still radically, for Luther the righteousness of God is nothing else but Christ himself. Such a conclusion imparts theology of the cross a virtual foundation as we have been emphasizing this theology to be radically Christocentric theology.

280 Bernard Lohse, *Martin Luther*, 150. In today's parlance distributive righteousness may seem to relate to the ethical practice of distributive justice of fair allocation and just distribution, which is the meaning in God's distributive righteousness. However, given the sinful nature of humanity it would not be inappropriate to call this the retributive righteousness for emphasis.

281 McGrath, *Luther's Theology of the Cross*, 100, 103.

282 *Preface to the Complete Edition of Luther's Latin Writings* (1545), *LW* 34: 336-7. For many it would seem awkward to call this passive because God's righteousness is active in declaring human being righteous. In his advent sermon, Luther explains the meaning of God's righteousness. He says, "it means the revealed grace and mercy of God through Jesus Christ in us by means of which we are considered godly and righteous before him." *Church Postils*, vol. 1. 33.

283 Bernard Lohse, *Martin Luther*, 260 note 31. Lohse contends that Luther never mentions this as causative yet it can be argued that Luther's acknowledged Hebrew way of thinking, however, does adequately render Luther's understanding of the term "justice or righteousness of God" and "love of God" as causative.

284 *First Psalm Lectures* (1513-1515), *LW* 10: 419. McGrath also concludes this, see McGrath, *Luther's Theology of the Cross*, 128.

285 Since the beginning of this century the tendency is to assign this discovery an earlier time than the more traditional view of 1519 in previous scholarship. E. Gordon Rupp argues that "it is clear, in all essentials, [that] his theology was in existence before the opening of the Church struggle in 1517." See Gordon Rupp, *Luther's Progress to the Diet of Worms* (London: SCM Press Ltd., 1951) 39; Roland Bainton seems to suggest the period of 1516-1517. See Bainton, *Here I Stand*, 45-46; McGrath concludes that Luther's new meaning of the righteousness of God occurred during 1515 possibly while he was still delivering his first lecture on Psalms. See McGrath, *Luther's Theology of the Cross*, 98. The debate continues, however.

286 *Four Psalms of Comfort* (1526), *LW* 14: 203.

[287] Ibid., *LW* 14:137-206.

[288] From the advantage of hindsight, Luther commented on this most important discovery that became basis for all he said and did. "At last, by the mercy of God, meditating day and night, I gave heed to the context of the words, namely, 'in it the righteousness of God is revealed, as it is written, 'He who through faith in righteous shall live.' Here I felt that I was altogether born again and had entered Paradise itself through open gates." See *Preface to Latin Writing* (1545), *LW* 34: 336-37.

[289] We will discuss Carl Braaten's criticism later in this section.

[290] John Doberstein quotes Friedrich Gogarten. See *LW* 51:XIX. This is in terms of the Biblical text that "becomes the living Word of God in the act of preaching, the voice of Christ himself addressing the hearer who cannot escape and must of necessity hear it and reject or accept it." *LW* 51:XIX.

[291] Martin Luther, *Church Postils*, vols. 1-2 trans. and ed. John Nicholas Lenker, reprint (Grand Rapids, MI: Baker Books, 1995) 3.

[292] Ibid. It was Frederick the Wise who requested Luther to write this for he desired to draw Luther from disputes to positive teaching of the gospel of which Luther was aware.

[293] Luther, *Church Postils*, vols. 1-2. 183-192.

[294] Ibid., 190-191.

[295] Luther, *Church Postils*, vols. 1-2. 21.

[296] Ibid.

[297] Ibid., 21-22.

[298] Luther, *Church Postils*, vols. 1-2. 34.

[299] Ibid.

[300] Ibid., 36.

[301] Ibid.

[302] Ibid.

[303] Tomlin, *The Power of the Cross*, 4.

[304] Førde, *On Being A Theologian*, 112.

[305] Tomlin, *The Power of the Cross*, 185.

[306] Walter von Loewenich, *Luther's Theology of the Cross* (Minneapolis: Augsburg Publishing House, 1976)

[307] Loewenich gives brief overviews of the work on the theology of the cross in the past literature including the work of Theodosius Harnack, Hermann Herring, Karl Bauer, Wilhelm Braun, Otto Ritschl, Reinhold Seeberg, Emanuel Hirsch, Karl Holl. Loewenich does not agree with their interpretation of Luther's theology of the cross as medieval and monkish. Lowenich, *Luther's Theology of the Cross*, 169 ff.

[308] Loewenich, *Luther's Theology of the Cross*, 12-13.

[309] Ibid., 17.

[310] Ibid., 22.

[311] Alister McGrath, *Luther's Theology of the Cross* (Oxford: Basil Blackwell, 1985) 149-150. McGrath follows von Loewenich in emphasizing the characteristics of Luther's *theologia crucis*; however, McGrath expands the original Loewenich's list.

[312] Tomlin, *The Theology of the Cross*, 114.

[313] Ibid.

[314] Loewenich, *Luther's Theology of the Cross*, 13.

[315] Ibid., 17,18.

[316] Ibid., 18.

[317] Ibid., 219.

[318] Ibid. Loewenich's commitment to this is seen in his treatment of the subject in pages 112-143.

[319] Loewenich, *Luther's Theology of the Cross*, 113.

[320] Ibid., 118.

[321] Ibid., 118-119.

[322] Ibid., 121.

[323] Ibid., 123.

[324] However Loewenich says that he is not concerned here about the ethic of Luther, Ibid., 113.

[325] Loewenich, *Luther's Theology of the Cross*, 114.

[326] Ibid., 21.

[327] Ibid.

[328] Loewenich, review of *Luther's Theology of the Cross*, by Lowell C. Green, *Lutheran Quarterly* 29 (May 1977) 197.

[329] *Heidelberg Disputation* (1518), *LW* 31: 52-53.

[330] Loewenich, review of *Luther's Theology of the Cross*, by Lowell C. Green, 197. Green finds many other scholars guilty of this aberration.

[331] Loewenich, *Luther's Theology of the Cross*, 120.

[332] Paul Althaus, *The Theology of Martin Luther*, trans. Robert C. Schultz (Philadelphia: Fortress, 1966)

[333] Ibid., 27.

[334] Ibid., 26-27.

[335] *The Magnificat* (1521), *LW* 21:317.

[336] Ruge-Jones, *Cross in Tension*, 19.

[337] Althaus, *The Theology of Martin Luther*, 28.

[338] Ibid., 277.

[339] Ibid., 278.

[340] McGrath, *Luther's Theology of the Cross*, 164 ff.

[341] Ibid., 164.

[342] McGrath follows E. Grilis account of *Deus absconditus*. See E. Grilis, "Martin Luther's View of the Hidden God. The Problem of the *Deus Absconditus* in Luther's Treatise *De servo arbitrio*," *McCormick Quarterly* 21 (1967) 81-94. Brian Gerrish also recognizes the two aspects of the hiddenness of God. He calls first of them "Hiddenness I" which is God hidden within

his revelation as in Luther's *theologia crucis*, and the second hiddenness is understood as "Hiddenness II" in which God is hidden behind the revelation as in *Bondage of the Will*. See Brian Gerrish, "To the Unknown God: Luther and Calvin on the Hiddenness of God," *Journal of Religion* 53 (1973) 263-293.

[343] For this McGrath refers to F. Kattenbusch, "Deus absconditus bei Luther," in *Festgabe für D. Dr. Julius Kaftan zu seinem 70*. (Geburtstag, Germany: Tübingen, 1920) 204.

[344] McGrath, *Theology of the Cross*, 165.

[345] Ibid.

[346] Ibid., 166.

[347] *LW* 33: 140.

[348] Ibid.

[349] McGrath, *Luther's Theology*, 167.

[350] Brian Gerrish, "To the Unknown God" 271.

[351] Althaus, *Luther's Theology*, 286.

[352] *LW* 51: 26.

[353] McGrath, *Luther's Theology of the Cross*, 167. (emphasis author's).

[354] Ibid.

[355] Førde, *On Being a Theologian of the Cross*, vii.

[356] Ibid., viii.

[357] Ibid.

[358] Ibid., ix.

[359] Ibid., x.

[360] Ibid.

[361] Ibid.,1, note 1.

[362] *Heidelberg Disputation* (1518), *LW* 31: 53.

[363] Førde, *On Being a Theologian of the Cross*, 18.

[364] *Heidelberg Disputation* (1518), *LW* 31:56-57.

[365] Førde, *On Being a Theologian of the Cross*, 111.

[366] Ibid., 110.

[367] *LW* 31:52.

[368] During Baptism (in ELCA tradition) the baptizer pronounces that the person being baptized is sealed by the Holy Spirit and marked by the cross of Christ forever.

[369] Regin Prenter, *Luther's Theology of the Cross* (Philadelphia: Fortress, 1971) 3.

[370] Ibid.

[371] Ibid., 4.

[372] Ibid., 5.

[373] Ibid., 4,7.

[374] Ibid., 5.

[375] *Heidelberg Disputation* (1518), *LW* 21: 56.

376 Ibid., *LW* 21: 57.

377 Prenter, *Luther's Theology of the Cross*, 6.

378 Ibid.

379 Ibid., 6-7.

380 Ibid., 7.

381 Rudolf Bultmann, "New Testament and Mythology," in *Kerygma and Myth,* ed. Hans Werner Bartsch (London: SPCK, 1953) 35.

382 Prenter, *Luther's Theology of the Cross*, 8-9.

383 Ibid., 10.

384 Ibid., 18.

385 *The Sermon on the Mount, LW* 21: 57.

386 Jürgen Moltmann, *The Crucified God*, trans. by R.A. Wilson and Herbert J. Bowden (New York: Harper and Row, 1974).

387 Burnell F. Eckardt, Jr., "Luther and Moltmann: The Theology of the Cross," *Concordia Theological Quarterly* 49 (1985) 19.

388 Moltmann, *The Crucified God,* 227.

389 Ibid., 72.

390 Ibid., 7.

391 David P. Scaer, "Theology of Hope," in *Tensions in Contemporary Theology,* ed. Stanley N. Gundry and Alan F. Johnson (Chicago: Moody, 1976) 213.

392 Moltmann, *The Crucified God,* 24 ff.

393 Moltmann says, "The political theology of the cross must liberate the state from the political service of idols and must liberate men from political alienation and loss of rights....It must prepare for the revolution of all values which is involved in the exaltation of the crucified Christ, in the demotion of relationships of political domination." See *The Crucified God*, 327.

394 Eckardt, Jr., "Luther and Moltmann: The Theology of the Cross," 23.

395 Moltmann, *The Crucified God,* 55.

396 Eckardt, Jr., "Luther and Moltmann: The Theology of the Cross," 23.

397 Moltmann, *The Crucified God,* 39.

398 Ibid., 19.

399 Ibid., 247, 255.

400 Ibid., 277.

401 Eckardt, Jr., "Luther and Moltmann: The Theology of the Cross," 25.

402 Ibid.

403 Moltmann, *The Crucified God*, 72-73.

404 Ibid., 246.

405 Ibid., 247.

406 Ibid., 72.

407 Ibid., 274.

408 Ibid.

409 Eckardt, Jr., "Luther and Moltmann." 22.

410 Moltmann, *The Crucified God*, 73.

411 Jürgen Moltmann, *Jesus Christ for Today's World* (Minneapolis: Fortress, 1994) 40.

412 Moltmann, *The Crucified God*, 106-107.

413 Winston D. Persaud, *The Theology of the Cross and Marx's Anthropology* (New York: Peter Lang, 1991) 176-180.

414 *Heidelberg Disputation* (1518), *LW* 31: 53.

415 Luke 23: 43.

416 Luke 23: 46.

417 Carl Braaten, "A Trinitarian Theology of the Cross," *Journal of Religion* 56 (1976) 120-121.

418 Ibid., 120.

419 *Prefaces to New Testament* (1545), *LW* 35: 370.

420 He is referred to as M. M. Thomas, M. M. T. or M. M. Thomas is the given name, Mammen the father's name and Madathilaparampil the surname or family name.

421 *Mar Thoma* is Syriac for Saint Thomas. Hence, it suggests that this Church traces its origin to the preaching of St. Thomas. St. Thomas is believed to have brought the gospel of Jesus Christ to the Malabar Coast in the State of Kerala in south India. Due to the connections with the Nestorians and then with the Monophysites (through immigrations from Syria in the fourth and the eight centuries) the Christians in Kerala are known as Syrian Christians today. The *Mar Thoma* Church was the result of a reform movement over liturgy and other practices within the Syrian Orthodox Church led by Abraham Malpan in 1836. As a result the *Mar Thoma* Church is a unique combination of Eastern and evangelical traditions with preaching and proclamation of the gospel oriented in sacramental piety.

422 Quoted from *The Guardian,* 5th June, 1975, 176 by Sunand Sumithra *Revolution as Revelation: A Study of M. M. Thomas' Theology* (New Delhi, India: Theological Research and Communications Institute, 1984) 2.

423 A list of his publications in English is given in the Bibliography.

424 Though Thomas has written about many creative and relevant issues and themes of Christian faith and witness both in Indian and in world context, the scope of this discussion is limited to these questions. Thus, his contribution to ecumenical theology, Indian Christian theology, his ethical thoughts, socio-political ideas and others will only be touched upon and discussed as it relates to our subject matter.

425 M. M. Thomas, *Salvation and Humanization* (Madras, India: CLS, 1971) 2.

426 Ibid., 8.

427 M. M. Thomas, *Towards a Theology of Contemporary Ecumenism* (Madras, India: CLS, 1978)185-186.

428 Ibid., 186.

429 Humanization is the central category to understand Thomas' theology which will be discussed in later sections.